The Frail Social Body

STUDIES ON THE HISTORY OF SOCIETY AND CULTURE
Victoria E. Bonnell and Lynn Hunt, Editors

The Frail
Social Body

*Pornography, Homosexuality, and
Other Fantasies in Interwar France*

Carolyn J. Dean

UNIVERSITY OF CALIFORNIA PRESS
BERKELEY LOS ANGELES LONDON

University of California Press
Berkeley and Los Angeles, California

University of California Press, Ltd.
London, England

© 2000 by the Regents of the University of California

Library of Congress Cataloging-in-Publication Data
Dean, Carolyn J. (Carolyn Janice), 1960–
    The frail social body : pornography, homosexuality, and
other fantasies in interwar France / Carolyn J. Dean.
        p.   cm. — (Studies on the history of society and
culture; 36)
    Includes bibliographical references and index.
    ISBN 0-520-21995-3 (alk. paper)
    1. Pornography—France.   2. Homosexuality—France.
3. Sex (Psychology).   I. Title.   II. Series.
HQ472.F8D43   2000
306.76'6'0944—dc21   99-13320
                                                          CIP
Manufactured in the United States of America
08   07   06   05   04   03   02   01   00   99
10   9   8   7   6   5   4   3   2   1

The paper used in this publication meets the minimum
requirements of ANSI/NISO Z39.48-1992 (R 1997)
(*Permanence of Paper*).

The following chapters are versions of materials published elsewhere: chapter 2: as "Pornography, Literature,
and the Redemption of Virility in France: 1880–1930,"
differences 5.2 (1993): 62–91, used by permission; and
chapter 3: as "The Great War, Pornography, and the
Transformation of Modern Male Subjectivity," *Mod-
ernism/Modernity* 3 (May 1996): 59–72, used by permission of The Johns Hopkins University Press.

To Rosa Villanueva Garcia

Contents

Acknowledgments

The writing and research of this work was generously subsidized by the American Council of Learned Societies, Brown University, a Harvard University Mellon Faculty Fellowship in the Humanities, a J. William Fulbright Research Fellowship, and the John Simon Guggenheim Memorial Foundation.

I am also deeply indebted to those colleagues who have invited me to present portions of this work for diverse audiences, including Nelly Furman, Steven Kaplan, Larry Kritzman, Dominick LaCapra, Mark Micale, Uta Poiger, Lawrence Rainey, and Liliane Weissberg.

My deepest thanks go to Bonnie Smith, Bryant T. Ragan, Carla Hesse, and Lynn Hunt, who offered detailed, thoughtful, and gentle commentary on the manuscript. Kermit Champa's intellectual generosity and critical acumen mark this book in crucial ways. I am also very grateful to Sheila Levine, Rachel Berchten, and Danielle Jatlow of the University of California Press, who shepherded this book through all the various stages and counseled its author with acuity, kindness, and good humor, and to Peter Dreyer, who copyedited the manuscript. My reading group at Brown—Christina Crosby, Mary Ann Doane, Karen Newman, and Ellen Rooney— generously read and helped out with different chapters, as did Elizabeth Francis, Mary Gluck, Martin Jay, and Tamar Katz.

As always, my deep gratitude to those who have made this book possible in many other ways: Laurie Bernstein, Volker Berghahn, Marion Berghahn, Amy Remensnyder, Camille Robcis, Michael Roth, Elisabeth Roudinesco, and Elizabeth Weed. The friendship of both Gretchen Schultz and Susan Bernstein has sustained me over many years and comforted me through the vagaries of this long project. And Rosa Villanueva's companionship has been essential in every way.

Introduction

> Though the earth, and all inferior creatures,
> be common to all men, yet every man has a
> *property* in his own *person:* this no body has
> any right to but himself.
>
> John Locke, *Second Treatise of Government,* sec. 27

In keeping with the legacy of the Enlightenment, most of us now believe that all human bodies are formally equal and equally dignified before the law. Of course, new liberal theories about equity before the law (or rather the presumption that all people were to be treated *as if* equal) did not immediately end the unequal treatment of different kinds of bodies in the West: women and poor men were excluded from the suffrage in most countries; colonists and slave owners justified the persecution of colonized peoples on the basis of their putative atavism. Nevertheless, this argument about bodily integrity remains so compelling that it is still invoked to demand equal treatment for all persons, and those arguments use the ideally dignified, impermeable body as a symbol for human rights in general.[1] In classical liberal theory,

---

1. This argument persists in spite of recent feminist and poststructuralist criticism that demonstrates with equal force that universal personhood and the universal body that houses it is an ideological fiction: one that renders mostly white, masculine, heterosexual, and upper-class bodies the standard against which all others are judged. Postcolonial theorists have often applied these insights to the structure of colonized subjects,

the body is a privileged metaphor for property relations, and for human rights conceived in terms of bodily
boundaries. Nation-states that destroy bodies thus do so,
according to the 1948 Geneva Convention on the Prevention and Punishment of the Crime of Genocide, to annihilate a "national, ethnical, racial, or religious group." [2]
State-sponsored killing, as Elaine Scarry eloquently argues, is never about numbers: it is, to paraphrase, about
the "making and unmaking of the world." [3] And arguments about rape similarly appeal to the trauma of ex-
propriation in order to describe the fundamental indig-
nity of the crime. In short, the destruction or mutilation
of the body is now a metaphor for the violation of human
dignity and the destruction or "unmaking" of the civilized
world.

How has this narrative about the inviolable body sustained its rhetorical forcefulness in spite of its unmet
promises and contradictions? Why is the symbolism of

---

and some legal and critical race theorists have also availed themselves of
conceptual tools implicit in this critique. This literature is diverse and
nearly endless: see the work of Willy Apollon, Leo Bersani, Homi Bhaba,
Teresa Brennan, Wendy Brown, Judith Butler, Drucilla Cornell, Luce Iri-
gary, and Renata Salecl, among others. Wendy Brown offers a forceful if
more general critique of liberalism's ability to resolve inequity in *States
of Injury: Power and Freedom in Late Modernity* (Princeton, N.J.: Princeton University Press, 1995). Moreover, many of these arguments come in
the wake of the poststructuralist discussion of the theoretical process by
which bodies are produced and naturalized. Poststructuralist theorists insist on the body's changing cultural status and do not presume that it has
intrinsic meaning or dignity. They never, however, deny its materiality. See
Judith Butler's defense of this position in *Bodies That Matter: On the Discursive Limits of Sex* (Routledge: New York, 1993).
    2. Convention on the Prevention and Punishment of the Crime of
Genocide (UN GAOR 260A [III], 9 December 1948).
    3. Elaine Scarry, *The Body in Pain: The Making and Unmaking of the
World* (Oxford: Oxford University Press, 1985).

the integral body so powerful that it constitutes different images of the social world? This book analyzes how interwar French cultural critics reconstructed the meaning of bodily integrity through the elaboration of fantasies about the body-violating qualities of pornography and homosexuality. It never presumes the self-evidence of the integral body but seeks to historicize its world-making powers in the context of four questions: How are shifts in the historical meaning of sexuality related to shifts in the fantasmic concept of bodily integrity? How, then, are discussions about sexual behaviors and representations constitutive of the integral body? Why were pornography and homosexuality invested with a psychic and cultural charge so forceful that critics perceived them as capable of unbinding the impermeable body, and with that body, the social world of metaphorical territories and boundaries fashioned in its image? How, finally (and most generally), was the varied, sometimes frail and porous human body transformed into this particular and particularly masculine, self-enclosed and inviolable image of ideally dignified humanity?[4]

4. Here and throughout the book, I use "body" in Giorgio Agamben's sense of the term. Agamben's major contribution has been to demonstrate that the relationship between the state and the body is always fluid (political life is defined by the citizen's willingness to expose himself to death before the sovereign, placing the body at the center of the political world and rendering clear distinctions between life and death and body and politics moot): "[T]he first foundation of political life is a life that may be killed, which is politicized through its very capacity to be killed" (89). For our purposes, this analytical move is crucial in establishing the historicity and fluidity of the state's relationship to the body and allows us to question how, given this fluidity, the modern social body was nevertheless fashioned after an impermeable, self-possessed one. See Agamben, *Homo Sacer: Sovereign Power and Bare Life* (Stanford, Calif.: Stanford University Press, 1998), 85–89, 109, 129.

But why pornography and homosexuality? After the Great War in France and elsewhere, pornography and homosexuality both symbolized culturally privileged links between bodily degradation and sexuality forged in the experience and representation of battles whose material and psychic costs historians have amply traced. In nuanced and not so nuanced ways, critics displaced the experience of war in discourses about so-called deviant sexuality. After 1918, a wide variety of French men and women used sexual deviance to discuss other concerns about the nation's declining "health." These discussions used old arguments about the monstrosity and degeneracy of sexual deviance in new ways. Since the late eighteenth century, medical men and legislators began to link the health of the individual body to the "health" of a metaphorical social body constituted by the "people": the impermeable, productive, and thus ideally masculine (or thoroughly sublimated feminine) body symbolized the nation's "health." The social body was thus no longer the sacred "body politic" of the Old Regime, imagined as a divinely ordained hierarchy in which the monarch (or princes or pope) was the metaphorical head and other "parts" symbolic (and symbolically located) extensions of that body.[5] Now, the body is a nation whose members are connected by their natural equality before the law: the 1789 declaration of the Rights of Man and Citizen declares that "men are born and remain free and equal in rights" and the Declaration of Independence famously asserts that "all men are created equal."

5. For a brief synopsis of the different uses of bodily metaphors for organicist conceptions of society, see Jacques Le Goff, "Head or Heart? The Political Use of Body Metaphors in the Middle Ages," in Marc Feher, ed., *Fragments for a History of the Human Body*, 3 vols. (New York: Zone Books, 1989), 3: 12–27. The king and the pope were Christ's intermediaries on earth.

By the mid nineteenth century, a medical model of the social body triumphed, meaning that cultural critics conceived of the nation's life in organic terms to be regulated by experts in the body's struggle against contamination and infection.[6] During that century, medical men increasingly identified sexual deviance as one of the most important sources of "infection" in a society overwhelmed by threats to the body's health presented by urbanization, democratization, demographic stagnation, military defeat in the Franco-Prussian War and their perceived symptoms: emasculation, nervousness, weakness, enervation. These concerns about emasculation led to new explorations of sexuality, themselves linked to convictions about the importance of healthy bodies in the making of civilization.

Interwar rhetoric about sexual deviance thus drew on the nineteenth-century preoccupation with the "undersexed weakling," the man whose body had lost its physical and thus moral fiber.[7] Most historians agree that the

6. Robert A. Nye, "Degeneration and the Medical Model of Cultural Crisis in the French Belle Epoque," in Seymour Drescher, David Sabean, and Allan Sharlin, eds., *Political Symbolism in Modern Europe: Essays in Honor of George L. Mosse* (New Brunswick, N.J.: Transaction Books, 1982), 19–41.

7. With the emergence of the science of sex or "sexology" in Britain, France, and Germany, medical men developed new taxonomies that classified persons according to sexual tastes: sadists, masochists, fetishists, homosexuals, and others. Angus McLaren argues, among others, that the new science of sexuality aimed to police the increasingly porous boundaries between normal and pathological sexuality as new sociopolitical conditions contributed to the erosion of normative manliness and womanliness. See id., *The Trials of Masculinity: Policing Sexual Boundaries, 1870–1930* (Chicago: University of Chicago Press, 1997), 155, 175, 176–78. On the invention of the "erotic imagination" and the way in which the "passional voice" became integral to the "rational, normal" one, see Vernon Rosario, *The Erotic Imagination: French Histories of Perversity* (Oxford: Oxford University Press, 1997), 160.

Great War exacerbated these concerns about masculinity and stress that many commentators thereafter perceived France as even weaker, more feminized, and more lacking in cohesion than they had at the end of the preceding century. In France, particularly, concerns about population decline produced alarm about natality that legislators used to justify severe measures against abortion and the exclusion of women from suffrage. The female body was thus part of the social body only to the extent that it played a part in species reproduction, so that legislators used the capacity to give birth oddly to deny women the rights supposedly inherent in being "born."[8] Finally, the evolution of a new political form, fascism, whose foundations had been laid in the late nineteenth century, is only the most obvious example of a virile, united, and impermeable image of the national body. But historians have said little about the war's impact on meanings attributed to sexuality and the social body, except obliquely in voluminous discussions about gender. They discuss the disillusionment of veterans, the diagnosis of shell shock that expressed the psychic trauma wrought by war on men who fought, and the political and cultural effects of the unprecedented exploitation and destruction of male and also female bodies in the interests of an ultimately Pyrrhic victory.[9]

8. For a provocative and suggestive feminist reading of the social contract, see esp. Carole Patemen, *The Sexual Contract* (Stanford, Calif.: Stanford University Press, 1988). Women's bodies were not constitutive of the social body except to the extent that they "belonged" to men and bore children. That is, women could not own their own bodies, as it were, and were only violable property by virtue of their subordination to men. Thus, for example, rape was not seen as rape unless the woman was someone else's property. See Georges Vigarello, *Histoire du viol* (Paris: Seuil, 1998), 105–6, 137.

9. Of the voluminous literature on this topic, see esp. Susan Kingsley Kent, *Making Peace: The Reconstruction of Gender in Interwar Britain* (Princeton, N.J.: Princeton University Press, 1993); Mary Louise Roberts,

But how was that trauma and exploitation symbolized? How was the experience of violence figured and inscribed in the social body? And what does it mean to assert that pornography became and still symbolizes a link between bodily degradation, violence, and sexuality? Pornography is conventionally defined as "the explicit depiction of sexual organs and sexual practices with the aim of arousing sexual feelings."[10] But in France and also in Europe and the United States, then and now, the category "pornography" also describes things not apparently sexual in content. This book is focused on France because during the tumult of the interwar years, it remained a liberal democratic state whose elites sought to reconcile individualism, secularization, and the rule of law with perhaps unparalleled, irrational fears and fantasies about national decline. Those same fantasies led other nations to extreme politico-legal solutions that repudiated liberal values and aimed to repress or annihilate sexual representations, sexual deviants, and other "assassins of the fatherland."[11] Thus France provides an ideal (if not the only) context within which to study a turbulent and decisive moment in the relationship between the liberal democratic state and narratives about the integral body, as well as the consequences of that relationship. Or, to put it another way, the French context provides a forum for

Civilization without Sexes: Reconstructing Gender in Postwar France, 1917–1927 (Chicago: University of Chicago Press, 1994); and Margaret R. Higonnet et al., eds., *Behind the Lines: Gender and the Two World Wars* (New Haven, Conn.: Yale University Press, 1987); Joanna Bourke, *Dismembering the Male: Men's Bodies, Britain, and the Great War* (Chicago: University of Chicago Press, 1996).

10. Lynn Hunt, ed., *The Invention of Pornography: Obscenity and the Origins of Modernity, 1500–1800* (New York: Zone Books, 1991), 10.

11. Jean-Paul Aron and Roger Kempf, *La Bourgeoisie, le sexe, et l'honneur* (Brussels: Editions complexes, 1984), 13.

exploring the role of fantasy in the life of liberal democracy and one in which to demonstrate that fantasy is not a frivolous or private matter unconnected to politics.[12] For the moment, however, I provide mostly American declarations about the meaning of pornography (as I shall in reference to homosexuality), to demonstrate the widespread and continued forcefulness of interwar themes and to make them as accessible and relevant as possible.

The scholar Alvin H. Rosenfeld, for example, has suggested that the Holocaust is being transformed into pornography through mass marketing, and in 1994 a French journalist called photographs of "ethnic cleansing" in Bosnia "pornographic."[13] In the United States, in 1997, a supporter of sex offender registries accompanied by police photographs of offenders bizarrely defended them on the grounds that they were not "pornography."[14] In 1994, the feminist legal theorist Catharine MacKinnon conflated modernity, war, pornography, and rape in Bosnia.[15] Here, she extends her otherwise controversial stance against pornographic material (that it *literally* violates women) to encompass a definition of pornography as that which represents the mutilation of both male and female bodies in war. Her interpretation thus resonates

12. For a brilliant theoretical and psychoanalytic discussion of the relation between fantasy and social reality, see Jacqueline Rose, *States of Fantasy* (Oxford: Oxford University Press, Clarendon Press, 1996), 1–15.

13. Alvin H. Rosenfeld, "Another Revisionism: Popular Culture and the Changing Image of the Holocaust," in Geoffrey Hartman, ed., *Bitburg in Moral and Political Perspective* (Bloomington: University of Indiana Press, 1986), 90–120. The journalist made his comments on French television.

14. William Claiborne, "'Outing' Former Sex Offenders on the Midway: California Officials Defend the Use of a Country Fair Booth Showing Where Convicted Felons Live," *Washington Post National Weekly Edition*, 29 September 1997, 30.

15. Catharine MacKinnon, "Rape, Genocide, and Women's Human Rights," *Harvard Women's Law Journal* 17 (Spring 1994): 5–16.

with those of other commentators for whom pornography seems to imply a modern violation of the body's architecture—its positive status as "property" in the Lockean sense: pornography represents the commodification of violence, the blurring of distinctions between different bodies, the ability of modern technology to capture these violations and our desire to see them.[16] Or, to put it differently, as Patrick McGrath writes in a review of Beth Nugent's novel *Live Girls:* "Its central metaphor, as the title suggests[,] is pornography. Its message is that when we live without hope, without spirit, and without art, relationships necessarily degenerate into rituals of mutual fear and exploitation, and identity turns lifeless and wastes away."[17]

Pornography here is nothing less than the destruction of life-giving, civilizing forces and the triumph of mistrust and tyranny over human community symbolized by the inner "death" of outwardly live girls—the spiritual flatness represented by the buying, selling, and display of women. Although both "high-" and "lowbrow" cultural critics have since the nineteenth-century invoked

16. In a recent *New York Times* article on "hedonism" in the former Yugoslavia, the author yokes the new pervasiveness of hard-core pornography to the appearance of "graphic pictures of mutilated and dead from the war." The article offers only this rationale for its odd coupling of pornography and photos of war dead, and it is gathered from a woman writing a book about sexual mores: "War and sex became stimulants used to keep people from examining what was happening." The assumptions that war is analogous to sex as a stimulant, that false nationalist promises and pornography have some relation to each other, and that pornography more generally symbolizes national decline are presented as utterly self-evident. For the history of such assumptions, see chapter 3. Chris Hedges, "Dejected Belgrade Embraces Hedonism but Still, Life Is No Cabaret," *New York Times*, 19 January 1998, sec. 1.

17. Patrick McGrath, review of *Live Girls*, by Beth Nugent, *New York Times Book Review*, 14 April 1997.

prostitution as a metaphor for an ethical world dimin-
ished by easy money and easy sex, the link McGrath implicitly draws between the public display and erotici-
zation of bodies and their "inner death" is absolutely
breathtaking in scope. It thus raises rather than resolves
questions about pornography's meaning. For "live girls"
is a metaphor for pornography, but pornography's referent remains unclear: is it merely the twentieth-century
version of prostitution and, if so, does it include a landscape that traverses commodity fetishism and the spectacle of wounded, violated bodies, whether they be Jewish victims of Nazi genocide, Bosnian victims of ethnic
cleansing or rape, or, in a less dramatic register, the purported humiliation of live girls? Is pornography the ac-
tual spectacle of corporeal abasement that symbolizes
ethical degradation, an image or description of that spectacle, or a fantasy about it? The question here is not
whether such fantasies should or should not have free
rein, or whether they are ethical. My point is that regardless of what we think about censorship, in all but a small
minority of marginal discourses, whatever earns the label
"pornography" signifies the symbolic (and for many anti-
pornography feminists, the literal) defilement of ideally
dignified humanity. "[William Phillips, writing in *Commentary*] nails the whole genre [of pornography] by dev-
astatingly describing [William] Burroughs's *Nova Express*
as 'the feeding almost literally of human flesh and organs
on each other in an orgy of annihilation. The whole world
is reduced to the fluidity of excrement as everything dis-
solves into everything else,'" an unsigned 1965 editorial
in *Time* magazine observed.[18] That is, pornography is a

18. "The New Pornography," *Time* 85 (16 April 1965): 29.

rhetorical figure that expresses the dissolution and violation of the inviolable social body.

If this concept of the meaning of pornography now is indeed correct, why should homosexuality have become a privileged moment of pornographic spectacle since the Great War? Homosexuality is now so often associated with pornography that legislators from France's President Jacques Chirac to U.S. Senator Jesse Helms claim that homosexuality is itself pornographic. To go back to the 1965 *Time* piece on pornography, the author makes a distinction between literature and pornography by noting: "However unconventional, [now canonized] writers found delight in sex; however critical of human folly, they were partisans of mankind. The new immoralists attack not only society but man and sex itself: Their writings add up to homosexual nihilism, and what Fanny Hill would have thought of them is made clear by her 'rage and indignation' when she observed a pair of 'male-misses scarce less execrable than ridiculous.'"[19] Or a 1982 anti-pornography tract that urged us to note that since "homosexual fantasies about forced sex are more violent and sadistic than those among heterosexuals [*sic*]," and that there is thus "an association between homosexuality and violence," it follows that a "link also can be suspected between much homosexuality and pornography."[20]

In 1986, a body no less august than the United States Supreme Court in *Bowers v. Hardwick* affirmed homo-

19. Ibid.
20. James Robinson, *Pornography: The Polluting of America* (Wheaton, Ill.: Tyndale House, 1982), 38–39. Chapter 4 will supply ample evidence of this link between homosexuality, bodily degradation, and self-abasement.

sexuality's status as pornographic (in the sense in which I am using the term here) by calling sodomy a "victimless crime" and linking it to the destruction of human community as embodied by family, nation, and tradition.[21] The case addressed the legality of Georgia's anti-sodomy law, which applies both to heterosexuals and homosexuals alike, although in this instance the law had been used to arrest a man for having private, consensual sex with another man. Critics have long associated homosexuality with sin, crime, and the moral decline of the populace, and this Court chose to interpret the sodomy statues as if they pertained only to homosexuality. But the Court's association of homosexuality with victimless crimes and hence with self-abasement is still more nuanced. The Court could not sanction homosexual sex, even in private, not only because homosexuals represent threats to social order (defective, criminal, sterile persons). They could not sanction same-sex practices because they conceived homosexual fantasies, oddly, as fantasies of bodily degradation as compelling and intoxicating as drugs— the Justices, after all, liken homosexual behavior to drug addiction. By legalizing those practices, the Court would effectively sanction the right to self-abasement (that is, after all, the implication of naming sodomy a "victimless crime": you only hurt yourself).[22] Homosexuality is thus

21. "Bowers v. Hardwick," in William B. Rubenstein, ed., *Gay Men, Lesbians, and the Law: A Reader* (New York: New Press, 1993), 135, 137.
22. Ibid., 135. Gay rights activists argue that the dissent in this case (authored by Harry Blackmun) acknowledged the link between desire and self-making and included same-sex sexual practices under this rubric. They tend not to discuss why the Court majority simply rejected the idea that for homosexuals desire could be intrinsic to self-making, except by reference to irrational prejudices. But it is challenging to try to make cultural sense of such prejudice. For the most recent expression of this point of view, see Morris Kaplan, *Sexual Justice: Democratic Citizenship and the*

an instance of the "pornographic imagination" not only because it marks sterile, non-reproductive bodies but also because same-sex desire is itself a violation of the body's intrinsic dignity.[23]

This book describes the process by which pornography and homosexuality came to symbolize the modern violation of human dignity and thus traces one of many complicated narratives that fashioned the liberal social body. That process was inextricable from the reconstitution of the integral male body in new terms after World War I. Although this reconstitution begins in the late nineteenth century, it is both more than a culmination and continuation of ongoing colonial wars and the political violence represented by the Great War, and yet it is not a dramatic break with the past. Instead, critics who reconfigured

---

Politics of Desire (New York: Routledge, 1997), 222–29. For a critique of *Bowers* that argues against using "privacy" in relationship to securing gay rights altogether, see Kendall Thomas, "Beyond the Privacy Principle," *Columbia Law Review* 92 (October 1992): 1431–1516. See also Carl Stychin, *Law's Desire: Sexuality and the Limits of Justice* (New York: Routledge, 1995), 16, 136, 135.

23. In 1975, German legislators legitimated discriminatory age of consent laws for gay men (making them higher than for heterosexual sex), on the grounds that such laws protected homosexuals from their own desire, implying that homosexuality was intrinsically degrading and unhealthy, Flora Leroy-Forgeot notes in *Histoire juridique de l'homosexualité en Europe* (Paris: Presses universitaires de France, 1997), 88–89. Moreover, the Supreme Court's ruling only represented the latest chapter in a long history: until the Middle Ages, Roman law referred to homosexuality as a "sexual abuse"; in the biblical tradition, homosexuality destroys man's dignity because it is associated with pagan practices and is antithetical to monotheism; between 1050 and 1300 it was deemed equivalent to murder, and, later, to bestiality (Leroy-Forgeat, 4, 25–31, 48, 82). See also John Boswell, *Christianity, Social Tolerance, and Homosexuality: Gay People in Western Europe from the Beginning of the Christian Era to the Fourteenth Century* (Chicago: University of Chicago Press, 1980). On homosexuality and the concept of addiction, see Eve Kosofsky Sedgwick, *Tendencies* (Durham, N.C.: Duke University Press, 1993), 130–42, and Stychin, *Law's Desire*, 134–39.

the integral body forged a new relationship between the metaphorically masculine social body and sexual politics that derived from a new and complex displacement of that violence into new and increasingly fantastic constructions of the dangers of so-called perverse sexuality. That is, the male body was not newly permeable after the Great War, but anxiety about that permeability expressed itself more intensively than ever. For the first time, the fortification of liberal democracy seemingly demanded the "liberation" rather than repression of male sexuality; the metaphorical integrity of the body required a new, ostensibly liberatory politics of the (male) body. On the other hand, we recall, that fortification required that the female body be continually sublimated in the interests of species reproduction.

Approach

By focusing on changing constructions of pornography and homosexuality, I shall analyze how a specific set of longings, fantasies, and male fears of bodily disintegration, expressed in narratives about sexual desire, was as central to the internal coherence of French ideas about who did and who did not qualify as "French" as other discussions about gender, about ethnicity, about race, about labor, political dissidence (anarchism and communism), and about other significant social categories. In other words, in the context of sexuality, the book historicizes one moment in the fraught passage from the body's birth to its assumption of or endowment with dignity. The construction of deviant sexuality was evidently only one way in which the social body was fortified after the war, but it tells us a great deal about how discussions of sexuality worked to include or exclude certain categories of people from the status of fully developed personhood.

And although such discussions necessarily overlap with other discourses, my analytical focus is on how sexuality was central in shaping who was and was not included in the category "French."

Of course, many historians have demonstrated how the scapegoating and eventual extermination of Jews, especially by the far right all over Europe, served the purpose of restoring an illusory virility to nations rhetorically emasculated by the war.[24] Similarly, although with less dire consequences, the scapegoating of women who transgressed normative gender roles expressed efforts to restore moral order through the reinscription of clearly defined male and female activities. Historians (among others) have also linked "Jewishness," femininity, and homosexuality by demonstrating how, by the end of the nineteenth century, these attributes became signifiers of bodily degradation and hence marks of racial "inferiority." My purpose here is to continue this work, and in particular to demonstrate how pornography and homosexuality were deemed emblematic of unregulated female sexuality. I do not, however, mean to add to this list by demonstrating how sexual deviants and pornographers were similarly scapegoated (although such scapegoating certainly occurred). Rather, I want to suggest not only that pornography and homosexuality have a degraded cultural status, but also that that degradation, at least since the war, is intrinsic to their cultural meaning. That is, neither homophobia nor anti-pornography sentiment are merely different sorts of prejudices against which tolerant people must struggle (or accommodate to); rather,

24. Although the literature is evidently vast, see George L. Mosse's synthetic account, *Toward the Final Solution: A History of European Racism* (Madison: University of Wisconsin Press, 1978).

they structure cultural norms that in turn inform institutional practices.[25] If both homosexuality and pornography have become metaphors for the violation of human dignity, can human rights arguments be made coherently in the context of sexuality? Many critics have argued that respect for the integral human body is a prerequisite for the elimination of torture, an argument against war, racism, sexism, and the violence they produce. But how, if certain sexual expressions or fantasies themselves intrinsically violate the body—if that is their cultural meaning—how can the "rights" of sexual dissidents be defined in terms of respect for the inviolability of their bodies?[26]

This book addresses this question implicitly by demonstrating how pornography and homosexuality became privileged (if not the only) repositories of the war's unprecedented violence—indeed, how they became synecdoches for sexuality itself, why, and with what effects. It argues that in spite of their differences, the two phenomena have comparable cultural functions in the often unacknowledged fantasy life of liberal democracy. Critics' discussions about pornography and homosexuality were really discussions about the social body's metaphorical masculinity and how to protect it from symbolic sexual violation—from shame, desecration, and subjugation.

25. Leroy-Forgeot, 61, 54–58, also notes that in spite of the separation of Church and state, homophobia persists: she calls this phenomenon "instinctive" homophobia, implying its irrationality. Similarly, she remarks that already in 1814 and 1815, Jeremy Bentham defended the depenalization of homosexuality on the grounds that legal strictures against it were irrational. Yet she never asks why liberal individualism, which has triumphed in promulgating the idea of tolerance generally, still meets "instinctive" resistance when the subject is homosexuality.

26. This question might also be asked in other contexts: I am thinking more specifically of race. On this question, see Ann Laura Stoler, *Race and the Education of Desire: Foucault's History of Sexuality and the Colonial Order of Things* (Durham, N.C.: Duke University Press, 1995).

After 1918, legislators, novelists, social and literary critics, and medical men no longer conceived of pornography and homosexuality as offensive public spectacles distinct and distinguishable from normal sexuality and civilized society. Instead, in different ways, both pornography and homosexuality became increasingly indistinct from normal sexuality. Commentators interpreted pornography's meaning as a threat to the masculine social body but could no longer locate that threat clearly in a specific collection of material. Pornography was no longer an offensive collection of too-visible texts and images; instead, it became a hidden repository of dangerous, annihilating, and undomesticated sexuality that lurked in the most benign bourgeois dwellings. Critics too reconceived the threat homosexuality posed to the social body now in terms of the *absence* of clear distinctions between homosexual men and women and the rest of the population. This book uses these changing definitions of pornography and homosexuality to understand how this imagined fluidity between the normal and the deviant was produced, interpreted, and resisted. In other words, both pornography and homosexuality became conceptually analogous, elusive repositories of social contamination whose identification and regulation were central to the defense and reconfiguration of the social body.

The published work to which I refer was penned primarily by journalists, novelists, legislators, and medical men who edited or wrote columns for (mostly) highbrow periodicals as well as by some men and women who challenged conventional wisdom—whom we would now label gay men and lesbians. Unless they were legislators, doctors, or policemen, I generally throughout the book refer to all of them as "cultural critics" or "critics" of various sorts. The chapters thus tease out different currents of thought concerning both homosexuality and pornography in this period; they refer to a wide variety of little-known texts and genres and sometimes unidentifiable authors in order to address intersections of many different levels of meaning. These critics defined the intellectual parameters of discussions in the postwar years and, in unexpected ways, traversed and linked diverse genres of material (where possible I indicate whether the work was for more elite or popular consumption).[27]

27. In order to sustain the multidimensionality of these discussions, then, I have sought to provide different kinds of writings, some of which were more marginal than others, mostly in the case of gay and lesbian voices. I should add that by using the terms "gay" and "lesbian" or "homosexual," I make a pragmatic rather than theoretical choice, for such language is more familiar and accessible than a term such as "queer." When appropriate, I use terms employed by the writers themselves, and when I move outside the specific historical context to speak more generally, I retain the more critically distant nouns. Finally, a few of my sources are foreign works that were seen as relevant enough to be translated—their themes clearly transcend national contexts, although for our purposes it is important simply that these works were translated.

The word "queer" has become increasingly popular among those scholars and others who repudiate the static concept of sexuality and sexual identity implicit in the use of the terms "gay" and "lesbian." That is, for some, since gay and lesbian identities were originally invented by medical men at the end of the nineteenth century, they bear the imprint of sexual regulation and define a person's character above all in the reductive terms of his or her sexuality. Moreover, many perceive them to validate gay monogamy and to invalidate other less normative sexual practices, such as sadomasochism or non-monogamy. Many gay men and lesbians, however, refrain from using the word "queer" because of its originally derogatory meaning—even though other pejorative words have been recuperated. Like "sexuality," "queer" is an analytic category that forces us to think about how cultural norms presume and conserve heterosexuality. Nevertheless, I think it wise to refrain from engaging in this debate here (except implicitly) and prefer to remain as straightforward and accessible as possible. For a brief discussion of terms, see the preface to Henry Abelove et al., eds., *The Gay and Lesbian Studies Reader* (New York: Routledge,

To the extent that commentators' rhetorical construction of pornography and homosexuality was interconstitutive, the work that follows is divided into two conceptually inextricable but analytically discrete sections. Both trace how the increasingly protean character of pornography and homosexuality became the dialectical point of departure for a new figuration of the integral body. Both sketch the changing construction of pornography and homosexuality in France from the late nineteenth century through 1940, using the late nineteenth century primarily as a backdrop to clarify or dramatize developments in the interwar period. The first section focuses on discourses about the proliferation of pornography, on discussions about the proper boundary between pornography and literature, and on debates about pornography's impact on patriotism. The second analyzes how critics forged a new image of the solid, heterosexual male body out of the newly fluid lines demarcating gay men and lesbians from straight men and women.

Together both sections aim to demonstrate how the mobility that defined both categories of meaning paradoxically constituted pornography and homosexuality as commensurate with the metaphorical degradation and violability of the integral body, and, in so doing, restored the ideally integral social body. The analysis focuses on the rhetorical construction of pornography and homosexuality rather than on the legal or social history of either term or with those bodies and materials thus labeled. Other scholars have recently begun to address the

1993), v–vii; see also Michael Warner, ed., *Fear of a Queer Planet: Queer Politics and Social Theory* (Minneapolis: University of Minnesota Press, 1993). For a trenchant critique of "queer" as a concept, see Leo Bersani, *Homos* (Cambridge, Mass.: Harvard University Press, 1995).

historical emergence of pornography and homosexuality. They analyze pornographic material, its criminalization and links to other forms of criminality, its networks of publication and distribution. Historians of homosexuality investigate the persecution of and community-building among gay men and lesbians as well as the constructions of erotic and gay identities.[28] I map another terrain: that of the collective fantasies that infuse and often generate the frameworks that define and regulate normative ethical communities.

This book focuses on an affective language about pornography and homosexuality that underlay medical, juridical, literary, and some popular discourses.[29] I trace

28. Among others, see Robert Darnton, *Edition et sédition: L'Univers de la littérature clandestine au XVIIIᵉ siècle* (Paris: Gallimard, 1991); Hunt, ed., *Invention of Pornography;* Annie Stora-Lamarre, *L'Enfer de la Troisième République: Censeurs et pornographes, 1880–1914* (Paris: Imago, 1990); Bryant T. Ragan and Jeffrey Merrick, eds., *Homosexuality in Modern France* (Oxford: Oxford University Press, 1996); (for a slightly more culturalist take) Aron and Kempf, *Bourgeoisie;* George Chauncey, *Gay New York: Gender, Urban Culture, and the Making of the Gay Male World, 1890–1940* (New York: Basic Books, 1994). For an interesting reading of the origins of modern pornography that is not, however, historical, see Frances Ferguson, "Sade and the Pornographic Legacy," *Representations* 36 (Fall 1991): 1–21.

29. In so doing, I draw on recent and methodologically varied studies of the modern theory and history of the body and sexuality, most, if not all, of which have in common a focus on the affective dimension of even the most resolutely "scientific" and secular constructions of the body (the nineteenth-century alignment, for example, of cultural memory with heredity). Such studies trace primarily what Michel Foucault termed "the cultural unconscious"—the sociopolitical desire that undergirds and constitutes the power of institutions but cannot be reduced to or centralized in them. For Foucault and his followers (to whom this book is indebted and from whom it parts), that desire resides in no necessarily visible location, but shapes human bodies by systematically and rationally yoking "biological existence" to "political existence" (in the image and interests of its own power). In so doing, that power transforms "the fact of living" into knowledge: its workings are embedded in specific "rituals of power" and discursive practices.

For an excellent study of discourses of biology and memory in rela-

one dimension of that language of collective fantasies, and reconstruct the sometimes intangible ideas that both engendered and informed them to analyze how those ideas became meaningful at a particular place and time.[30]

---

tionship to a fantasmic social body, see Laura Otis, *Organic Memory: History and Body in the Late Nineteenth and Early Twentieth Centuries* (Lincoln: University of Nebraska Press, 1994). Otis argues that by the mid nineteenth century, thinkers before and after Darwin produced their own vision of the social body that viewed the state in terms of the history of biology, and memory in terms of the biological transmission of "race" and heredity from body to body. Rose, *States of Fantasy*, 8, claims that the "inner life" of the state has always been present but never adequately explained, consisting of "the factors which [Max Weber] lays out as most recalcitrant to sociological [and one might add historical] explanation . . . ends which defy intellectual grasp, hidden 'motives' and 'repressions.'"

Foucault uses the term "cultural unconscious" in "Rituals of Exclusion," in *Foucault Live (Interviews, 1966–84)*, trans. John Johnston (New York: Semiotext(e): 1989), 71. He uses the term "biopower" to describe this process in *The History of Sexuality*, vol. 1: *An Introduction* (New York: Random House, Vintage Books, 1980), 140. As many scholars have noted, Foucault never clarifies how individual bodies are shaped by the sociopolitical desire of sovereign power. There is now a voluminous interdisciplinary literature on the history of bodies in both early modern and modern Europe, usually but not always intertwined with other discussions of race, sexuality, and gender. See, among others, Agamben, *Homo Sacer;* Antoine de Baecque, *Le Corps de l'histoire: Métaphores et politique (1770–1800)* (Paris: Calmann-Lévy, 1993); Julia Epstein and Kristina Straub, eds., *Body Guards: The Cultural Politics of Gender Ambiguity* (New York: Routledge, 1991); Feher, ed., *Fragments for a History;* Thomas Laqueur, *Making Sex: Body and Gender from the Greeks to Freud* (Cambridge, Mass.: Harvard University Press, 1990); Phillipe Perrot, *Le Travail des apparences: Le Corps féminin XVIIIe–XIXe siècle* (Paris: Seuil, 1984); Barbara Maria Stafford, *Body Criticism: Imaging the Unseen in Enlightenment Art and Medicine* (Cambridge, Mass.: MIT Press, 1991); Klaus Theweleit, *Male Fantasies*, 2 vols. (Minneapolis: University of Minnesota Press, 1987). The classic anthropology text is Mary Douglas, *Purity and Danger: An Analysis of the Conception of Pollution and Taboo* (New York: Routledge, 1995).

30. Of course, many theorists have sought to interpret the meaning of sexual deviance by reference to the psychic dimension of culture. As productive as psychically grounded discussions of culture are, they usually proceed by analogy—nationalism, for example, is like paranoia, of which homophobia is a form—rather than explaining how nationalism, racism, or homophobia is constituted as paranoid. Victor Burgin remarks that he has begun "to look at nationalism, at racism, *as if* they might

Most important, the book tries to understand how they expressed a seemingly inexpressible fear about the social body's fluidity. As cultural theorists have argued in other contexts, such fantasies are a means of constituting the meaning of sexual deviance and hence consequential ways of imagining the normative body. Of course, perceptions of deviant sexuality are embedded in institutional modes of action (e.g., censorship, penal laws). I cannot here demonstrate exactly how those perceptions led to the implementation of social policies, but I do analyze how those perceptions were constituted and speculate about how they facilitated the formation and maintenance of social norms, at least on a symbolic level.[31]

---

indeed be paranoid structures." Here psychoanalytic theory takes the role of elaborating the "as if." The empirical link between the logic of paranoia and of culture, of the psychic and the cultural, thus remains elusive. See Burgin, *In/Different Spaces: Place and Memory in Visual Culture* (Berkeley and Los Angeles: University of California Press, 1996), 137. Other examples might include Judith Butler, *The Psychic Life of Power* (New York: Routledge, 1997); Eric Santner, *My Own Private Germany: Daniel Paul Schreber's Secret History of Modernity* (Princeton, N.J.: Princeton University Press, 1996); Eve Kosofsky Sedgwick, *Epistemology of the Closet* (Berkeley and Los Angeles: University of California Press, 1990), Slavoj Žižek, *The Plague of Fantasies* (London: Verso, 1997), 3–44. The difficulty of reconciling arguments rooted in the logic of the psyche and historical arguments that require specific contextual frameworks is wonderfully exemplified by two of Kendall Thomas's essays: one insists on the permeability of the social body and the other, in which he tries to make a case for the legal protection of consensual gay sex, argues for the body's fundamental impermeability. Remember too that Giorgio Agamben argues most persuasively that the body has always been permeable. See Thomas, "Corpus Juris (Hetero) Sexualis: Doctrine, Discourse, and Desire in Bowers v. Hardwick," *Gay and Lesbian Quarterly* 1 (1993): 33–51, and id., "Beyond the Privacy Principle."

31. The methodological problem of linking social, economic, and political trends to cultural ones while respecting the complexity of each dimension of institutional formation has not been confronted successfully by any historian or cultural theorist yet. Wendy Brown has recently articulated the problem as the necessity of theorizing the relation between "subject formation" and "social positioning." Roger Chartier, *On the Edge*

Cultural fantasies about sexuality are very difficult to explore, not only because sexuality itself is so intangible a category of historical meaning, but because our investments in normative sexuality are often not clearly related to socioeconomic or political interests and intersect in extremely complex ways with race and gender. This book seeks to interpret those fantasies in order to understand why and how homosexuality and pornography came to mean what they did and to speculate about the effects of those meanings. I shy away from any psychoanalytic paradigm because of the overwhelming methodological complexity such an analysis poses, and thus leave that task to others. I offer a less theoretically constrained but I hope no less rigorous argument. More specifically, historians of sexuality generally neglect the interwar period or analyze its preoccupations as extensions of nineteenth-century concerns. Although this emphasis on continuity is historically accurate, I hope to show that fantasies about sexual deviance (or, here, pornography and homosexuality) during the interwar years deserve the scrutiny conventionally restricted to fascism and the effects of war on politics, class, and gender relations.

The history of the shifting definitions of pornography and homosexuality after the Great War more specifically captures one unwritten dimension of the story about how cultural critics envisioned and reconstructed the

---

of the Cliff: History, Language, and Practices, trans. Lydia G. Cochrane (Baltimore: Johns Hopkins University Press, 1997), terms that relation one between "discourse" and "practice." See Brown, *States of Injury,* 119, 142 n. 13, and the discussion of Chartier's *On the Edge of a Cliff* by Bonnie Smith, Jonathan Dewald, William Sewell, and Chartier himself in *French Historical Studies* 21 (Spring 1998): 213–64. For an interesting but problematic effort to link culture and society in a methodologically revealing way, see Dominique Kalifa, *L'Encre et le sang: Récits de crimes et société à la Belle Epoque* (Paris: Fayard, 1995).

meaning of bodily integrity in liberal democratic states. By tracing the changing constructions of homosexuality and pornography, this book traces the process by which legislators and cultural critics rhetorically restored expropriated bodies to their rightful owners, and thus seeks to explain how symbolic property is divided and distributed, and, perhaps most important, to whom.

1

Pornography and Perversion

Mens sana in corpore sano.
Juvenal, *Satires* 10.356

A sound mind in a sound body, is a short but full
description of a happy state in this world.
John Locke, *Some Thoughts on Education* (1693)

How did interwar commentators reconceive the meaning
of pornography such that it thematized new fears about
sexual deviance and more generally, moral decline? What
is the relationship between fantasies about pornography
and the remaking of the integral body after the war?
This chapter begins to address these questions by demonstrating how the perception that pornography was an
identifiable body of material slowly dissipated as critics
became increasingly alarmed at pornography's proliferation. Historians have recently conceived of this proliferation as a symptom of democratization. In so doing, they
challenge an older vision, best represented by the historians Montgomery Hyde and Giuseppe Lo Duca, who both
argued that pornography was the product of repressive
social attitudes and policies: the "unenlightened," "irrational," and prudish views of cultural or religious conservatives forced sexuality into "aberrant" channels, blinded
us to the real value of great art and literature deemed

"obscene," and thus distorted, repressed, and ruined the natural beauty of human sexual expression.[1]

Recent accounts call into question this progressive liberal vision because it treats pornography ahistorically as a symptom of repressed and hence unnatural sexuality. In so doing, newer histories insist that the categories of natural and unnatural are themselves historical, that pornography's meaning is never univocal and self-evident, and link its modern forms more specifically to the dissemination of democratic ideas. This challenge to the older progressive vision has come primarily from scholars of the early modern period but also, to a lesser extent, from historians of contemporary Europe and the United States.[2] "If we take pornography to be the explicit

1. See Havelock Ellis, *More Essays of Love and Virtue* (London: Constable, 1931). H. Montgomery Hyde, *A History of Pornography* (New York: Farrar, Straus and Giroux, 1965); Giuseppe Lo Duca, *L'Histoire de l'érotisme* (Paris: Le Jeune Parque, 1969); Steven Marcus, *The Other Victorians: A Study of Sexuality and Pornography in Mid-Nineteenth-Century England* (New York: Norton, 1964). More recently, a similar argument has been extended in several directions. Susan Sontag tries to make a case that not all literature heretofore deemed pornographic necessarily deserves that label. But she also retains the distinction between pornography and literature on the grounds that the former is an inferior literary form and the product of Judeo-Christian repression. The arguments of anti-pornography feminists such as Andrea Dworkin and Catharine MacKinnon must be distinguished from the kinds of liberal arguments cited above, because they conceive of pornography as the product of patriarchal power rather than repression. But they do share with those arguments the conviction that pornography is the product of a culture that distorts the "truth" about human sexuality. In the first case, the distorted truth is sexuality generally; in the second, feminist, case, it is female sexuality. Sontag, "The Pornographic Imagination," in id., *Styles of Radical Will* (New York: Farrar, Straus and Giroux, 1969), 35–73; Dworkin, *Pornography: Men Possessing Women* (New York: Putnam, 1981). There is now an increasingly voluminous feminist literature about pornography contesting both Dworkin and MacKinnon. The "sex wars" are not immediately relevant to this study, however, so my account of the debate is necessarily reductive.

2. Of course, many American literary and film theorists have addressed pornography in the United States; but for the most part such studies are not historical.

depiction of sexual organs and sexual practices with the aim of arousing sexual feelings, then pornography was almost always an adjunct to something else until the middle to the end of the eighteenth century," Lynn Hunt argues.[3] Her suggestion provides pornography with historical context and its meaning with texture. For until the mid nineteenth century, pornography, as Hunt puts it, "used the shock of sex to criticize religious and political authorities." The Enlightenment emphasis on nature rendered "the material fact of sex" a particularly useful device to attack the artificiality of so-called divinely ordained hierarchies: "political" pornography in the form of verses and pamphlets against royal figures not only humanized them but transformed them into particularly bestial and corrupt specimens of humanity who indulged rather than constrained the most unspeakable desires. In short, pornography's emergence was coincident with the emergence of democratic ideals and harnessed sex explicitly in the service of political critique.

Hunt notes that the link between democracy and pornography became particularly evident by the 1880s, when the consolidation of liberal governments and the development of a popular press itself dependent upon mass literacy made possible a new audience for pornography and variations in the forms of its consumption.[4] In keeping with this insight, Annie Stora-Lamarre and Walter Kendrick, among others, do not conceive of pornography as the product of Victorian hypocrisy or censorship, as did their liberal predecessors, but rather as the product of late-nineteenth-century secularization.[5] According to

3. Lynn Hunt, ed., *The Invention of Pornography: Obscenity and the Origins of Modernity: 1500–1800* (New York: Zone Books, 1991), 10.

4. Ibid., 23.

5. Annie Stora-Lamarre, *L'Enfer de la Troisième République: Censeurs et pornographes, 1880–1914* (Paris: Imago, 1990); Walter Kendrick,

them, upper-class elites defined pornographic literature
as all material likely to distract women and working-class
men from their national duty: from combat, reproduction, and productive labor. It included implicitly and
explicitly sexual texts and images, pacifist literature,
and contraceptive information.[6] Pornography threatened
the lifeblood of the nation and undermined good and
healthy citizenship by encouraging loose morals, especially among those groups that elites deemed most susceptible to its influence. In France—but also in England,
Germany, and the United States—the modern concept of
the pornographic was solidified by the 1880s, and its
emergence was concomitant with the threat posed to
elites by workers and women in a period of increasing wealth, consumption, and literacy. Pornography was,
then, a category of material created, invented, and produced as a means to regulate and target the moral behavior of certain populations. The seizure of and legislation against so-called pornographic work provided a
means of increasing the surveillance of working-class
people and all women. For pornography to exist, "a public which might be corrupted by obscene publications
had to exist."[7]

The Secret Museum: Pornography in Modern Culture (New York: Penguin
Books, 1987).

6. Annie Stora-Lamarre, "Plaisirs interdits: L'Enfer de la Bibliothèque
nationale," in Pascal Ory, ed., *La Censure en France à l'ère démocratique*
(Brussels: Editions complexes, 1997), 43–52, claims that three strains predominated in sexually explicit texts in France: scenes took place in Russia
or in the colonies, reflecting racist beliefs about the presumably more
erotic nature of "Eastern" peoples; they unfolded in closed spaces cut off
from the outside and so free from regulation (convents, brothels); and they
privileged England as the locale of sadomasochism.

7. Ian Hunter, David Saunders, and Dugald Williamson, *On Pornography: Literature, Sexuality, and Obscenity Law* (New York: St. Martin's Press,
1993), 88.

The chapter that follows presumes this relationship between pornography and democratization but argues that
under the increasing pressure of modernization (democratization, urbanization, technological changes), whatever solidity the pornography concept possessed began
to dissolve. The chapter begins with a broad historical
overview of the increasingly malleable meanings attributed to pornography between 1880 and 1940 by critics of
all sorts, and proceeds to a discussion of interwar police
and trial records registering the effects of that mutability.
I use the discussions about pornography's perceived proliferation to demonstrate how critics eventually constituted pornography as intrinsically elastic and yet oddly
definable, as a fluid category and yet as a specific genre.
In so doing, their discussions generated and manifested a
newly emerging formation of sexuality in which desire
was, paradoxically, difficult to locate. Later chapters trace
this formation, whose contours I begin to outline here.

The Emergence of Pornography

In July 1881, the same year they codified freedom of the
press, French legislators passed an anti-pornography law
that substituted a secular social contract for the moral
absolutes of the old regime. Now texts and images were
no longer to be judged according to their depictions of
religion and monarchy, but condemned or approved
based on whether they conformed to received ideas about
proper moral life in a liberal state. Thus, legislators sought
to regulate "les outrages aux bonnes mœurs" as an intentional infraction (*malignité d'intention*) against the social
body that offended "decent and honest citizens in a civilized society."[8] As early as 1806, Etienne-Gabriel Peignot

8. Daniel Bécourt, *Livres condamnés, livres interdits, régime juridique
du livre, liberté ou censure?* (Paris: Cercle de la Librairie, 1972), 111. In

(in the first modern use of the term "pornography") asserted that pornographic books could be censored for
moral as well as religious and political reasons (i.e., blas-
phemy or satire).[9] In 1819, the Napoleonic Code officially
censored written work, songs, and pamphlets. But the
Code still distinguished between the regulation of acts
and of ideas, between the censorship of "offenses against
public decency" (*outrages à la pudeur*) and the expression
of "bad morals" in texts. All press censorship (excepting
dramatic work) was abolished in the Charter of 1830, and
censorship of the theater was finally eliminated in 1906.
In 1836, the "Enfer" ("Hell") section was established at
the Bibliothèque nationale as a repository for seized or
condemned licentious books. In the absence of explicit
censorship laws concerning books, editors published at
their own risk, knowing that they might be prosecuted
under other statutes relating to the preservation of morality—hence the spectacular obscenity trials of Gustave
Flaubert and Charles Baudelaire in 1857. Until 1881, censorship in practice was aimed primarily at politically in-
flammatory melodrama with potentially corrupting social themes. But by the early years of the Third Republic
(1870–1940), legislators were already arguing that a wide
variety of writing constituted an intentional infraction
against social order and sought to regulate it in more precise legal terms.[10]

1791, the French revolutionaries had for the first time ushered in legislation that repudiated censorship in the name of individual liberty (except
regarding images and illustrations),

   9. Hunt, ed., *Invention of Pornography*, 14.

   10. Films were first censored in 1909, and all films had to be approved
by a jury of censors between 1936 and 1945. See Jean-Pierre Jeancolas,
"Cinéma, censure, controle, classement," in Ory, ed., *Censure*, 213–21,
and, on the Second Empire, Odile Krakovitch, "La Censure des spectacles
sous le Second Empire," in ibid., 53–76.

This paradox whereby legislators at once codified freedom of the press and sought to censor a certain rather nebulous genre of material in these very expansive terms was thus an effort to produce a normative framework within which to regulate behavior. But it also reflected new social pressures. For the metamorphosis of pornography in France as a category of meaning coincided with the consolidation of liberal government and its gender and class interests and was articulated in the rhetoric of "degeneration" (*dégénération*), a term first used by the French doctor Bénédict-Auguste Morel in 1857 to define metal pathology. Degeneration eventually symbolized the self-indulgence, excess, and individualism associated with (too much) democratization, urbanization, and mass culture—with its department stores, its advertising, films, and promises of luxury to increasing numbers of people.[11]

Such fears about democratization and the so-called emasculation of the nation intensified after France's humiliating defeat in the Franco-Prussian war, which led to the Commune uprising of 1870–71 and hence to the failed overthrow of a conservative regime by heirs of the *sans-culottes*. Moreover, the demographic decline in which France's population was rising at a lower rate than that of her neighbors fueled anxiety about French weakness compared to her German rival, and generated other concerns about feminist demands for the vote and women seeking alternatives to careers as wives and mothers. All of these developments, then—unruly mobs challenging state authority, the so-called natality crisis, and the threat of feminism—were blamed on a perceived

---

11. Bénédict-Auguste Morel, *Traité des dégénérences physiques, intellectuelles et morales de l'espèce humaine* (Paris: Ballière, 1857).

unraveling of social discipline explained by reference to the overstimulation of nerves that doctors believed to be peculiar to modern urban life. The perception that pornography was dangerous thus reflects anxieties summed up concisely by Albert Eyquem in 1905. Eyquem bemoaned the "softness" of French society in the aftermath of the Franco-Prussian War and gave several reasons for the proliferation of pornography: moral crisis, including the weakening of family ties; the lack of systematic prosecution of pornographers; the lack of national solidarity and consensus; the early freedom given to children; and the degradation of working-class morality facilitated by divorce and alcoholism.[12] Degeneration was thus both cause and effect of cultural decline, a metaphor for cultural dissolution and a descriptive term applicable to various social groups—in particular "degenerate" working-class radicals, prostitutes, homosexuals, and feminists—who threatened to undermine the productivity and stability of the social body.

Across the professional spectrum, elites, whatever their ideological differences, thus represented social order and disorder in terms of a medical model of the social body. Legislators aimed quite specifically to censor "pornographic" material because so-called degenerates had unbalanced nervous centers and were extremely susceptible to external sense impressions. Doctors insisted that susceptible men who read the marquis de Sade would become sadists, and defense lawyers for the writer Marguerite Coppin claimed she was a deranged woman whose pornographic work reflected her mental disar-

12. Albert Eyquem, *De la Repression des outrages à la morale publique et aux bonnes mœurs ou de la pornographie au point de vue historique, juridique, législatif et social* (Paris: Marchal & Billard, 1905), 195, 188.

ray.[13] They imagined a vertiginous spiral in which the proliferation of pornography led to the proliferation of degenerates and eventually to the dissolution of culture itself. In so doing, they used an excessive, undisciplined sexuality to symbolize the loosening of social bonds implicit in the concept of degeneration.

Legislators accordingly defined pornography as material that undermined the normative, productive, and hence healthy sexuality of the ideal social body, and the category "pornographic," recall, included birth control information and pacifist literature as well as sexually explicit texts and images. Grassroots groups formed to fight pornography and consistently low birthrates, including the Fédération des Groupements de familles nombreuses, and the Alliance nationale pour l'accroissement de la natalité, among others. Such groups defined their common struggle as a battle to protect "the sanctity of the home, youth, [and] women from immorality," and to abolish "state-regulated prostitution, debauchery, libertinage, and propaganda advocating abortion and contraception."[14] For the most part these "hygiene" groups formed after the law permitting the creation of associations was passed in 1901. Inspired in part by Swiss Protestant leagues struggling against immorality, French versions similarly attracted both Protestants and militant Catholics.[15] But they also aligned themselves with the

13. Jacobus X (Augustin Cabanès), *Le Marquis de Sade devant la science médicale et la littérature moderne* (Paris: Carrington, 1901), 225; Stora-Lamarre, *Enfer de la Troisième République,* 162.

14. Emile Pourésy, *Le Bilan de la pornographie* (Paris: Bibliothèque nationale, 1934), 2.

15. For a full discussion of the leagues against immorality in France and their origins, see Stora-Lamarre, *Enfer de la Troisième République,* 80–81.

fight against "depopulation" waged since the end of the century, and traversed both the left and the right of the political spectrum, since both conservatives and republicans were concerned, for different reasons, with the effects of moral decline and a low birthrate. In short, they aimed to combat the threat of venereal disease and alcoholism and organized to cleanse France of prostitution and pornography: moralists believed both "scourges" were responsible for the dissemination of immorality and the ill health of the national body. In 1894, Senator René Bérenger introduced a bill to prevent the "teaching of immorality through the eyes" aimed largely (but not exclusively) at prostitution. The Chamber of Deputies passed a watered-down version of the bill in 1885.[16]

Under the leadership of Bérenger, known by his detractors as Père-la-Pudeur, legislators had already passed laws against "les outrages aux bonnes mœurs" in 1881, and in new, expanded versions in 1882, 1898, and 1908, all of which were promulgated in the name of a "défense de la famille." "Outrages" included selling pornographic images, texts, and material about contraception. In order to extend the law's repressive arm as far as possible, lawmakers defined "outrages" in 1898 to include all material that "provoked," "incited," or "stimulated debauchery," and used these concepts to prosecute texts that were not evidently "obscene" because they did not contain *explicitly* sexual or offensive words or images. Penalties were much more severe for infractions in newspapers or in pamphlets than for pornographic books, and included both hefty fines and the abrogation of the right to vote for

16. Bérenger quoted in Alain Corbin, *Women for Hire: Prostitution and Sexuality in France after 1850*, trans. Alan Sheridan (Cambridge, Mass.: Harvard University Press, 1990), 317.

up to six months. Between 1899 and 1907, the number of those condemned for violations quadrupled. Many of the violators were working-class hustlers out to make easy money, but many were poor Jewish immigrants who sold obscene literature to feed their families.[17] Targets of censorship ranged from Jean Richepin's highly politicized, scatological popular songs to reproductions of Antoine Watteau's *Embarquement pour Cythère* (Voyage to Cythera), which members of the elite could view at the Louvre with impunity.[18]

The Meaning of Pornography

The danger posed by pornography was thus inseparable from anxieties about democratization, and rhetoric about pornography as a symptom of democracy and degeneration abounded in the late nineteenth century and into the early twentieth.

One fin-de-siècle critic noted that pornography had escaped the confines of the brothel where it had originated (since pornography in Greek originally meant writing about prostitutes). The scholar Etienne Bricon's entry for pornography in the *Grande Encyclopédie* compared pornography to a prostitute, not to explain its origins but to clarify its modern meaning: pornography was above all an act of making private sentiments and behaviors inappropriately public; pornographic representations "divulged the mystery of love." Thus, what made pornography pornography was that it put things "on scene." Love, Bricon declared, keeps its beauty only as long as it retains its secrets. By revealing secrets meant to remain secret,

---

17. Stora-Lamarre, *Enfer de la Troisième République*, 164–66.
18. Lionel d'Autrec, *L'Outrage aux mœurs* (Paris: L'Epi, 1923), 92.

pornography was no different than a woman who sells herself on the street.[19]

Bricon used prostitutes as an analogy because they also confused the spatial symbolism of private and public. Nineteenth-century critics often invoked the specter of prostitution to symbolize the dissolution of boundaries between public and private spheres, since women who sell their bodies transform themselves into "public" spectacles and mock the sanctity of the private spiritual bond upon which marriage is founded. At the fin-de-siècle, the consensus about pornography's meaning (in spite of varying attitudes toward censorship) was really a consensus about the proper boundary between public and private. Annie Stora-Lamarre argues that "for there to be an infraction [of the law] the obscene book had to receive publicity."[20] Echoing the idea that there was now a "public" unconstrained by the ethical imperatives that allowed elites to view all art without dangerous consequences, the art critic Georges Fonsegrive wrote in 1911 that art could not be held morally accountable except when it was exhibited publicly. Before a broad audience, art lost its immunity from prosecution and was answerable to those worried about its effects on the individual, the community, and hence on the "species."[21]

But still, what constituted indecent literature? Why was its traversal of the boundary between private and public inappropriate? Why was publicity given to some representations so dangerous? The answer was, apparently, self-evident. In his treatise on "public morality," Al-

---

19. Etienne Bricon, "Pornographie," in *La Grande Encyclopédie* (Paris: Société Anonyme de la Grande Encyclopédie, 1895), 27: 321–22.

20. Stora-Lamarre, *L'Enfer de la Troisième République*, 133.

21. Georges Fonsegrive, *Art et pornographie* (Paris: Blond, 1911), 57; Stora-Lamarre, *Enfer de la Troisième République*, 113.

bert Eyquem noted that for material to be subject to the laws of 1881, 1882, and 1898, it had to be "contraire aux bonnes mœurs." Yet, at the same time, he insists that no "legislator, however, could provide [a] definition [of what that infraction would consist]." He quotes Senator Devaux, who apparently claimed that "it is not possible . . . to define [this crime] and the commission of the Chamber of Deputies has sought vainly to do so." Eyquem himself argues that "in the end, there is an 'outrage aux bonnes mœurs' where there is an obscene publication." While he recognized clearly that the laws were imprecise, he still asserted confidently that "though this leaves the meaning of [the crime] rather arbitrary, it nevertheless permits us to affirm that the law tolerates publications that take a certain license but do not push the limits of the obscene," and, moreover, that "between the licentious and the obscene, it is easier to feel the difference than to explain it."[22]

In France, even civil libertarians who criticized the new censors and the new legislation had no problem "feeling" the difference between art and pornography and worried only that philistines charged with enforcing the law would confuse art and obscenity. Hence in 1905 several writers founded the League for the Liberty of Art to fight the anti-pornography crusader René Bérenger, but its members confined themselves to attacking the imprecision of "bonnes mœurs," not to defending pornography. What, asked a writer for the satirical journal *L'Assiette au beurre,* makes my journal obscene? The publisher, Hachette, had received a request to forbid sale of the magazine in the Orléans train station for no other reason than that it was offensive, but the law, he claimed,

·

22. Eyquem, *De la répression,* 34.

provided no means for determining the criteria by which it could be judged offensive.[23] And in a reference to the idea that a pornographic writer always intended to commit an infraction against social order, another author writing in the same magazine noted that the law provided no clear distinction between good and bad morals, and asked: "Is it possible that a citizen can commit a crime without realizing it and be punished for an unconsciously committed infraction?"[24] Clearly, another concluded, "for these gentlemen [anti-pornography crusaders] so-called pornography is only a convenient pretext for suffocating thought and persecuting Art."[25]

Most of the writers for the journal go on to protest the purity campaign waged by Bérenger on the grounds that the lawmaker targeted great art while ignoring "real" pornography. They were echoed by commentators elsewhere, who denounced Bérenger and his allies for not recognizing the difference between pornography and art. Maurice Hamel noted that Bérenger "pursues those works that constitute the glory of French art but lets . . . pornography breed in the Palais Royal and ignores all the purulence of the café concert."[26] Another columnist insisted that censorship was problematic unless a real distinction could be established between pornographers and artists.[27] In short, while they denounced censorship, all these writers had a pretty good idea of what constituted pornography, even though, like Eyquem, they constantly

23. *Assiette au beurre*, January 1906, n.p.
24. Ibid.
25. Ibid., February 1906, n.p.
26. Maurice Hamel, "La Pornographie au café-concert," *Courrier français*, 15 February 1913, 8.
27. Curnovsky, "Sur la progrès de la pornographie," *Vie parisienne*, 11 November 1905, 904.

allude to the fundamental imprecision of the category. Sources thus do not suggest that contemporaries had any doubt about what constituted pornography, even if they could not explain its meaning clearly, even if, as Senator Devaux remarked, the entire legislature had sought to define pornography "in vain." Though it is true that anti-pornography legislation covered a wide array of texts, prosecution was typically conducted with genuine confidence in the solidity of the pornography concept.

The Proliferation of Pornography

At the same time, this solidity came under pressure in the context of the perceived proliferation of pornographic material. As some historians have demonstrated, this increased focus on pornography's dangers displaced other anxieties about gender boundaries, about the degeneration of a nation that many bourgeois Frenchmen believed had been sapped of its vital energy because of population decline, feminism, and democratization. These late-nineteenth-century themes were reiterated over and over in commentaries about pornography, primarily by critics, as we have seen, who sought to delineate clear boundaries between the muck of pornography and uplifting "art." And, as I have argued, many critics "knew" when material was pornographic (they simply did not trust legislators to make that determination), and others associated it with the decline of the spiritual bond forged by domesticated heterosexuality and symbolized by the increased commercialization of sex. That association between moral decline and pornography remained prominent.

Pornography increasingly replaced prostitution as the privileged metaphor for moral decline, commodity culture, and the loosening of spiritual bonds that threatened to undermine the mind's defenses against the "hot and penetrating" power of sensuous stimuli.[28] The increase in nudity at popular theaters, and later the popularity of radio and cinema, also provided new symbols for the vulnerability of the tremulous private body and hence new symbols for the rhetorical destruction of the impermeable social body as well.[29] There were plenty of popular theatrical productions, from the Grand Guignol to the café-concert to the music hall, that used nudes as public entertainment. Moreover, on the eve of 1914, most of the café-concerts had been transformed into larger music halls that mixed classes and genres and thus created an even larger audience for such spectacles.[30] One of the most popular forms of entertainment were "tableaux" consisting of white women with their bodies bound by flesh-colored cloth to look nude, posed in imitation of classical statuary. This immobility was morally respectable, but such respectable performances were becoming increasingly rare. "[S]ince the beginning of this century, the nude has little by little affirmed its indispensability to revues, while also becoming increasingly scabrous and pornographic, increasingly audacious— no longer spiritual," two contemporary commentators noted.[31]

Critics worried less about pornography's effects on women, children, and working-class people (although

28. Edmond Haraucourt, *La Démoralisation par le livre et par l'image* (Paris: Ollendorff, 1917), 16–17.
29. For a recent overview of popular culture in the interwar period, see Charles Rearick, *The French in Love and War: Popular Culture in the Era of the World Wars* (New Haven, Conn.: Yale University Press, 1997).
30. Concetta Condemni, *Café-concerts: Histoire d'un divertissement* (Paris: Quai Voltaire, 1992), 61.
31. G. Witoswki and Lucien Nass, *Le Nu au théâtre depuis l'antiquité jusqu'à nos jours* (Paris: Paragon, 1909), 212.

they did worry) than on how the means of pornography's transmission had multiplied in the past two decades, reaching and ruining even the hardiest souls. "[W]e are drowning in garbage. It takes all forms: texts, images, novels, newspapers; it exhibits itself brazenly on the cover[s] of magazines, hides hypocritically under the aegis of art. . . . [I]t transforms itself into postcards, classified ads, . . . approaches passersby. . . . The virus operates . . . the slow poison does its work," Adolphe Brisson observed.[32] There was "no longer any vice that has not become the object of a specialized monograph," another critic asserted, and those monographs could be found everywhere.[33] In a series of articles penned for the journal *L'Oeuvre* in the early 1920s, the critic Gustave Téry denounced the perceived proliferation of pornography in even more dramatic terms: "[T]he pornographic tide threatens to engulf respectable bookstores"; "all honest citizens recoil before this rising tide of refuse now overwhelming French literature . . . we now have a new 'pornographic school.'"[34]

Transitions

In the years before the war, pornography thus became increasingly identified with the expanding public sphere and with moral decline itself. The ordinary citizen and anti-pornography activist Emile Pourésy defined pornography as the insatiable demand for increasing thrills ("all the vices contrary to life and *contre nature*"), and characterized that demand in general terms, associating it with no one social group, gender, or particular "type" of

32. Adolphe Brisson quoted in Emile Pourésy, *Sous la fléau de l'immoralité: Cris d'alarme* (Paris: Relèvement social, 1936), 246.
33. Curnonsky, "Sur le progres," 904.
34. Gustave Téry, *L'Ecole des garçonnes* (Paris: L'Oeuvre, 1923), 17, 13.

person. In 1898, Senator Bérenger penned and pushed through a law that extended the 1881 and 1882 laws to cover classified ads and exhibitions in music halls. The law thus not only regulated pornography but identified it with an extended public sphere that included new forms of popular advertisements, leisure activities, and a large reading public. Pornography was so omnipresent that it was perceived to be not only coextensive with the public sphere, but also the cause and effect of moral decline. Pourésy attributed its origin to a generalized "moral corruption," but at the same time, attributes moral corruption to pornography.[35] The philosopher Edmond Goblot noted that "pornography is the effect of moral corruption rather than its cause," but also that "pornography caused moral corruption."[36] The nationalist social critic Georges Deherme declared that society was in a state of moral dissolution when "ethical principles are weakened, ideas confused, rules unknown, and souls no longer have direction." In such a society, he claimed, pornography finds a haven, and it is therefore a symptom of social and economic "anarchy." But even though he argued that this anarchy created the demand for pornography, he also insisted that "literature alters morals," as if bad literature could cause the social dissolution of which he claimed it was an effect.[37] Pornography was the eerie symptom of a society in the process of dissolution, a process of which pornography was also supposed to be the primary cause.

35. Pourésy, *Sous La fléau*, 248.
36. Quoted in Stora-Lamarre, *Enfer de la Troisième République*, 93.
37. Georges Deherme quoted in [Abbé] Louis Bethléem, *La Littérature ennemie de la famille* (Paris: Blond & Gay, 1923), 110; Georges Deherme, *Les Classes moyennes: Etude sur le parasitisme social* (Paris: Perrin, 1912), 309.

This tautology and its attendant imprecision eventually began to metamorphose into the meaning of pornography. Indeed, critics eventually identified pornography not only with the public sphere but with the wholesale possession of the private body by the public spectacle. Pornography "taught immorality through the eyes" and entered the body in spite of itself. It was thus no longer dependent for its destructive consequences on a particularly weak or unformed mind or state of nerves. Critics began to dispense with allusions to nerves and inherited pathologies and emphasized instead suffocation, disgust, and nausea in particular as a way of describing pornography's effects and their dissemination. They now drew almost exclusively upon these terms, which were originally used by medical men to link physical and moral hygiene by reference to the body's need for clean air to combat the suffocation, stagnation, and malodorous atmosphere of decaying urban centers.[38] In 1903, for example, the critic Ernest Charles wrote that after meandering in certain theaters, spectators leave "nauseated and disgusted."[39] According to the critic Flers in 1909, contemporary scenes of nudes provoke "the most brutal and the most undisguised immorality, which leads to disgust."[40] Or, as Adolphe Brisson wrote in reference to another performance: "At certain moments this lugubrious furor, this frenzy went so far that a real malaise took over the audience . . . the dialogue exhaled an odor so bestial that more than one spectator felt secretly nauseous."[41]

38. Jean-Paul Aron and Roger Kempf, *La Bourgeoisie, le sexe, et l'honneur* (Brussels: Editions complexes, 1984), 230.
39. Ernest Charles quoted in Eyquem, *De la répression*, 147.
40. Quoted in Witowski and Nass, *Le Nu*, 213.
41. Quoted in ibid., 216–17.

The morals of the brothel, he continued, had ceased to be confined to brothels and had now "penetrated" the theater, and this penetration, as it were, quite literally seemed to make audiences dizzy, vertiginous, ill, and nauseous. The critic Etienne Lang wrote in *L'Echo de Paris* that the only way to sustain the spiritual effects and hence the "chaste stimulus" of true art was to immobilize women's bodies; women's animate movements on stage produced a state of vertigo that began as excitement and ended as nausea and a sense of intolerable abjection and self-hatred.[42]

Georges Deherme reiterated predictable themes about pornography as a symptom of moral decline in his 1912 work on "social parasitism." He also noted that "art propagated by such measures" (art that sold by appealing to sexual sensations), was "reduced to describing" the "battle of the sexes, undressing, [and] the lovers' embrace" and provoked "nausea."[43] Immoral novels leave the reader "disgusted," in a state of "lassitude," according to Abbé Louis Bethléem, a moral crusader and editor-in-chief of the Catholic *Revue des lecteurs,* who was arrested several times for destroying magazines he believed corrupted youth.[44]

This rhetoric persisted in the interwar years, and expressed what nineteenth century critics feared all along: that efforts to contain the dissemination of pornography would fail, and the entire population would fall under its spell. Although the unhealthy "degenerate" body continued to signify moral dissolution, newer discourses even-

42. Ibid., 32.
43. Deherme, *Classes moyennes,* 156–59.
44. Abbé Louis Bethléem, *Romans à lire et romans à proscrire* (Cambrai: Masson, 1908), 50–51. By 1938, Bethléem's *Revue des lecteurs* reached 10,000 readers a month, a modest but influential circulation.

tually effaced any discussion of how the body processed external sensations, so that every body was potentially an unsuspecting victim of pornography's lure.[45] In the postwar context of newly intensified fears about population decline, Victor Margueritte's racy 1922 novel *La Garçonne* and the pornography that alluded to it in one way or another only confirmed such anxieties. The book sold 25,000 copies the first month after it was published, and a quarter of postwar forbidden titles alluded to *La Garçonne*, whose heroine challenges stereotyped female behavior and engages in same-sex sexual relations. Gustave Téry, commenting on the novel, likened it to pornography, and described pornography as a deleterious, sickening exhalation, a leakage of poisonous gas that, he wrote elsewhere, "suffocated" honest people.[46] Pourésy wrote that "disgust entered the hearts" of those who witnessed pornographic spectacles, and that the most visible manifestation of our "saturation" by pornography was collective nausea.[47] Sylvain Bonmariage, the author of many novels and commentaries and a critic of moral purists,

45. For example, at a 1908 conference of hygiene associations, M. de Lamazelle said: "Immorality will always be with us. We must not fight immorality but its contagiousness, the continual excitement that immorality produces, and hence [we must] fight the exploitation of immorality [that resides in us all]." At the same conference, Edmond Goblot echoed this sentiment in other words: "Modern psychology has discovered that the domain of sexual emotions is much more significant than we had suspected. . . . It is no longer possible to live as if we had no sexuality." Therefore, he said, we must seek, not to fight pornography, but to build resistance to it among an ever more diverse array of people. That is, these groups sought to fight the *transmission* of seemingly airborne immorality, of which pornography was one privileged vehicle. See *Fédérations des Sociétés contre la pornographie: Assemblé*, 21 May 1908, 18, 63.

46. Téry quoted in Anne Manson, "Le Scandale de *La Garçonne*, 1922," in Gilbert Guilleminault, ed., *Le Roman vrai des années folles, 1918–1930* (Paris: Denoël, 1975), 109; Téry, *Ecole des garçonnes*, 13.

47. Pourésy, *Sous la fléau*, 246.

wrote nevertheless that "the atrocious spectacle of vice becomes intolerable" when performed in bad neighborhoods and by poor people. When the hero of one of his 1938 short stories, once the leader of moral purity campaigns, and perhaps modeled after Pourésy, visits Pigalle, he is overcome by nausea and sickened even more by his own apparently uncontrollable arousal.[48]

Nausea gradually became less a description of pornography's effects than a metaphor for its vertiginous circularity. Nausea, of course, was a metaphor for vertigo, for movement, for the effect of mobile bodies on stage in contrast to the female statues of the tableaux or to the restrained movements of classical actresses, and it was this that writers who had long used the term now began to emphasize. Moreover, when various critics wrote about pornography, nausea was also a metaphor for the seemingly indecipherable relationship of cause and effect (was pornography the cause or the effect of moral decline?) discussed earlier. Bonmariage's hero wants to vomit, but finds himself nevertheless aroused by a young girl on stage. His illness is not caused by pornography but by the propagation of a virus whose symptoms make it difficult to detect: does the hero become sick because he is uncontrollably aroused, or is he aroused because his body is already sick and thus especially susceptible to arousal? In fact, he kills the woman indirectly responsible for his state as the only means to escape a condition he deems incurable. And yet a jury acquits him, believing him to have temporarily lost his mind, and hence the ability to discern the relationship between cause and effect and right and wrong.

48. Sylvain Bonmariage, *Les Plaisirs de l'Enfer* (Paris: Raoul Saillard, 1938), 231, 220.

Here, murder is not the symptom of a clear cause—the deleterious effects of pornography and the victim's particular susceptibility to its stimuli. Instead, murder is the effect of an indeterminate cause, and our hero slips down the slippery slope from nausea to arousal to murder because he has, as the book implies, denied his own susceptibility to sexual stimuli. Pornography is deleterious because the hero does not know how to defend himself against it, because it is not at all clear how to recognize pornography.[49] We do not know why or if pornography produces the effects we assume it does. In contrast to nineteenth-century accounts, pornography is no longer a clearly recognizable category of material and meaning; rather, it is simultaneously pervasive and opaque. Moreover, this simultaneous pervasiveness and opacity—this invisible circulation—defines pornography itself.

As pornography became increasingly visible (or was perceived as such), it also became increasingly protean, intangible, and so promiscuous that it traversed the threshold between private and public, especially after the war. The Paris lawyer Adolphe Théry wrote that consumers of pornography had at an earlier time "them-

---

49. If the cause of illness can be identified or located at all, it is in the repressed body of the man exposed to sexual spectacles. There was a voluminous discourse during the interwar years about how sexually repressed male bodies in particular responded more to "bad" sexual stimuli than sexually educated and hence hence presumably healthy ones. This particular logic perhaps explains why anti-pornography activists for the first time advocated a double strategy of repression and education to combat such material, although they believed that the public had to be taught that pornography was bad in the first place. "Without education, the repression of pornography is not even possible, because the state, obliged to take public opinion into account, cannot militate against that which the public considers innocent and venial," Edmond Goblot said. "Educational work is essential" (quoted in Stora-Lamarre, *Enfer de la Troisième République*, 93). I address this reversal of turn-of-the-century logic extensively in chapter 2.

selves recognized that material that crudely addressed
the senses . . . [or] 'obscene' work . . . must be hidden,"
precisely because it suffocated and sickened those whom
it touched. Today, however, "pornography is everywhere,
and no place, however sacred it is, remains completely
closed, because [pornography] is a supple, rich, intelligent enemy who hesitates at nothing." It is as if nausea
no longer described only pornography's effects but also
its faceless, nameless character.[50] Georges Fonsegrive
claimed that pornography was like a prostitute: it pre-
tends to love without loving, "its expressions are those
of a body emptied of its soul, expressions without meaning or purpose, expressions that define the singular-
ity of pornography." He suggested that pornography
was dangerous because it had permeated all aspects of
culture, so completely that culture itself had become
pornographic.[51]

After the war, then, pornography defined material
that no longer remained behind the closed doors of rich
men's studies and infiltrated locales where it had no business being. No longer hidden, pornography nevertheless
eluded identification. The perceived pervasiveness of pornography thus rendered the enemy so omnipresent that it
infested otherwise dignified settings, and was not always
distinguishable from "culture" itself. Many writers accused pornographers of trying to conceal their "real"
message from readers: Abbé Louis Bethléem claimed that
pornographers were mercenaries who hid the message
of their work under the cover of characters who seemed
to have "grandes âmes."[52] In a commentary on Victor

50. Adolphe Théry, *Manuel pratique de lutte antipornographique* (Paris:
Spes, 1927), 11–12.
51. Fonsegrive, *Art et pornographie*, 12–13.
52. Bethléem, *Littérature enemie de la famille*, 33.

Margueritte's *La Garçonne,* one critic wrote that the novel was pornographic trash masquerading as literature that "moralizes and contemplates contemporary social vices."[53] And Gustave Téry noted that *La Garçonne* was pornographic because it was "dishonest" and "treasonous."[54] But this approach to the problem already implied that pornography was something that could be concealed, that could conceal, as it unfolded before your eyes. Indeed, in most accounts, pornographic authors now counted for little, because they had become no more than agents of contamination, symptoms of an epidemic that spared no one. Pornography took on a life of its own; it appeared, as I have noted, in different guises—Bethléem was upset because pornography so often passed for literature.

Pornography was thus an effect with no discernible cause, a virus that mutates for no explicable reason except its tendency to mutate. The tension between pornography's apparent visibility and its apparently surreptitious infiltration of postwar culture—Théry wrote that it enters the sanctity of the home "under a benign appearance"—produced the narrative structure of an "open secret" in which the increasing visibility of pornography intensified cultural fantasies about (and surveillance of) its now protean character.[55] If social commentators of all sorts defined pornography as a mobile vehicle of contagion with no substance except its contagiousness, if they conceived pornography as a virus that is both the cause

53. Jean de Pierrefeu quoted in Manson, "Scandale de *La Garçonne,* 1922," 109.

54. Téry, *Ecole des garçonnes,* 6.

55. I take the now well known term "open secret" from Eve Kosofsky Sedgwick's reworking of D. A. Miller's phrase in her *Epistemology of the Closet* (Berkeley and Los Angeles: University of California Press, 1990), 67.

and effect of social dissolution, and hence one whose origins could not be clearly identified, how could society protect and arm itself against this deadly disease? Most of the police records and legal exertion on behalf of stemming the proliferation of pornography testify to this perception of its increasingly mutable character. Moreover, they manifest efforts to target pornographic material with a precision not present in nineteenth-century sources. Paradoxically, pornography's conceptual mobility depended on an increasingly rigid link between pornography and non-normative sexuality, so that laws aimed at preventing the proliferation of pornography became increasingly indistinct from or intertwined with laws against "unnatural" sexual acts.

Pornography and the Police

In the only book devoted to the social history of pornography in modern France, Annie Stora-Lamarre argues that the prosecution of pornography quintupled in the years directly preceding the Great War as a means of ideological preparation for the national "regeneration" to come (75 trials between 1910 and 1914, 14 between 1881 and 1910). But she also notes that between 1920 and 1930, police activity directed against obscene work declined dramatically.[56] Although she is correct, this decline remains mysterious, and it is difficult to explain why police pursued most pornography less relentlessly than before. Alain Corbin and J. H. Morel have argued that after 1907, the police were given greater powers to combat the "venereal threat" purportedly menacing the population. The expansion of police powers to "clean the streets"

---

56. Stora-Lamarre, *Enfer de la Troisième République,* 192–93, 206.

evoked periodic protests against the abuse of power in a Republican regime that were directed primarily against those officers responsible for regulating prostitution. Although such protests had been responsible for a relative harnessing of police harassment of prostitutes over the years, they had little effect on the prosecution of pornography distributors.[57]

Moreover, there was little change in the institutional structure whereby pornographic material was condemned. In the late nineteenth century, the seizure of pornographic material was facilitated by anonymous and non-anonymous letter writers, and some bookstores were perpetually under surveillance. Obscene books and obscene texts and images more generally were deemed as such either by juries made up primarily of middle-class professionals (for books) chosen by judges and mayors, or by judges alone (for all other material).[58] Perhaps the confusion produced by demobilization after the war, the heightened focus on the dangers of venereal disease, the destruction of records, and an atmosphere of general chaos in which a return to economic and political stability were priorities, contributed to the decline in zealous pursuit.

Laws against pornography became increasingly complex and were enforced in an increasingly haphazard manner. It was as if pornography were a clear enemy but, as Théry noted, a "surreptitious" one that entered unlikely places under the most "benign appearance."[59] Evidence does suggest that police found the work of arresting

---

57. J. H. Morel, *La Police des mœurs sous la Troisième République* (Paris: Seuil, 1992), 159–61; Corbin, *Women for Hire*, 340.
58. Stora-Lamarre, *Enfer de la Troisième République*, 80–81.
59. Théry, *Manuel pratique de lutte antipornographique*, 12.

pornographers tiresome by the interwar years and, moreover, that the targets of censorship and surveillance had changed. In some documents, police sound positively weary. In 1939, the prefect of police in Paris wrote that "as far as pornography is concerned, there is no question of depriving Paris of this lively and frivolous [*léger*] art, which has always found a favorable climate in the capital. It is instead a matter of removing from the view of honest and cultivated citizens [*gens du goût*] all the stupid and unwholesome productions now the subject of illicit commerce."[60] For example, the Paris police received numerous petitions in 1933 complaining about an annual nude beauty contest entitled the "Concours de la Vénus moderne" from several Catholic and "family" organizations. The police finally attended in 1935 and concluded that the soirée passed without incident and that there was nothing obscene about it: "Then the candidates began to walk on the stage. Twenty-three young women, entirely nude, their sexes shaven and covered only with a fig leaf, exhibited themselves in nonlascivious poses. . . . The evening was, to resume, very calm at every instant. . . . In effect, at no moment did the audience ever express any sentiments contrary to those that only the love of beauty might inspire." And another layer of irony might be added to this description: one of the main organizers of the contest was the son of a former commissioner of the Paris police.[61]

Police did seek to control material meant to attract buyers and thus displayed too brazenly. In an increasingly moralizing political climate, the police also had to respond to legislators seeking to appease those associa-

---

60. Archives de la Préfecture de Police de Paris, BA 383.
61. Ibid., BA 382.

tions whose members complained about explicitly displayed texts and images and claimed that the state did not
take sufficient action against pornography in spite of the
laws at its disposal.[62] Moreover the anti-pornography
leagues inundated the police with letters demanding action against this or that bookseller—taking their cue directly from their "Anglo-Saxon" counterparts, as well as
from their Swiss brethren. Upper-level police administra-
tors put the (exaggerated) number of condemnations between 1928 and 1939 at 115 for "outrages aux bonnes
mœurs" by the Tribunal of Correction of the Seine (Paris)
totaling 40,000 francs in penalties and 98 months of
prison: roughly ten a year in that decade.[63] As in the late
nineteenth century, prosecutions were consistent with
the fin-de-siècle censorship of contraceptive information,
political dissidence, and "perversions." Thus, condemned
texts included everything from a special issue of the
Communist newspaper *L'Humanité* issued in 1933, to a
work on sexual perversions by the German sexologist
Magnus Hirschfeld, to a book entitled *Maternité* that the
authorities decided was to be sold exclusively in medical
bookstores.[64]

62. For one of the first articulations of this view, see Paul Nouris-
son, *Etude de la répression des outrages aux bonnes mœurs au point de
vue de la nature de l'infranction, de la penalté et de la jurisdiction* (Paris:
J. B. Sirey, 1905). This complaint continued to be widespread in the anti-
pornography associations during the interwar years. See Téry, *Ecole des
garçonnes,* 46; Pourésy, *Sous la fléau,* 240.
63. I have not been able to confirm this number. The *Recueil des
Gazettes des Tribunaux* contains about twelve trials explicitly related to
"bonnes mœurs" throughout this entire period, indicating that the police
inflated the numbers.
64. Archives de la Préfecture de Police de Paris, BA 383. On efforts
to shut down Communist Party publications, see Jean-Yves Moller, "La
Survie de la censure d'etat (1881–1949)," in Ory, ed., *Censure,* 81. Magnus
Hirschfeld's *Geschlechtsübergänge: Mischungen männlicher und weibli-
cher Geschlechtscharaktere (Sexuelle Zwischenstufen)* (Leipzig: W. Malende,
1905), was translated into French in 1936.

The pursuit of work exhibited too publicly was consonant with widely expressed anxieties about the increasing volume of pornography available through new forms of media and a predictable effect of perceived moral decline as it had been defined since the late nineteenth century. Interwar policy thus seems generally consistent with nineteenth-century themes, except for less rigorous prosecution and a greater disjunction between the rhetoric and practice of the law. At the same time, however, I want to speculate that specific texts and images related to "mœurs speciales" (that is, to all non-normative sexuality, including prostitution) were increasingly targeted by narrowed police investigations. Of course, books about homosexuality and "perversion" had always been the object of prosecution. But the list of condemned books in police files from 1925 to 1938 reflects an intensified pursuit of non-normative sexuality rather than explicit, "public" heterosexuality per se; forbidden books included plain nudity, but overwhelmingly concerned homosexuality, flagellation, and nude spectacles, reiterating an old association of the female dancer or actress with the prostitute. From the years 1920–37, very few condemnations of a work containing female nudity appear in the *Gazette des Tribunaux,* and those judgments were motivated less by the content of the material ("photographs of women in lascivious poses") than by its display ("the display of such images so that they could be seen by anyone who enters").[65]

The lists of condemned books, which were expanded every year and determined for the most part by tribunals rather than juries, were divided into two parts: those

65. *Recueil des Gazettes des Tribunaux,* 18 November 1936.

works that could neither be displayed nor sold and those that could simply not be displayed in public view. Most of the material that could not be sold at all described so-called sexual perversion (including pseudo-scientific books), male and female homosexuality more specifically, or was particularly scabrous in its presentation of nude women. The intellectual gay magazine *Inversions* (though it contained no sexual imagery) figured on the list, as did books with titles such as *Pederastie, Elle et elle, Notre Dame des* [*sic*] *Lesbos, Mesdames les garçons, Ces dames de Lesbos,* and *Ouvrages traitant de la flagellation et de la perversion sexuelle.* Those works merely to be hidden from the public were very explicit descriptions of sexual orgies or those containing extreme nudity.

Moreover, several other commentators replicated the police's informal definition of pornography as perversion and more specifically homosexuality and, for different reasons, prostitution. The law professor Maurice Gand noted that it was virtually impossible to define clear distinctions between obscenity, infractions against *bonnes mœurs,* and mere licentiousness. It was extremely difficult in particular, he claimed, to find judges willing to condemn the work of artists nominally considered "great." Yet one criterion did link two incidents: the tribunal's 1931 acquittal of a Belgian editor in Paris accused of selling engravings by the artist Felicien Rops and a jurist in Poitiers agonizing over how to define *bonnes mœurs.* The judge in the Rops case noted that the most offensive thing about his work was its "representation of acts *contre nature* such as lesbian practices, masturbation scenes, acts of pederasty as well as bestiality." And the jurist confidently noted that "we can say that there are certain vices so monstrous (pederasty, homosexuality) that without being directly prohibited by legal texts, are so contrary to nature that we would not hesitate to condemn them."[66] Edmond Haraucourt suggested that while censorship must always respect art, "sadistic and homosexual" publications and those concerned with "prostitution" must always be prohibited.[67] A 1927 decision by the Cour de Paris narrowed the offense against good morals down by insisting that a work was pornographic if it in any way constituted "an apology for pederasty, an appeal to homosexual passion, or a provocation to exercise unwholesome curiosity," the latter a reference to non-normative sexuality more generally.[68]

Of the many prosecutions for offenses against decency in the interwar period, the contrast between the decision against the new magazine *Inversions* (the first in France dedicated solely to gay men's concerns) and the acquittal of Georges Anquetil, the editor of a satirical left-wing journal, of selling obscene work by mail is most revealing. In 1926, a M. de Bourmont accused Anquetil of sending unsolicited obscene work to his home in the hope of increasing sales of Anquetil's book, *L'Amant légitime,* among others. He claimed to have been offended by the material and afraid that it might have fallen into

---

66. M. Saratier quoted in Maurice Gand, *Guide juridique et pratique pour la lutte contre la license des rues* (Paris: Librairie de Recueil Sirey, 1932), 17, 15. To be fair, Saratier also mentions adultery as contrary to decency, but the mention only highlights the importance of homosexuality in making his case. He uses homosexuality to highlight the slippery slope now implicit in the law. Adultery is a minor infraction, but homosexuality is the only thing we know with certainty is obscene. If we sanction adultery, however distasteful, we run the risk of relativizing our sure knowledge of homosexuality's aberrant character. Finally, Gand also provides a list of books condemned in France from 1913 to 1914 (89–96) and of various cases concerning the condemnation of periodicals and theatrical productions (96–128).

67. Haraucourt, *Démoralisation par le livre et par l'image,* 76.

68. Bécourt, *Livres condamnés,* 111.

the hands of one of his children. The judge noted that Anquetil's text treated sexual matters in a far from morally uplifting manner, but asserted that because "no term is specifically obscene, and [none] is so vulgar as to offend decency," the work was not technically "contraire aux bonnes mœurs."[69]

In the same year, the publishers of *Inversions*, which contained no sexual content, were prosecuted under the same laws and condemned. The judge (the same man who had acquitted Anquetil) conceded that "the journal had at no moment used a term that might offend decency" but nevertheless claimed that it offended decency just the same: "Each page constitutes a cynical apology for homosexuality and a systematic appeal to homosexual passions and unwholesome curiosities; thus even though the authors have taken great care to be absolutely decent, their articles constitute not only an offense against decency and propaganda that might . . . compromise the future of the race, but are obscene, if not by words, then by the indecency of the subjects they treat and the general allure of the publication."[70] The reluctance to prosecute heterosexually explicit material was matched only by the vigor with which homosexually oriented literature was pursued. In the nineteenth century, both heterosexual and homosexual representations had been prosecuted with similar if not equal vehemence, but by the interwar period, homosexual material was increasingly demonized, while heterosexually oriented publications and images were more or less tolerated, if occasionally censored. That is, although there existed no (if any) monolithic concept of gay identity or behavior

69. *Recueil des Gazettes des Tribunaux,* 30 November 1927.
70. Ibid., 27 October 1926.

and certainly many texts in which readers could read between the lines escaped censors, police targeted perceived representations of explicit homosexual relations or affirmative discussions of same-sex desire.

The police spent a great deal of time scanning the classified ads. To the extent that the classified ads imply commercial transactions or themselves represent a form of publicity for otherwise private matters, they were considered "pornographic" (as the 1898 law clearly stated). The ads were defined as such because they made otherwise legal private behavior public, but police rarely deemed forms of public heterosexual solicitation or imagery except prostitution offensive. And prostitution appears frequently in such lists because, as mentioned, the war and interwar years witnessed a draconian and repressive campaign against prostitution in order to stem the dissemination of venereal disease among soldiers and thus ostensibly to protect public health more generally.

A 1929 condemnation of the magazine *Gens qui rient* on the grounds of its obscene classifieds makes clear that the police cracked down on "personals" because they associated them generally with prostitution. The judge, Petit, ruled that even though classified ads were not technically obscene, they were indecent because they formed a "provocation" and encouraged licentious behavior: Anquetil's fairly scabrous, public, and equally non-obscene work apparently did not.[71] In any case, the sheer expansiveness of the categories and materials deemed infractions of the law makes a mockery of police efforts to pursue "pornography," since it defined almost every type of sexual relationship imaginable except (technically speak-

71. Ibid., 20 April 1929.

ing) married heterosexuality. Police were directed to look
for the following categories, however covert: perverts;
men looking to purchase women (an allusion to the
imaginary white slave trade); prostitution; women looking for a man to "keep" them; pimps who arranged con-
tacts between men and men, women and women, men
and women; masseuses; flagellants or flagellators; those
with "modern tastes"; pederasts; and sellers of obscene
photos.[72] At the same time, law-enforcement lists also
oddly distilled pornography as a category of meaning
by defining it in terms of all the non-normative forms
of hetero- and homosexuality figured in the ads. The criterion for pornography's solidity was less the publicity
given to sexuality in general than "unnatural" public sex
and prostitution (here, in classified ads).

Sylvain Bonmariage declared in 1938 that the difference between previous centuries and our own was that
ours was a century of "self-interested perversity." Although he defended pornography against prosecution, he
claimed that the public presentation of homosexuality
exemplified this dangerous, "self-interested" perversity,
which did not respect the necessary relationship between
sexuality and civilization. Civilization, he believed (quite

72. Archives de la Préfecture de Police de Paris, BA 383. Narratives
about the white slave trade in which young girls were abducted, bought,
and sold into prostitution, often by foreigners, first developed in England
in the 1880s. They continued to flourish during the interwar period in
France as well. See René de Bérénger "La Traite des blanches et le commerce de l'obscenité: Conférences diplomatiques internationales du 15
juillet 1902 et du 18 avril 1910," *Revue des Deux Mondes* 58 (1 July 1910):
75–111; Maurice Gand, *Une Forme moderne d'esclavage: La Traite des
femmes* (Lyon: Chronique sociale de France, 1930). The latter is a summary of the League of Nations investigation into the so-called white slave
trade. According to Bécourt, an international anti-trafficking law was
signed at Geneva in 1923.

conventionally), depended on the veiling of the sexuality
that animated much of its productions, and homosexuality blatantly displayed was a symbol of the self-interested
sexuality that led to cultural decline.[73] In his work, homosexuality was pornographic because it represented a
state in which "pleasure took the place of love" and devoured the healthy, loving sexuality that distinguished literature from pornography. Moreover, to the extent that
civilization depended on "suggestion" rather than publicly exhibited sexuality, homosexuality represented "that
which is precise": that which proclaimed itself too loudly
and was thus pornographic.[74] Bonmariage only made
clear what was still implicit in judicial claims: that homosexuality (but also sadomasochism and other "unnatural" pleasures) now more than ever defined the content
of pornography. As obscenity law focused increasingly on
protecting the "race" and defending the "family" between
the late 1920s and the late 1950s, it also focused more extensively on perversion and prosecution was more suc-
cessful if books contained depictions of so-called unnatural acts. While not of course ruling out other genres of
obscenity as pornographic, legal and other critical discourses transformed perverse sexuality into a synonym
of pornography. This particular transformation effected
a clear delineation between the pornographic and nonpornographic that enabled the law to function effectively,
or at least to have the illusion of a clearly defined target.
But it did so oddly at the very time that laws mimicked
the elasticity that rendered pornography so imprecise a
category: as the content of pornography became increas-

73. Bonmariage, *Plaisirs de l'Enfer,* 23–24.
74. Ibid., 226, 23–24.

ingly singular (if broadly defined), laws expanded to cover an ever more diverse array of texts and images. For example, anti-pornography laws expanded in 1930 to cover all material deemed an "outrage aux bonnes mœurs" except books, and another law of 1939 aimed at protecting the "race," and hence in "defense of the family," no longer spared books. For now that books were printed in vast numbers and were thus more accessible, it became harder and harder to distinguish them from other sorts of publications.[75]

In a departure from late-nineteenth-century laws, then, this legislation covered, not books deemed to have been written with ill intent, but all those persons involved in manufacturing pornography, at every stage of production, from those who wrote it to those who printed the magazines or images, without regard to the author's intention. The concept of authorial intention became more diffuse as new technologies and increased readership expanded the distribution of "pornography" into a transnational industry (hence international laws against "trafficking" signed in Geneva in 1923). In January 1940, before the French defeat by the Nazis in June, the government convened a special commission in "defense of public morality" consisting of seven men: law professors, judges, educators, and members of associations in defense of public morality. This commission made an

75. Legislators passed a new anti-pornography law in April 1939. The law expanded the 1882 and 1898 provisions to extend not only to the sale, distribution, or display of pornographic material, but to the pursuit of those engaged in "trafficking" in all sorts of pornography, including "engravings, photographic paintings, snapshots, reproductions, emblems, and all objects contrary to good morals." In addition to this law passed in April, the government issued a decree regulating all material deemed to threaten "the race," for the first time including books. Archives de la Préfecture de Police de Paris, BA 384; Bécourt, *Livres condamnés*, 111.

official distinction between pornography and erotic literature in order to focus more precisely on the "vulgar" content of specific sorts of texts and images, and predictably deemed all "perverse" (non-normative) and homosexual representations vulgar.

My purpose here, however, is not to recount all the complex details concerning changing pornography law but to make a more general point: the increased focus on perverse literature occurred at the same time as the definition of pornography became entirely mutable. As we have seen, pornography became a specific repository of homosexuality and also of non-normative sexuality more generally at the historical moment when new forms of media enabled sexuality to traverse the boundary between public and private and corrupt even the most stolid men and women. Everyone was potentially possessed of a "pornographic imagination," a phenomenon both real and imagined to which lawmakers responded by extending laws to cover almost every imaginable sort of image and text, every possible form of distribution, and every conceivable hiding place.

Pornography now deeply threatened the public sphere and metaphorically overwhelmed, suffocated, and poisoned reason: pornography was a symptom and cause of cultural decline. How could the social body be cleansed of pornography against such overwhelming odds? The targeting of non-normative sexuality provided some reassurance that that body could be thus cleansed, but the heated debate, and the continued lack of clarity about what constituted obscenity in spite of an emphasis on non-normative sexuality, meant that the issues of pornography's boundaries and immorality's triumph persisted. Moreover, the continued lack of clarity underlines the disseminating of pornography throughout the social body, and hence that body's real permeability.

The Great War, in which veterans and others, both intellectuals and not, believed politicians and legislators to be guilty of slaughter, brought this question to the fore in other contexts as well. Rhetoric about the war helped critics, police, and lawmakers anchor pornography in specific, female and feminized bodies that enabled the law to retain its legitimacy and the social body its imaginary purity. The relationship between pornography and perversion constituted a new rhetorical strategy to preserve the boundaries between a purportedly pure social body and pornography, which came most dramatically under siege after the Great War. The next chapter addresses the relationship between pornography and femininity and pornography and gender more generally in the context of debates about the boundary between literature and pornography, in order to understand why, in this case, the feminized and even sexualized body was always a pornographic one, and why, moreover, it could never be rescued from its degraded corporeal and psychic state.

2

Pornography, Literature, and the Redemption of Virility

> Unfortunately this book will have to chronicle
> a sad story of unwarranted interference in the
> natural processes by which the standards of the
> public are formed and executed. It is a tale of
> literature emasculated while books on crude
> sexual athleticism are encouraged.
>
> David Loth, *The Erotic in Literature*

Voluminous evidence from the interwar period thus suggests that the solidity of the pornography concept was compromised by the increasingly widespread perception that its omnipresence and power threatened even the most hardened and rational spirits. In order to salvage moral order, social critics still evoked pornography's capacity to damage women, children, and working-class men, and sought to censor and repress it. But Sylvain Bonmariage suggested that a sexually knowledgeable person was more able to fend off pornography's ill effects than a sexually ignorant one, and Edmond Goblot insisted that "educational work" was the antidote to por-

Epigraph: David Goldsmith Loth, *The Erotic in Literature: A Historical Survey of Pornography as Delightful as It Is Indiscreet* (New York: Dorset, 1961), 10.

nography's power, indicating that combating this enemy was a problem repression alone would not resolve. But why was repression deemed ineffective, and how would education resolve the problem? How would sexual education restore the now compromised boundary between the pure social body and pornography? In this chapter, I address how the turn away from repression as a weapon in the fight against pornography's perceived proliferation, mobility, and influence was part of a new strategy to restore the integral body. I address this shift within the framework of debates about the elasticity of the boundary between literature and pornography: how did elites in the literary world challenge the traditional, and until then rather unproblematic, divide between the inappropriate exposure that characterized pornographic texts and the discreet and subtle suggestiveness proper to literature?

In order to analyze their construction of this controversial debate, I shall look more precisely at the shift from one to another sort of discussion about pornography: from 1880 to 1918 cultural critics, journalists, and medical professionals forged a link between the proliferation of pornography and the presumed emasculation of the nation; after the Great War, cultural commentators instead linked emasculation to the overzealous repression of pornographic material. The continuity between these apparently contradictory discussions about how best to restore the nation's manhood makes clear to what extent discussions of pornography were at the time really discussions about the masculinity and "health" of the social body. The discourse about pornography shifted from the repression of harmful material to the derepression of those erotic texts deemed to be in harmony with a new concept of the male self. The damage inflicted by pornography was no longer figured as a medical harm (although this notion persisted) but as the destruction of a romantic, expressive integral self necessary to the maintenance of productive, fulfilled individuals.

How then, was pornography used rhetorically to symbolize social pathology and hence to figure the threat represented by moral decline in both of the periods discussed? The chapter that follows describes how some (mostly naturalist, realist, and decadent) "pornographic" books, first conceived of by critics as metaphors for emasculated bodies, eventually came to represent virile ones, and thus how fantasies about the properties of differently gendered bodies were embedded in and shaped the boundary between literature and pornography. It demonstrates, moreover, how critics expanded the realm of the nonobscene by defining pornography as the rhetorical container of an uncontainable, excessive femininity. In so doing, they cemented the divide between literature and material deemed unworthy of civilized readers.[1]

---

1. In *On Pornography: Literature, Sexuality, and Obscenity Law* (New York: St. Martin's Press, 1993), Ian Hunter, David Saunders, and Dugald Williamson and others also address this question, using a different conceptual framework. They argue, after Foucault, that pornography is not produced by the repression of true, real, or healthy sexuality. It no longer mirrors unhealthy sexual practices. Rather it *is* a sexual practice produced within the context of what they call a perpetually shifting and multiple "pornographic field." The divide between aesthetics and pornography is the regulatory effect of a complex set of overlapping disciplinary apparatuses—the law, the police, literary standards, and so forth (the "pornographic field")—whose form and content necessarily changes over time. That divide must thus always be mutable; or rather, that mutability is the dialectical point of departure for a rigid drawing of boundaries between the two. Although the unspeakable pleasure or subversive power associated with pornography paradoxically extends the tentacles of regulatory power, the boundary between the aesthetic and the pornographic also marks what Abigail Solomon-Godeau refers to as "the failure of a discursive *cordon sanitaire:* an attempt at segregating the licit from the illicit that constantly founders." But how can the divide between aesthetics and pornography be an expression of cultural hegemony so totalizing that

Gender and Pornography

As noted in chapter 1, legislators and doctors used non-procreative sex as a symbol of industrial and sexual non-productivity and justified censorship in the name of regulating the sexuality of women and working-class men in the interests of the state. But they also conceived of this "degenerate" sexuality—and hence the dangerously seductive effects of pornographic material—in gendered terms. Literary men used women's seductive powers to figure the specter of cultural dissolution, and in so doing established a powerful symbolic association between degeneracy, sexuality, femininity, and pornography. That is, fantasies about the proliferation and seductive power of pornography were, as we shall see in the course of this chapter, inseparable from fantasies about the power of women and the threat posed by undomesticated femininity to the state regulation of sexuality.[2] The critic

---

pleasure becomes merely an extension of power and yet a site where presumably subversive pleasures can be imagined? Hunter et al., *On Pornography*, 138; Abigail Solomon-Godeau, "The Legs of the Countess," *October* 39 (1986): 95; Linda Williams, *Hard Core: Power, Pleasure, and the Frenzy of the Visible* (Berkeley and Los Angeles: University of California Press, 1989), 89–91; 151–52.

   2. These trends were transnational and quite predominant in Germany. At this time, German medical literature about the "science" of sexuality (dubbed *Sexualwissenschaft* [sexology] by Iwan Bloch in 1904) was broadly influential. Of these, the works of the Austrian doctor Otto Weininger (a Jewish anti-Semite who killed himself while still in his early twenties after his book *Geschlecht und Charakter* [*Sex and Character*] was published in 1903), the Hungarian Zionist Max Nordau, and the sexologist Alfred Eulenburg were among the most widely read by specialists in France, although only Nordau had been translated. In his *Sex and Character*, Weininger famously equated sexuality with femininity, and femininity with immorality, solipsism, self-loss, and delusions. Albert Eulenburg had argued that "many men look upon the sleeping woman at their side . . . with a feeling as if they could thrash [her], if not stab her or choke her to death in cold blood." Nordau claimed that the "normal man" feels only "indifference toward the female sex once his desires are satiated," whereas

Victor Barraud wrote in the art journal *La Revue blanche* in 1895 that woman, "with a simple undulation of her rump . . . was able to trouble man's brain; and with her slowly insinuating ability to fascinate, she picked apart futures, the arts, creeds. Venus-Pandemos triumphed over idealistic aspirations; she ridiculed chastity, the family, the fatherland." [3]

The historian Michelle Perrot claims that many influential voices "denounced the social and domestic power of women . . . [they were] perceived as an occult, diffuse, and secret power for which men are mere playthings." She speaks of a "masculinity crisis" around the turn of the century in which antifeminist literature flourished on both the Right and the Left: writers as diverse as Emile Zola, Octave Mirbeau (an anarchist sympathizer), and Maurice Barrès (France's most prominent protofascist) all believed that "loss of virility is a sign and cause of the social degeneracy and decadence" they perceived to be "prevalent during the period." The liberation of female sexuality from its procreative function would, Barraud claimed, eventually destroy family and father-

---

pathological men were incapable of cool, neutral, "indifferent" emotion. Weininger, *Sex and Character* (London: Heinemann, 1910 [1903]), 297–98; Eulenburg, *Algolania: The Psychology, Neurology, and Physiology of Sadistic Love and Masochism*, trans. Harold Kent (1902; New York: New Era, 1934), 31, 33–35; Nordau, *Degeneration* (New York: Appleton, 1895), 125. For recent overviews of the threat represented by female sexuality at the end of the century, see Bram Dijkstra, *Idols of Perversity: Fantasies of Feminine Evil in Fin-de-Siècle Culture* (New York: Oxford University Press, 1986), and *Evil Sisters: The Threat of Female Sexuality in Twentieth-Century Culture* (New York: Owl Books, 1996); Elisabeth Bronfen, *Over Her Dead Body: Death, Femininity, and the Aesthetic* (New York: Routledge, 1992); Maria Tartar, *Lustmord: Sexual Murder in Weimar Germany* (Princeton, N.J.: Princeton University Press, 1995). There are many works that touch on this theme; these are most relevant to our concerns.

3. Quoted in Dijkstra, *Idols of Perversity*, 358.

land, and Charles Richet, a doctor, claimed that the New Woman was engaging in a sinister because "voluntary sterility." In 1905 the antifeminist Théodore Joran won a prize from the Académie Française for a book of essays on *Le Mensonge du féminisme* (The Lie of Feminism).[4]

Mainstream critics objected above all to literature they believed was unmediated by the cerebral force necessary to mold impressions in the interests of a higher moral and intellectual purpose. That literature reflected the "masculinity crisis" provoked by the specter of the unregulated female body. The Hungarian doctor and journalist Max Nordau wrote that the proponents of such writing were "intellectual eunuchs" and male masochists who could only escape from their sexual obsessions through "self-mutilation."[5] In the 1880s, Nordau studied in Paris under the psychiatrist Jean-Martin Charcot, during which time he gathered material for what was to become the most popular treatise on the effects of "degeneration" in artists all over Europe. In France, *Degeneration* (1892) was translated in 1894 and went through at least seven editions in that year alone. According to the historian George Mosse, the book "caused a stir in all nations," "typif[ied] one aspect of [its] age and the men [*sic*] who made it," and is "one of the most important documents of the *fin-de-siècle*."[6] Nordau interviewed many of the decadent, symbolist, and naturalist writers who dominated the Parisian avant-garde, including, among others, Emile Zola and Laurent Tailharde. A Zionist, Nordau's

4. Michelle Perrot, "The New Eve and the Old Adam," in Margaret R. Higonnet et al., eds., *Behind the Lines: Gender and the Two World Wars* (New Haven, Conn.: Yale University Press, 1987), 58–59.
5. Nordau, *Degeneration* (1895), 296, 31, 169.
6. George L. Mosse, preface to a recent English edition of Max Nordau's *Degeneration* (Lincoln: University of Nebraska Press, 1993), xiv.

real purpose was to represent all of these "degenerate" artists as heirs of German romanticism, with which the resurgent anti-Semitism in Germany was infused. But he also aimed his attack at avant-garde literature for what he perceived as its mirroring of cultural decline—for what he called its "unbounded egoism" and "emotionalism." Avant-garde writers celebrated luxury and decadence and had nothing but contempt for the customs that fostered social cohesion. They could not distinguish the real from the illusory, right from wrong, or good from evil: the degenerate artist "does not see things as they are, does not understand the world, and cannot take up a right attitude towards it." Nordau predictably identified France's debauched capital as home to the largest number of degenerates, who "satisfy their unhealthy impulses" with "pen and pencil" rather than with the "knife of the assassin."[7]

Degeneration articulated systematically and in pseudo-scientific language the categories used to delineate "pornography" and literature that were already implicit in other late-nineteenth-century attacks on "obscene" works. Nordau argued that "eroticism" was the "most characteristic and conspicuous phenomenon of degeneration." Sexual pathology, he contended, was "at the heart of all perverse literature"—and here he meant Baudelaire, Zola, Swinburne, and others—which all the "new French pornographers rely [on] . . . for proving the artistic *raison d'être* of their depravity." He placed pornography alongside "realism, mysticism, symbolism, and diabolism," and argued that what all these so-called "doctrines" had in common was their point of departure: it was "where normal sexual relations leave off. Priapus has become a symbol of virtue. Vice looks to Sodom and Lesbos, to Blue-

7. Nordau, *Degeneration* (1895), 9, 243, vii.

beard's castle and the servants hall of the 'divine' Marquis de Sade's *Justine* for its embodiments."

Nordau argued quite conventionally that behind great literature was a virile male body whose virility provided the necessary energy needed to transcend and hence redeem man's creaturely status through literary production. "Degenerate" writers were instead eunuchs and masochists because their work was feminized by its proximity to sex and hence to earthliness. They were weak, nervous men with deteriorating bodies, evidence of a sterile, agonized manliness symptomatic of cultural decline.

In the context of fears about national decline and emasculation, French critics after Nordau attacked avant-garde works across the spectrum, making little distinction among decadent, symbolist, and naturalist literature. Echoing medical opinion, they saw such literature as the product of hypercivilized cultures in which men had grown weary of "normal" sexual relations and were tempted by new thrills unconnected to the procreative purpose of sex. The avant-garde insistence on art's autonomy in particular mirrored the sterility of these men lured into perversion: like the pervert, art was absolutely self-reflexive and repudiated a productive sexual economy in favor of another perverted (because unproductive) one of its own making. As men sought pleasure for its own sake (hence the resurgence of "pederasty" and "tribadism," of Sodom and Lesbos), so the modern writer, as Achille Ségard put it, had lost sight of the transcendent goal of literary production and was incapable of "dominating the intensity of his impressions" and "directing his vision."[8] Hugues Rebell called such writers

8. Achille Ségard, *Les Voluptueux et les hommes d'action* (Paris: Société d'éditions littéraires et artistiques, 1900), 105–6.

"eunuchs" and "incomplete beings."[9] Men wrote as if
they were women.

In the context of this narrative, it is perhaps not surprising that so-called pornographic texts were figured as
feminized bodies.[10] The pornographic text mimicked the
presumed emasculation of the author in two different
and yet interrelated ways. First, critics conceived of the
pornographic text as a narcissistic extension of the feminized body, sensual and overwrought. The text was expe-
rienced as flesh, and thus transformed into a dangerously
seductive and hence feminized body. As Achille Ségard
wrote, because sex was the most "imperious of all instincts," decadent writers like Jean Lorrain could not
extricate themselves from their own obsessions. Ségard
attributed Lorrain's troubles to his assimilation of "dangerous" because "excessively sensual" books: "It was toward adolescence—that age when impressions are still
vibrant and tenacious—that the dangerous books of Baudelaire and Poe were put in M. Lorrain's hands. He read
them . . . in the way one imbibes drugs."[11] And, conclud-
ing this typical scenario, Lorrain's health worsened, his

9. Hugues Rebell, *Le Culte des idoles* (Paris: Bernard, 1929), 12.
10. I should note that I have found little discussion among women of
pornography, except for those members of hygiene movements who sought
its elimination. The small scale of the feminist movement in France (compared with England) and its heavily Catholic and bourgeois membership
make it unlikely that French feminists supported derepression. In the texts
I have read, so-called "bohemian" women's opinions did not differ in any
recognizable way from men's, although they sometimes employed a different sort of rhetoric, the analysis of which is beyond the scope of this study.
Annie Stora-Lamarre, *L'Enfer de la Troisième République: Censeurs et pornographes, 1880–1914* (Paris: Imago, 1990), 130, notes that there was very
little pornography written by women, and that the few pornographic
works they did write were treated as far more scandalous than those written by men.
11. Ségard, *Voluptueux*, 97.

heart began to give him trouble, and he started writing sensuous books that fully expressed his "feminine" character.

But pornographic works were also, and more frequently, conceived of as repulsive *repudiations* of sensuality—they repelled as well as seduced. That is, if pornography represented, on the one hand, a metaphorical extension of the feminized because seductive body, it also represented, on the other, the stripping away of the metaphors separating culture from nature and hence was again aligned with femininity. Pornography was an exposed, unadorned body and this implicit distinction between "nude" (cultural) and "naked" (natural) recapitulated conventional distinctions between the literary and the unliterary—between texts that were or were not morally redemptive. Hence, although authorities refrained from censoring the naturalist Zola because of his popularity, he was always called a pornographic writer because of his detailed descriptions of all kinds of "vices." Zola was consistently attacked by both the Left and the Right as an "enemy of the Republic" because he wrote "filthy and unwholesome" books: he was deplored by the Left because he represented manual work as "repugnant" and detested on the Right because he "redefined disgust as a form of morality," "scandal as glory," and "cynicism as genius."[12] Zola, however, always the moralist, insisted

12. René-Pierre Colin, "Les Naturalistes à l'assaut de la morale 'honnête,'" in Pascal Ory, ed., *La Censure en France à l'ère démocratique* (Brussels: Editions complexes, 1997), 146. These are all quotations from various nineteenth-century critics of Zola. Colin argues that the state threatened lesser novelists with censorship, too, although he also notes that, in the end, naturalism was eventually not perceived as a tremendous threat. Although this is true, my focus is on the process by which naturalism was transformed into an acceptable genre.

that his exposure of vice was good for moral order, that "in order to dress . . . wounds it would be necessary to study them, to expose them and to care for them!"[13]

The historian Hippolyte Taine only approved of sensuality in literature when "ennobled by genius," but not if love was "deprived of all adornments. . . . All . . . noble sentiments." An artist like Giulio Romano, he claimed, could turn orgies into "works of art," while John Wilmot, earl of Rochester, wrote works of "frozen obscenity," in which "all that is left is satiated lust, jaded sensuality."[14] Stefan Zweig wrote that Paul Verlaine's pornographic writings were inferior to his poetry because they were "repulsive in self-revelation," "naked," and hence "utterly obscene."[15] And the critic Robert Sarcey insisted that the naturalist Belgian writer Camille Lemonnier's *Un Mâle* was "pornography" because Lemonnier depicted an unmarried peasant couple making love in lush fields. Sarcey denounced Lemonnier for being "faithful to the poetics of today's naturalists. . . . in love he sees absolutely nothing but this carrying away of the senses . . . which throws the male . . . on the female. He reduces love to nothing more than bestial heat [*rut*]." Too much "virility" in texts—for in *Un Mâle* the protagonist is unmistakably virile—in effect meant not enough.[16]

---

13. Emile Zola, preface to Dr. G. St. Paul, *Thèmes psychologiques* (Paris: Vigot Frères, 1930), 1.

14. Quoted in Iwan Bloch, *Sexual Life in England Past and Present*, trans. William H. Forstern (London: Aldor, 1938), 513.

15. Quoted in Henry Marchand, *Sex Life in France* (New York: Panurge Press, 1933), 268.

16. Robert Sarcey, "Un Grain de pornographie," *XIXᵉ Siècle* 4 (October 1881), n.p. Sarcey quoted in Gustave Vanwelkenhuyzen, *Histoire d'un livre:* Un Mâle, *de Camille Lemonnier* (Brussels: Palais des Académies, 1961), 102. The French word *mâle* in this context signifies virility.

That distinction between literary and unliterary was thus also almost always gendered. When the critic Octave Uzanne remarked that the seventeenth-century erotic writer Nicolas Chorier's "style was too male to be pornographic," he echoed Alcide Bonneau's insistence that truly erotic writing repudiated our "animal origins."[17] Bonneau, himself a connoisseur of libertine literature, wrote that what made a writer virile was his distance from sex, his ability to name it without naming it explicitly. He argued that even Montaigne, an opponent of puritanism, could not bring himself to call a spade a spade, and, because of his greatness, used words like *cela* to designate the unspeakable, thereby "obeying the very prejudice he denounces."[18]

This is not to say that bad literature and pornography are the same thing, or that pornography has no recognizable formal features. I only want to note to what extent pornography at that time was perceived to reflect a writer who deviated from the disciplined, "healthy" masculinity required for social stability. But a 1912 medical text by the prominent psychiatrists Paul Voivenel and A. Rémond, *Le génie littéraire* (Literary Genius), challenged the pornographic characterization of many literary works, and in so doing pioneered the expansion of the non-obscene already under way in avant-garde writing. The book merits extensive analysis, for the authors sought

17. Lionel d'Autrec, *L'Outrage aux mœurs* (Paris: L'Epi, 1923), 90. D'Autrec's book is a compendium of hundreds of contemporary views on pornography. He wrote up a questionnaire and requested that respondents write a few paragraphs expressing their views about the category of "obscenity" in particular.
18. Alcide Bonneau, *Curiosa: Essais critiques de littérature ancienne ignorée ou mal connue* (Paris: Lisieux, 1887), 331.

explicitly to provide a solid scientific basis for the fundamental distinction nineteenth-century critics had established between "cerebral" and hence masculine literature
and sexualized and hence feminine "pornography." In so
doing, they drew out some of the contradictory implica-
tions of avant-garde writing itself. How, they asked, did
literary form express manhood and what did it take to be
a (literary) man?

Le génie littéraire is a long description of cerebral functions and neuro-anatomy that sought to prove, among
other things, that because of the proximity of the sexual
and linguistic functions in the brain, the genius who
wrote a violently sensual work was not necessarily a degenerate. In fact, Voivenel and Rémond argued, literary
genius is a *"progénéréscence synérgique* of the whole of the
centers of the frontal system [of the brain]"—that is, degenerates are incapable of literary genius.[19] They go on to
suggest that the main criteria for distinguishing between
a genius's and a degenerate's work is virility. Women cannot demonstrate the same literary genius as men because
women's literary work reflects female physiology: it is
passive, unfocused, and exteriorizes rather than tran-
scends the confusion that inspired it. But then, apparently contradicting the connection between sexuality and
femininity to which they and other critics adhered, they
claim that women are "poorly gifted from the point of
view of sexual sensibility." Now it is not the presence
but the absence of sexuality that precludes women from
giving their literary productions an express purpose. Or

19. Paul Voivenel and A. Rémond, *Le Génie littéraire* (Paris: Alcan,
1912), 266. In many turn-of-the century medical texts, Cesare Lombroso's
among them, degeneracy was often associated with the genius suffering
from nervous exhaustion and heightened sensibility.

rather, since Voivenel and Rémond insisted elsewhere on a conflation of femininity and sexuality, women have the wrong kind of sexuality, one that is incompatible with literary genius.[20]

Echoing critics of the self-reflexivity of avant-garde art, Voivenel and Rémond insisted that Stéphane Mallarmé, because of his "feminine" tendency to confuse means and ends, to present his thought in terms of an "unintelligible" and hence mystical veil, was degenerate and probably "impotent." They argued further that if feminine literature sought to achieve a "nervous equilibrium," and masculine literature manifested its genius in "conquest and struggle," then surely Gabriele d'Annunzio (whom Nordau had denounced as a degenerate) was a literary man. But in so doing, they inadvertently extended the parameters of the literary to include a writer normally dismissed along with Mallarmé as impotent: "The union of the genius of language and of sexuality, the intimate, complete, splendid fusion, is to be found in Gabriele d'Annunzio." His oeuvre "expresses a violent but never indecent sensuality, such that the magic of the verb predominates over the most unfettered instincts."[21]

Here, in d'Annunzio's work, Voivenel and Rémond privileged sexual experience as a mode of consciousness insofar as it is a "psychic excitation" that manifests itself in the literary equivalent of a male "genital response"— the desire to conquer. They excerpt this passage to prove their point:

> The male had already thrown himself at her, had forced her to the ground . . . and with his fist he struck her face, her

20. Ibid., 275, 277.
21. Ibid., 283, 266.

arms, her chest. . . . . She neither cried out nor defended herself, but at each blow moaned a weak moan almost with
a breathless entreaty. Then she felt his mouth crush hers,
weightier than his fist, and the blows ceased, his hands
passed to another violence, flesh penetrated flesh as a sword
that eviscerates. A panting rose in the throat swollen by veins
waiting to be slit, a furious shudder of he who strives to tear
the reddest roots of life from the depths of being and to cast
them beyond the limits imposed on men's desire.[22]

In their view, this passage quite literally conveys the
man's "desire to conquer" and sexuality is dominated by
the language used to express it. This positive interpretation of the link between language and sexuality was thus
possible only insofar as Voivenel and Rémond read the
passage as a literal celebration of normative virility, of
a glorious, phallic tumescence. They literalized the excerpt's sadomasochism: it does not refer to a desire for
self-fulfillment through self-annihilation but to a normative male sexuality driven by the "natural" desire to dominate a woman. Voivenel and Rémond entreated their
readers to recognize the beauty and hence "decency" of
d'Annunzio's work, although they offer no formal analysis of why his work is more "decent" than, say, Nordau
perceived it to be. The verb and the phallus are indistinguishable vehicles of a "psychic excitation" that moves us
with the enormity of its (literary) power.

Voivenel and Rémond were squarely within late-nineteenth-century categories even as they sought to expand
the forms through which the body could be symbolized,
so that at least one text previously deemed pornographic
could now have the same redemptive function as literature. In their (rather wishful) view, these sexual images

22. D'Annunzio quoted in ibid., 267.

ensured redemption because they accurately represented normal and hence virile male physiology exaggerated by the heightened virility of genius. Genius was thus manifest in a hyperbolic masculinity untainted by perversion and hence sterility, and literature served moral order by example: genius dominated sex, tied sexual sensations inseparably to ideas, and in so doing guaranteed that immorality would not lead to debauchery and sterility.

This paradox—that literature could be at once of the flesh and absolutely "pure," that it could be both womanly *and* manly—meant that the spatial symbolism of "lower" sexual pleasures and "higher" intellectual ones had to be reformulated. In the psychiatrists' opinion, d'Annunzio's passage no longer smelled of beasts or of exotic perfume, but evoked grandiose monuments to man's greatness, his disciplined struggles and conquests. Hyperbolic tumescence was no longer the sign of an effeminate male body, no longer expressed the author's desire to "be a woman," and hence his sterility and desire for self-dissolution. In their view, tumescence is well regulated and always in our best moral interests, like Emile Zola's pristine, philanthropic motives in "exposing," and "tearing apart" our "natural being."[23] It is as if they sought to theorize above all Zola's paradoxical insistence that the purpose of naturalist literature was not to corrupt but to cleanse, that the purpose of writing novels about vice (as medical men had long claimed in books about so-called sexual deviance) was to prevent it.

To the extent that Voivenel and Rémond used d'Annunzio, not as an example of, but as an antidote to,

23. Zola quoted in Deborah Silverman, *Art Nouveau in Fin-de-Siècle France* (Berkeley and Los Angeles: University of California Press, 1990), 80.

the overwrought nerves that left men weak and trembling, they sought to put phallic tumescence in the service of moral order: to establish a medical ground for using erotic language in society's interest. Their book is at once a tirade against feminists and an effort to put genius back into the service of improving the species. They claimed to have proven scientifically that feminists who sought equality and the vote were wrong: "the brain of a woman cannot be identical to that of a man." Furthermore, they claim that literary genius has "an intimate correlation with the propagation of the species." After all, they insist, "nature condemns monsters to sterility," while genius is nature's way of perfecting "man's" neuro-anatomical structure. In short, healthy reproduction is dependent on male supremacy.[24]

But how exactly does this after all quite conventional assertion that the genius's language dominates sex work here? How is d'Annunzio's text "nude" and not "naked?" How do we know (in aesthetic rather than neuro-anatomical) terms that the indecent phallus is different from the "never indecent" one? And if the phallus and the verb are finally (or formally) indistinguishable, how is d'Annunzio's text literature and not "pornography," the apparently transparent transcription of sex? If the genius's work merely represents male physiology in perfect working order, what ultimately distinguishes the genius's glorious (and hence literary) phallic conquest from the transparent (and hence pornographic) representations of male virility condemned, among others, by Sarcey? Or, for that matter, what distinguishes this phallic conquest from the irresistible seduction of the reader condemned by Ségard? How would this literature in fact represent a

24. Voivenel and Rémond, *Génie littéraire*, 268, 273, 291.

body redeemed by a higher purpose and hence a properly virile—chaste, manly, erect—virility? Because they offer nothing other than a rather literal and quite conventional reading of d'Annunzio not shared by other, sharper if less tolerant critics, the flesh-bound virility of "eunuchs" (as Hugues Rebell called writers like d'Annunzio) is in fact hard to distinguish from the potency of the genius whose sensual language redeems our creaturely status. Literature is the metaphorical extension of a bestial, sterile, insatiable body, as well as of a noble, productive, and hence properly "civilized" one, an ambivalence Benedetto Croce captured when he noted that d'Annunzio was both "too virile" and "too feminine" to be a truly great writer.[25]

Voivenel and Rémond thus reiterated the ambiguity between a chaste, sanitized and hence "masculine" and a purely sexualized and hence "feminine" virility (already implicit in d'Annunzio's text) in their own inability, finally, to find solid grounds on which to differentiate literature from pornography. To repeat Benedetto Croce's comment in lengthier terms, the literary depiction of a glorious hardness (for that is precisely how d'Annunzio "never indecently" names perfect manliness) is not necessarily compatible with social equilibrium, does not necessarily restore virility to literature without at once threatening to undermine it, to render it sterile and feminine. D'Annunzio's less sympathetic contemporaries could not ignore the bestial imagery in the long passage quoted above, the vulnerable, swollen "veins," the smell of the slaughterhouse, the longing for castration and obliteration.

---

25. Benedetto Croce quoted in Barbara Spackman, *Decadent Genealogies: The Rhetoric of Sickness from Baudelaire to D'Annunzio* (Ithaca, N.Y.: Cornell University Press, 1990), 67.

Voivenel and Rémond failed then to show how literature could be something other than a tautology of pornography, how literature could be of the flesh without being feminized, how literature that named virility could remain virile. Or rather, on a more abstract level, their work failed to show how "exposure," to use Zola's word, did not seduce, tantalize, repulse, nauseate, and hence threaten social order, but rather neutralized and contained pleasure; how it was no longer a supremely feminine loss of perspective but a manly effort to set things right; how, finally, exposing nature could be the sine qua non of cerebral mediation (which medical men who wrote about vice claimed all along). But this ambiguity between femininity and masculinity, and hence between pornography and literature, eventually broadened the definition of the literary so extensively that "literature" no longer consisted solely of those texts in which sexuality was clearly absent, suggested, or even repressed. In their paradoxical efforts to provide a stable basis for the divide between literature and pornography, interwar critics, as we shall see, rendered the eroticized "pornographic" body indistinct from the impermeable male body.

From Repression to Derepression

Although some historians have noted that the invention of modern pornography required a mechanical concept of the body not developed until the Enlightenment (Sade is a case in point), it was not until the late nineteenth and early twentieth century that pornography was denounced *because* it depicted bodies as machines.[26] Pro

26. See Antoine de Baecque, "The 'Livres rempli d'horreur': Pornographic Literature and Politics at the Beginning of the French Revolution," in Peter Wagner, ed., *Erotica and the Enlightenment* (New York: Lang, 1990), and Margaret Jacob, "The Materialist World of Pornography" in

gressive advocates of derepression often drew analogies between war, pornography, and consumer capitalism and insisted that they were synonymous with the dissolution of masculinity, and hence with the dissolution of the fragile moral fiber that held the social body together.

As the legal scholar Paul Lapeire noted, in regulating men's "genital activity" in the name of the national interest, the state robbed them of their individuality and hence of their virility, so, for example, censorship laws did not preserve the nation from emasculation—as the authors of such legislation in France had hoped—but instead encouraged it. After the Great War, critics such as Lapeire demonized the forces of repression for constraining the so-called instinctive currents that made nations and races great. Lapeire argued that with the institution of democratic government and its secular foundations under the Third Republic, morality had lost its anchor in a higher religious purpose. For him this was a welcome change, and he celebrated the end of the Church's power in moral matters. But in his opinion, politicians who rightly rejected religious doctrine had replaced it with equally repressive censorship legislation that made no distinction between erotic and pornographic material.[27]

For rather than acting as a constraint that guarantees the freedom of all—and hence balancing individual and social needs, as the liberal state must—repression sapped morale and reduced "man" to nothing other than a "lowly cog" in a "gigantic machine . . . less and less free to do what he will with his activity and his body." After

Lynn Hunt, ed., *The Invention of Pornography: Obscenity and the Origins of Modernity, 1500–1800* (New York: Zone Books, 1991), 157–202.

27. Paul Lapeire, *Essai juridique et historique sur l'outrage aux bonnes mœurs par le livre, l'écrit, et l'imprimé* (Lille: Douriez-Bataille, 1931), 22–23.

all, had not thousands of men become the disposable material parts of a war machine whose rationale was proven false? Had they not been seduced by a "grand illusion" that blinded them to their real spiritual degradation? Was not the repression of so-called pornographic material in the name of social order and the war effort only a surreptitious means by which politicians emasculated young men while feeding them delusions of virility? In short, did not repression encourage rather than inhibit moral degeneration, now conceived of as the bankruptcy of the political system and as the hypocrisy and tyranny of established elites?[28]

As Lionel d'Autrec noted, the repression of pornography effected under the Third Republic had not driven pornographers out of business. Instead, it had been used to condemn "those writers who denounce social decay"—writers like Zola and Lemonnier, whom legislators had deemed exemplars *of* that decay. Furthermore, the same politicians who permitted detailed descriptions of murder and who glorified war suppressed the "most normal and most beautiful of all human acts." The same men who denounced moral laxity "die while being caressed by a prostitute . . . die in the arms of a pederast." "All the democracy's elite," d'Autrec declared, "smoke opium and have themselves flagellated in the houses on the rue Miromesnil."[29]

28. Ibid., 23.
29. Autrec, *Outrage aux mœurs*, 288, 92, 287. By the mid nineteenth century already, satirists allegorized the censor as "Anastasie," figured as a shrew with an enormous pair of scissors. Thus, not only was pornography gendered feminine, but the state's effort to censor was represented as feminine as long as censors could be seen as prudes and hypocrites. In spite of its popularity, even in the nineteenth century, the most common

Thus in the name of restoring virility, politicians were said to have undermined it, to have turned some men into passive instruments of a war machine so that others could indulge themselves in luxury, perversion, and pornography. This rather paradoxical insistence that the derepression of sexuality would lead to the end of this immorality meant that derepression was not really about freeing so-called instincts but about socializing them in the name of helping men to remain men. Understood in this way, derepression did not refer to the dissolution of corporeal boundaries, the loss of discipline and hence to the acting out of dangerous longings, but to the restoration of an expressive, integral male self that had been commodified in pornography, in consumerism, and especially in war. Pornography thus symbolized the fragmentation of the male psyche.[30]

Most critics stressed the beauty and naturalness of sexuality, now seen as an uplifting spiritual force, signifying profundity and power, rather than as undisciplined and feminine.[31] "Sensuality is the mysterious but necessary and creative condition of intellectual development. Those who have not gone to the limits of the flesh, whether to love or to damn it, are incapable of understanding the entire range of the spirit," according to the poet and novelist Pierre Loüys (1870–1925), Lapiere notes, adding:

---

symbol of the censor remained the candle-snuffer, and hence an image of repression. See Christian Delporte, "'Anastasie': L'Imaginaire de la censure dans le dessin satirique (XIXe–XXe siècles)," in Ory, ed., *Censure*, 89–99.

30. See, e.g., Hunter et al., *On Pornography*, 190–95.

31. "The appeal to 'sheer sensuality' is supposed to 'purify and quicken the mind,'" noted D. H. Lawrence, who is cited as exemplary of an "ethical elite" using erotic literature to "practice facing up to their sexuality and achieving its aesthetic sublimation" by Hunter et al. (*On Pornography*, 113, 192). The shift away from repression I am describing was thus hardly limited to France.

"[D]oesn't [Loüys] affirm that all the powerful cities that have reigned in the world have been . . . as licentious as they were powerful, as if their dissolution was necessary to their splendor?"[32]

The histories of the cities to which Loüys referred—Alexandria, Athens, Rome, Venice, and Paris—were allegories for a process of literary creation in which "only the virility of the body fertilizes the brain." At first reading, this paradox of creation through dissolution sounds much like the theory of literary production articulated by decadent artists, and that is presumably how Loüys meant it. "Decadent" nations necessarily produced the greatest artists, "sterile but refined," according to Paul Bourget (1852–1935), the foremost theorist of decadence, echoing Baudelaire and echoed by Paul Valéry. But, as Lapeire saw it, there was no decadent celebration of corporeal dissolution in Loüys's statement, no sterility, no degeneration. He asked rather: is it "necessary to be as pessimistic as Valéry? What is certain is that it is not in the power of any authority to contain these powerful and subterranean forces that unceasingly exercise nations and races." In his view, great works of art derived rather from a healthy, natural virility, and texts deemed pornographic fifty years before had not necessarily signaled the degeneration of culture but, on the contrary, had affirmed its manliness.[33] "Everywhere, always, in eras of progress as in eras of decadence, in peace as in war, sexuality is the origin of all events and actions," Charles-Noël Renard similarly concluded.[34]

32. Lapeire, *Essai juridique*, 25.
33. Ibid., n. 25; Paul Bourget, *Essais de psychologie contemporaine* (Paris: Lemerre, 1883), 27.
34. Charles-Noël Renard, *Les Androphobes* (St. Etienne: Imprimerie spéciale, 1930), 57.

The regenerative impulse implicit in the new emphasis on derepression is especially clear in the claim that all great male writers were what one commentator called "les grands génitaux," which became one of the commonest defenses of writers put on trial for "obscenity." Overzealous regulation of literature on moral grounds was thus necessarily a bad thing. If you "castrate the sexes . . . you castrate thought," d'Autrec insisted.[35] Sylvain Bonmariage, too, denounced repressive constraints on sexual feeling: "To the same degree that social conventions . . . force writers to conform to a narrowly defined framework of morality, natural law pushes them to find an outlet for their repressed instincts. As soon as they no longer fear criticism, their self-expression issues from that force that dominates man: sex." Bonmariage also argued that the link between art and sexual pleasure was part of the evolution of civilization and, when satisfied, "provokes . . . the flowering of the highest thought by adding to sensibility and imagination unhoped for riches."[36]

All these writers were repelled by the "puritanism" they claimed followed on the heels of the war. Instead, the writers, artists, and journalists who called for the formation of a "League Against Puritanism" in 1923 believed that ["Anglo-Saxon"] prudishness impeded the restoration of "all the traditions of the *génie latin . . .* [its] *esprit,* lightness, and gaiety" and prevented the "rehabilitation of love." As Georges Anquetil, put on trial in 1922 for obscenity, expressed it: "[A]ll that touches on the sexual question must be held to be natural and consequently

---

35. Autrec, *Outrage aux mœurs*, 280.
36. Bonmariage quoted in ibid., 290; Sylvain Bonmariage, *Les Plaisirs de l'Enfer* (Paris: Raoul Saillard, 1938), 12, 9.

freed of all hypocrisy that surrounds it, because that hypocrisy encourages the libidinal perversions now killing our race." When tried for another infraction against obscenity law in 1927, Georges Anquetil defended himself by employing a now familiar argument: he advertised sexual material, he claimed, in order "to moralize . . . to expos[e] the brutal portrait of certain social horrors to readers . . . so that they could protect themselves against vices that might otherwise tempt them."[37]

The novelist Armand Charpentier, a great opponent of censorship and a staunch anti-Catholic, argued that "perversion" was born of the repression of "natural" instincts by our puritanical culture.[38] And in perhaps the most elaborate argument against repression, Frédéric Paulhan claimed that in attempting to tame the sex instinct, man had created barriers to sexual satisfaction which only increased the allure of forbidden pleasures. He suggested (echoing Freud) that mores be relaxed to accommodate sex outside of reproduction in order to preserve social order both from depopulation and from even more "severe" deviations (as from heterosexuality). In other words, the so-called sex instinct had been repressed at great cost to social order.[39]

The liberation of the male sex instinct thus did not signal the dissolution of culture but was necessary to its survival: it guaranteed the quality of thought itself. That is, a "higher" or civilized perspective could only be sustained through a vigorously proclaimed virility. Nature and sex-

37. Quoted in Autrec, *Outrage aux mœurs*, 290, 253. *Recueil des Gazettes des Tribunaux*, 30 November 1927.
38. Quoted in Autrec, *Outrage aux mœurs*, 247.
39. Frédéric Paulhan, *Les Transformations sociales des sentiments* (Paris: Flammarion, 1920), 240–41.

uality were thus no longer equated with the female body and degeneration, but with masculinity and cultural grandeur. Critics paradoxically believed that the maintenance of order required the liberation of virility, liberation from the now feminizing constraints on what Bonmariage had referred to as "natural law." Derepression did not lead to the sterility of unproductive lust but sustained productive manliness. The influential British sexologist Havelock Ellis (1859–1939) testified to the transnational nature of these views when he endorsed rational sexual education rather than censorship as the most effective means of combating perversion. He assumed pornography would hold no temptation for the well-educated mind, and that taboos only made things more desirable; "secrecy and repression," he argued, are "against nature."[40] The French left-wing writer André Lorulot called pornography "the *useless* [emphasis in original] display of all the details of sexual functions." Pornography, he continued, had no effect on healthy, informed minds, but inevitably corrupted the naive and uninformed.[41]

Moral order was now conceived to be the logical fulfillment of a liberated, virile "nature," and openness and liberty rather than repression and secrecy were the prerequisites of health. This logic defined what readers might now perceive as a conventional distinction between literature and pornography. As Alexander Zévaès protested, censorship laws could not distinguish between the "vigorous and virtuous indignation of a poet" and "shame-

40. Havelock Ellis, *More Essays on Love and Virtue* (London: Constable, 1931), 124, 137.
41. André Lorulot, *"Ma 'pornographie' et . . . la Votre!" Réponse à l'Abbé Bethléem* (Herblay: Idée libre, 1930), 6.

less and depraved lewdness."[42] Zola's defenders, Have-lock Ellis among them, asserted that his work was not the "raw" material of pornography, but represented "the rawness of truth and indignation."[43] And the surrealist Robert Desnos claimed that, in contrast to pornography (which was writing confined to the "inferior faculties"), erotic literature from Baudelaire to Apollinaire was great because it was both liberated and manly: Baudelaire's work was "male," and "virile"; Apollinaire was too cerebral but did manifest "a liberty of spirit and especially a masculine quality without which a man cannot produce an erotic [hence aesthetic] work whatever the form in which he expresses his passion."[44]

But how does liberating the sexuality once associated with pornography (remember d'Annunzio) serve to regulate it? How exactly does the abolition of censorship ensure the preservation of moral order? In other words, embedded in the peculiar idea that writing was literary to the extent that it fulfilled the dictates of nature was that other question: how does the genius's phallic tumescence ensure rather than undermine virility, and thus how does naming virility serve rather than subvert social order? What really marks the distinction between aesthetically acceptable literature and pornography? Thus it was that by the interwar years, the question of how to differentiate between literature and pornography was inextricable from another question central to a newly secularized moral order: how could the state at once retain social

42. Alexandre Zévaès, *Les Procès littéraires au XIXème siècle*, 3d ed. (Paris: Perrin, 1924), 146.
43. Ellis quoted in Marchand, *Sex Life in France*, 265–67.
44. Robert Desnos, *De l'érotisme considéré dans ses manifestations écrites et du point de vue de l'esprit moderne* (1923; reprint, Paris: Cercle des Arts, 1952), 67, 76, 112.

equilibrium by keeping men virtuous and liberate nature by keeping them potent? And how, then, could it ensure that men would remain men?

One could argue that this political question was precisely the unarticulated one underlying the work of many academic aesthetic theorists after 1900 who sought to steer a third way between neoclassicism and aestheticism, between what the critic Paul Gaultier perceived as an overvaluation of reason (the "objectivists") and an overvaluation of sexual instinct (the "subjectivists"), respectively. Gaultier argued conventionally that art was amoral, meaning that it could not be linked to its author's morals or "race." Art is independent of morality and yet cannot help but contribute to heightening moral sensibility: nudity when sculpted or painted is chaste, according to Gaultier; even Ingrès's *Odalisque* does not elicit desire.[45]

Another, more explicit effort to theorize anew precisely how the rendering of sex in aesthetic production immunizes us from sex's necessarily "immoral" effects won a prize in 1920. The competition was sponsored by the Académie des Sciences Morales et Politiques on the theme "Should Art Be Independent of Morality?" and the winning essay by Charles Lalo was partially published under the title *La Beauté et l'instinct sexuel* (Beauty

---

45. Paul Gaultier, *Le Sens de l'art* (Paris: Hachette, 1911), 149–53. Writing under the pseudonym "Dr. François Nazier," Henri Drouin claimed: "I think it is easy to find literary equivalents of all modes of sexual activity" (*Trois Entretiens sur la sexualité* [Paris: Editions du Siècle, 1926], 46). "[A]rtistic creation incontestably possesses a sexual substratum," according to Drouin; a woman's intellectual work reflects her excessive, insatiable sexuality, whereas a man's is the equivalent of his sexual satisfaction (*Femmes damnées* [Paris: La Vulgarisation scientifique, 1945], 71–72). Drouin's comments reflect contemporary scrutiny of the relationship between sexuality and aesthetics.

and Sexual Instinct) by Flammarion in 1922. Lalo argues that art is a necessary corollary to morality, but not in the way traditionally conceived. Reproduction is a social obligation, while artistic creation derives from an instinctive sexual longing that has no place in family life. Art represents the "deployment" of eroticism outside of the family and should not cross "the threshold of the legal household, where the reign of morality begins."[46]

But this does not mean that art has no positive social function. "Does art," Lalo asks, "have to distinguish itself from our instincts in order to render itself a superior cultural form?" In his search for a more precise understanding of the relationship between art and sensual pleasure, Lalo polemicizes against those spokesmen of culture (aimed specifically at the reactionary editor of the *Revue des deux mondes,* Ferdinand Brunetière) who, in "refusing to recognize eroticism cannot recognize art itself." Thus, against those who would "mutilate and corrupt art with . . . proscriptions," Lalo proposes an "erotic theory of beauty." He conceives of art as a "remembering" of sexual instinct that would at once give form to and discipline the eroticism incompatible with family life and hence moral order: "The raison d'être of aesthetic life is to discipline and to socialize these excessive expenditures that, if left entirely to the individual, would . . . be a source of perpetual anarchy."[47]

In Lalo's view, sex is not transformed into art through a creative will, through sublimation and hence by way of an escape from sexuality, but by somehow appropriating

46. Charles Lalo, *La Beauté et l'instinct sexuel* (Paris: Flammarion, 1922), 127, 156.
47. Ibid., 22, 29, 25–26, 126. See also Charles Lalo, *L'Expression de la vie dans l'art* (Paris: Felix Alcan, 1933), 253.

sexual arousal.[48] Thus, whereas "great" empires had really dissolved through excessive licentiousness, in literature self-dissolution is "remembered" and yet somehow purged or forgotten, as in a dream (although Lalo never explains how). Literature's redemptive and purifying function is thus no longer manifested in what literature says about the way we *should* live, but in its perpetual evocation of an erotic longing or dream at once remembered and purged from consciousness. As the surrealist Robert Desnos put it: what real poet "does not like to withdraw into that spiritual retreat where love is at *once pure and licentious* [emphasis mine] in the absolute?"[49] In Lalo's emphasis, by that time hardly original, on what literature did (remembering) rather than on what it meant, virility lies in the eloquence of literary form—not in the thing represented but in the writing through which it is evoked. The literary critic Louis Estève insisted conventionally that all higher art forms bear a "warm reflection of their original [erotic] ardor" even as they are purified by their formal properties. Art still bears the expurgated traces of sexuality.[50] In this context, as Laurence Bertrand Dorléac puts it, modern censorship eventually concerned itself less with questions of sexual or political morality and more with forms of representations themselves: "form in itself became a moral question."[51]

48. For recent theoretical elaborations of this concept of sublimation deemed closer to Freud's texts than received wisdom, see Jean Laplanche, *Problématiques III: La Sublimation* (Paris: Presses universitaires de France, 1980), and Leo Bersani, *The Freudian Body* (New York: Columbia University Press), 1986.

49. Desnos, *De l'érotisme*, 14.

50. Louis Estève, "L'Amour androgyne," *Bon Plaisir*, February 1923, 45.

51. Laurence Bertrand Dorléac, "Art et censure" in Ory, ed., *Censure*, 191, 194–95.

Realism and naturalism expand their availability, and the male spectator's sexual pleasure is now desublimated and yet difficult to locate, manifest and yet hard to detect, so that sexual pleasure remains proper to art but (properly) elusive.

Lalo's work thus merely culminates a movement in which mainstream art criticism expands the realm of the nonobscene to incorporate previously nonliterary texts. Although I can only offer speculations based on this criticism, we have seen that eroticism in writers such as d'Annunzio and Zola was recognized as a formal property of art, so that texts originally perceived as "naked" became "nude." Virility, then, was still embedded in the transcendent meaning of the text, but now within forms that both disclosed and purged what was seductive or repellent. Critics extended the nonobscene as part of a broader effort to rethink the nature of the relationship between literature and sexuality in accord with a new cultural imperative to sustain literature's virility by "liberating" it. That is, again, they inadvertently legitimated earlier, avant-garde ideas about the nature of aesthetic redemption, not in an effort to revolutionize poetry, but on the contrary, in their effort to preserve moral order, to cleanse and purify the nation.

With the exception of the fascist d'Annunzio, and perhaps Zola, most avant-garde artists would never have conceded this interpretation. Literature could now function both to "liberate" and regulate men's virility in the interests of a patriarchal moral order: it would be at once chaste and seductive, restrained and revelatory, a metaphorically male body in which those "feminine" qualities denounced by critics of pornography would be neutralized. But this interpretation also points to a symmetry between avant-garde texts and the bourgeois culture they sought to repudiate—the latter's puritanism and morality, its own "neutralization" of libidinal excess.[52] As Desnos says of Sade: "Throughout the vicissitudes of an extreme fantasy, in the laudatory sense of the word . . . sadists, masochists, masturbators, sodomites, and flagellants are revealed without baseness or filth."[53]

High-culture writers neither all agreed with Charles Lalo and Alexander Zévaès nor shared their motives in defending literature from censorship. There was not immediately a new and uniform judgment about what literature was or was not, and I have no desire to reduce modernist works to the vulgarization of critics or to deny the truly revolutionary nature of the French avant-garde(s). I wish simply to suggest that the long-term shift from pornography to literature was made possible because avant-garde texts could be coded as masculine ones and because critics expanded the literary forms in which virility could be expressed and embodied. By analyzing the historically specific process by which male bodily integrity was "restored" in new terms, we can perhaps begin to explain something about how literary forms produce and are themselves produced by cultural norms, and how pornography comes to mean what it does.

Among the intellectual elite after the war, many works previously deemed pornographic were redefined as literature, and pornography was still a form of sexual mercantilism that reduced human beings into things and

52. On this question, see Rita Felski, "The Counterdiscourse of the Feminine in Three Texts by Wilde, Huysmans, and Sacher-Masoch," *PMLA* 5 (1991): 1094–1105.

53. Desnos, *De l'érotisme*, 110. On the conventional distinctions between high and low art, see the discussion between Rosalind Krauss, Yves Bois, Hal Foster et al., in "The Politics of the Signifier II: A Conversation of the *Informe* and the Abject," *October* 67 (1994): 3–21. The abject, as Krauss notes, can be traced to Georges Bataille's *informe*. Bataille would have opposed Desnos's "recuperation" of Sade here, in which the writer's work is purified. As Krauss puts it, "I take it to be a way for Bataille to group a variety of strategies for knocking form off its pedestal" (4).

undermined the virile integrity of the social body. Maurice Dekobra defended independent artists and writers against censorship on condition that they "do not devote themselves to commercial pornography," and Hans Ryner, declaring his desire to join the League against Puritanism, asserted that his "adherence to this League does not mean I hold pornographers in any esteem." Again, pornography became for the twentieth century what prostitution had been for the nineteenth: a metaphor for contamination, for a world in which money was the measure of all things, and in which a popular inability to discriminate between dreams and reality, refined and vulgar pleasures predominated—in short, for consumer culture. After all, only "impotent bigots," "old maids," and the feeble-minded more generally adored pornography.[54]

The League's members, echoing their 1905 forefathers, thus did not seek to abolish censorship altogether but to reduce its scope to protect artists and writers, but not "pornographers," from condemnation. They and other critics consequently protested less against the regulation of things obscene than against the confusion of literature with pornography. Pornography remained coded as feminine, as unmediated nature and unproductive libidinal expenditure understood, in an interesting although perhaps not unexpected analogy with men's dehumanizing experience in the Great War, as the reduction of human beings to body parts (recall the "useless details of sexual functions" and the body in its utter "nakedness"). Lionel d'Autrec, who wrote a passionate tract against censorship, distinguished carefully between acceptable and unacceptable erotic works in reference to Léon Daudet's

54. All quoted in Autrec, *Outrage aux mœurs*, 273–74, 195.

L'Entremetteuse: "M. Daudet is morbid. Haunted by sexual perversion. . . . His book is written by a pervert incapable of an audacious and powerful virility and only excited by contact with spicier things." The naturalized Frenchman Giuseppe Lo Duca, a historian of pornography, claimed that unlike the erotic, pornography was "non-symbolic" and hence not worthy of protection.[55]

The pornography of the late nineteenth century began to be seen as literature by a widening circle of critics when the exposure of virility was reinterpreted as upholding moral order. Pornography became literature when that exposure was conceived as central to the neutralization and hence containment of femininity, when libidinal excess was refigured as a healthy, spiritual, masculine force rather than a diseased, material, and feminine one. In other words, I have sought to show how literature once deemed pornographic was recast as a masculine body that transcended sexuality, and pornography became a repository of that sexuality. When critics brought sex into the open, they sought, oddly, not to tell all, but to sanitize and purify it. Again, this shift was transnational and remains current: as late as 1960, Montgomery Hyde, a passionate British opponent of censorship and one of the first historians of pornography, argued that the lifting of taboos would lead to the end of pornography and the celebration of the erotic: "Obscenity and pornography are ugly phantoms which will disappear in the morning light when we rehabilitate sex and eroticism."[56]

55. Giuseppe Maria Lo Duca, *L'Histoire de l'érotisme* (Paris: Le Jeune Parque, 1969), 21.

56. H. Montgomery Hyde, *A History of Pornography* (New York: Farrar, Straus & Giroux, 1964), 204.

When Havelock Ellis announced in 1931 that today's obscenity is the future's propriety, and Alexandre Zévaès insisted that what shocked people in the past would seem timid today, they meant that all pleasures must become permissible—that is, all pleasures must conform to the requirements of social order and hence of virility.[57] In this vision, pleasure only ever furthered the aims of reason, the liberation of nature always regulated social order, and femininity was only ever visible as a glorious phallic tumescence. When the morning light bleached pleasure of its impurities, pornography would become literature. The majority of these commentators were confident that derepression would lead to the elimination of all so-called sexual aberrations, including the use of pornography and homosexuality.[58] This confidence perhaps explains why some sexual fantasies were not accorded the same protection or approbation as others, or why so many French intellectuals defended certain sexually explicit material while obeying a cultural imperative to regret that pornography existed.

The process by which modernism began to gain mainstream acceptance—by which many works, from those of Jules Barbey d'Aurevilly (1808–1889) to Zola's, were no longer deemed obscene and unliterary by a wider audience of critics (if not legislators)—was thus inextricable from a broader revision of the gendered terms that defined the relationship between the body and the literary. Thus, the expansion of the nonobscene does not only reflect, as Walter Kendrick argues, the increasing estrangement of art and society and the self-proclaimed "otherness" of art. That expansion does not only testify to

57. Ellis, *More Essays*, 129; Zévaès, *Procès littéraires*, xi.
58. See Autrec, *Outrage aux mœurs*, 247, 263.

the "relegation of 'literary value' to the province of experts" and underscore the fact that so few people now read books like *Ulysses*.[59] Cultural critics revised the symbolism of masculinity and hence reconstructed the relationship between masculinity and moral order. Masculinity no longer symbolized the darkness and secrecy of repression, but the glare of the morning light, the glorious hardness of reason. It no longer neutralized threats to the social body by repressing libidinal excess—its diseased, feminized components. Instead, masculinity sustained virtue by sustaining sexual potency, regulated moral order by removing repressive constraints on nature. That is why critics so often saw (and see) the consumers of pornography as pitiable victims of sexual repression.

If this argument is correct, then the shift from repression to derepression fashioned the sexual drive as an expression of culture rather than of nature, or, rather, rendered the two indistinct. In a dramatic shift, critics rendered the body integral and impermeable *because* it was sexually "liberated," and came to see sexual liberation as oddly continuous with the transcendence of sexual desire. In nineteenth-century aesthetic production, virility was transcended and occupied a status to be over-

59. Walter Kendrick, *The Secret Museum: Pornography in Modern Culture* (New York: Penguin Books, 1987), 170–72, 195, 178. Kendrick mourns the presumed dethroning of words in favor of the power of images. He does not resent mass culture, however, but is sorry that literature can no longer play the subversive role it once did. He blames this development both on an increasingly estranged avant-garde and on cultural shifts that favor other sorts of media. While interesting, his book is primarily descriptive and begs the question of why and how literature loses its power, or why texts once deemed pornographic are no longer called literary. It also entirely neglects gender as a category of analysis, an omission Linda Williams has sharply criticized in her own reading of Kendrick (Williams, *Hard Core*, 11–15).

come even as it informed creativity. Now virility occupies a transcendent status, but it cannot be located metaphorically "under" the creative process. This logic raises a question left unresolved by interwar critics: if they had liberated the body's sexuality, and desire was a force equivalent, and indeed, indistinct from reason, how could sexuality be identified or described or located? The same critics who celebrated sexual liberation saved the body's integrity by reinterpreting the body's desire as the very force of reason and by relocating sexuality in pornography, the output of feeble and feminized minds and bodies. Pornography, in Hyde's words, was the repository of "ugly phantoms," which would be eliminated when everyone was properly educated: reason would then be absolutely uncontaminated by the vagaries of desire (as if reason and desire did not always intersect in complex ways). The expansion of the nonobscene thus represents a redefinition of the relationship between the body and culture, mediated through gender, that now makes even the marquis de Sade's work acceptable to judges. When Robert Desnos said that "erotic literature could not lie," he meant that the truly literary work names or "liberates" and thereby purifies its virility, proudly proclaiming its higher truth. What judge could ask more of a defendant?

3

The Great War, Pornography, and the Violated Social Body

> Dear body, poor body, magnificent body,
> oh matter!
>
> Charles-Ferdinand Ramuz,
> *Présence de la mort* (1922)

As the preceding two chapters have demonstrated, pornography's increased elasticity depended, paradoxically, on its transformation into a rhetorical container of abject sexuality. In this chapter, I shall make the same argument in the context of a discussion about how interwar critics used pornography to dramatize the unprecedented violence of the Great War. Writers, artists, doctors, and others found themselves challenged to explain the war's psychological symptoms as they manifested themselves in a wide variety of contexts and in "culture" more generally, and pornography became one symbol of the dismembered, traumatized, susceptible male body and psyche. These traumatized souls and their psychic symptoms perpetuated the dissolution of faith in human reason and progress throughout western Europe, sustaining the per-

---

Epigraph: Charles-Ferdinand Ramuz, *Présence de la mort* (1922; reprint, Lausanne: L'Aire, 1978), 58.

ception of the postwar period that T. S. Eliot so aptly described as "the immense panorama of futility and anarchy which is contemporary history."[1]

Proponents of war in France promised that it would regenerate a nation debilitated, as they perceived it, by a
low birthrate, feminist demands for equality (which the
war would obliterate), a lack of vigor, and, in their most
dizzy fantasy, by tainted blood. Instead, by the end of
1916 more than a million Frenchmen had given their
lives in battles with little substantial territorial recom-
pense. For the first time, combat produced apparently
incurable psychological symptoms that undermined the
virility the war was supposed to restore: nightmares, in-
somnia, anxiety, and paranoia were all diagnosed in England as "shell shock"—the consequence of exposure to
repeated trauma. In France, doctors interpreted the same
symptoms using the lexicon of hysteria, but in both contexts the symptoms shook conventional expectations of
manliness as embodied in the modern young warrior.
Young men quite literally lost control of their reason and
fell prey to deep psychic forces that compromised their
rationality and their ability to face the enemy with un-
daunted courage. In contrast to England, where doctors
gradually accepted psychological explanations for shell
shock, in France, medical men generally saw it as a deficit
of will.[2] "[T]hese pseudo-impotents of the voice, of the

1. T. S. Eliot, "Ulysses, Order, and Myth," *The Dial*, November 1923, reprinted in Frank Kermode, ed., *Selected Prose of T. S. Eliot* (New York: Harcourt Brace Jovanovich, 1975), 177.
2. On the treatment of shell shock in England, see, most recently,
Joanna Bourke, *Dismembering the Male: Men's Bodies, Britain, and the
Great War* (Chicago: University of Chicago Press, 1996), 107–23, and Eric
Leed's classic, *No Man's Land: Combat and Identity in World War One* (Cambridge: Cambridge University Press, 1979).

arms, and of the legs, are really only impotents of the will," the intern André Gilles wrote. Doctors would teach such men to "police their own nerves."[3] Moreover, some French doctors oddly enough thought of shell shock as contagious, and thus presumed, contrary to all national-ist rhetoric about the innate courage of the male patriot, that all soldiers were potentially weak-willed—that an entire generation, in a word, might lose its nerve.

In this chapter, I shall suggest that "pornography" rep-resented a fantasy about the destruction of the body and psyche that metaphorically linked the trauma of the indi-vidual male soldier to collective cultural trauma. In so doing, I participate in an ongoing historical discussion about how postwar France coped with wartime trauma by focusing on a little-known and yet extensive discussion about pornography that intersects with all kinds of dis-cussions about postwar efforts to redeem masculinity; I address fantasies about the seductive powers of violence and efforts to define and combat those forces, rather than patriotic discourse per se.[4] These fantasies about por-nography emerged in the wake of the Great War, when so-

3. André Gilles quoted in Marc Roudebush, "A Battle of Nerves: Hyste-ria and Its Treatment in France during World War I" (Ph.D diss., Univer-sity of California, Berkeley, Department of History, 1995), 17. I thank Mark Micale for calling my attention to this dissertation. Céline (Louis-Ferdinand Destouches), himself a doctor, writes about shell shock in his novel *Voyage au bout de la nuit* (Paris: Denoël et Steele, 1932), but he evi-dently did not suffer from it personally.

4. There is a voluminous literature on the effects of the war, most re-cently in debates about historical memory and commemoration. I men-tion many of the works on gender relations in the Introduction; see also, among other books, George Mosse, *Fallen Soldiers: Reshaping the Memory of the World Wars* (Oxford: Oxford University Press, 1990). For a gendered perspective on commemoration, see Daniel Sherman, "Monu-ments, Mourning and Masculinity in France after World War I," *Gender and History* 1 (April 1996): 83–107.

cial commentators and analysts began to postulate a significant link between the wartime proliferation of pornography and the unprecedented violence of modern
combat. Only then did pornography and violence became
continuous descriptions of assaults on the integrity of
the human body. It is not a coincidence, in other words,
that during the years since 1920 *nonviolent* heterosexual "pornography" has gradually been exempted from
obscenity prosecution in the United States and western
Europe. Nor is it surprising that anti-pornography feminist activists believe that pornography *is* violence against
women. This link between pornography and violence gave
and gives pornography the epistemological stability on
which such a claim can be founded, while simultaneously
establishing a sense of continuity that remains essential
to the idea that pornography is an increasingly elastic,
mobile category of meaning, with few fixed referents.
How to have it both ways?

Pleasure and Violence

In the popular writer Armand DuBarry's book *Les Flagellants* (one of a series he wrote on "abnormal" psychology*)*, he describes flagellation as a degrading spectacle
in which the man at the center is reduced to an infant, often crying out for his father and mother.[5] The discourse
about flagellation was one of the primary medical, literary, and popular discussions about sexuality before and
after the war that explicitly combined sexual violence and
sexual pleasure, and critics later used the logic of such
scenarios to thematize and understand the war's vio-

---

5. Armand DuBarry, *Les Flagellants* (Paris: Chameul, 1898), 21.

lence.[6] Already before the war, in 1905, Sigmund Freud had suggested that "the history of human civilization shows beyond any doubt that there is an intimate connection between cruelty and the sexual instinct."[7] In France, in 1904, the critic Pierre Guénolé insisted that for a variety of reasons, flagellation in the modern, sexualized sense had become so widespread that it could not be ignored. The press allegedly gave it a great deal of publicity (although Guénolé provides no examples), the influx of foreigners contributed to its proliferation, it was increasingly practiced in specialized brothels, and most important, the taste for the whip reflected, not only the pathological desires of "erotomaniacs," but the normal person's quest for psychological pleasure. In a rather confusing distinction, Guénolé claims that individuals who enjoy real pain are "purely and simply crazy," whereas those who enjoy it in the interest of sexual stimulation

6. Contemporaries generally viewed pleasure in pain as a manifestation of its authors' and readers' weakness of moral will, although the unfolding of this view is complex. Some recent work has addressed the development of eroticized violence in England and the United States. In a fascinating essay, Karen Halttunen argues that eroticized violence emerged as the underside of the new late-eighteenth-century culture of sentimentalism: as violence became increasingly taboo, it emerged in eroticized, pornographic form. Halttunen claims that "the pornography of pain" ultimately represents a new means, paradoxically, of expressing recent cultural taboos *against* pain. See Karen Halttunen, "Humanitarianism and the Pornography of Pain in Anglo-American Culture," *American Historical Review* 2 (April 1995): 303–34. See also Anne McLintock, *Imperial Leather: Race, Gender and Sexuality in the Colonial Context* (New York: Routledge, 1995), 142–43. On the link between sex and violence in the late nineteenth century, see Angus McLaren, *The Trials of Masculinity: Policing Sexual Boundaries, 1870–1930* (Chicago: University of Chicago Press, 1997), 170. In this chapter, I am interested in a different historical moment in which pornography's meaning becomes indeterminate.

7. Sigmund Freud, *Three Essays on the Theory of Sexuality* (New York: Basic Books, 1975), 25.

are found everywhere, both among the working class, where corporal punishment produces pleasurable humiliation, and among the bourgeoisie and the upper classes, where flagellation is more self-consciously used as a sexual stimulant.[8]

Hugues Rebell, a prolific author of literary criticism, of "legitimate" second-tier novels, and of flagellation pornography under the pseudonym Jean de Villiot, also noted that the numbers of flagellants had proliferated in the fin-de-siècle. According to him, they no longer resembled the highly ritualized, disciplined practitioners of flagellation in "mystical sects," "leaving the field free for the libertine spirit of a new generation, which . . . believes itself far too superior to bow to the . . . dignified rituals of time passed." Although "democracy has released us from old superstitions," he wrote, our epoch is nevertheless "perverse," and Max Nordau's *Degeneration* tells us how and why. Villiot thus disingenuously (since his primary writings are flagellation pornography) associates flagella-

8. Pierre Guénolé, *L'Etrange Passion: La Flagellation dans les mœurs d'aujourd'hui* (Paris: Office central de Librairie, 1904), 97, 110–11, 121. In his 1886 compendium of sexual perversions, *Psychopathia Sexualis*, the Austrian sexologist Richard von Krafft-Ebing used the example of the Austrian aristocrat and writer Leopold von Sacher-Masoch to describe male masochism, to which he assimilated flagellation. "Krafft-Ebing's invention of masochism appeared at the moment when juridical discourses no longer found it possible to condone corporal punishment without somehow countering the sexual stimulation that medical discourse identified with flagellation," according to John K. Noyes, *The Mastery of Submission: Inventions of Masochism* (Ithaca, N.Y.: Cornell University Press, 1997), 92–93. See also Suzanne Stewart, *Sublime Surrender* (Ithaca, N.Y,: Cornell University Press, 1998), and Jean de Villiot (Hugues Rebell), *Les Mystères de la maison de la Verveine, ou Miss Bellasis Fouettée pour vol (tableau de l'education des jeunes Anglaises)*, traduit de l'anglais par Jean de Villiot (Paris: Carrington, 1901), v. Jean de Villiot in fact wrote the book he claims to have translated; see Dr. L. R. Dupuy, *The Strangest Voluptuousness: The Taste for Lascivious Corrections* (Paris: Medical Library, n.d.), 50.

tion with the proliferation of perversion in a decadent age; increasing numbers of people are engaged in the practice, he says.[9] Villiot argued elsewhere that sadism (sadism and flagellation are sometimes blurred in his writings and sometimes not) is a fact of life, nothing other than "obeying an instinct to destroy" common to man and animals and tied, as science has demonstrated, to the "sexual instinct." And, in yet another text, he claims that "flagellation, in sum, is merely one more means to provoke the stimulation of the senses, such that it has been used at all times . . . to quench carnal appetites."[10]

Many other writers expressed the same sentiments about the proliferation of a once highly ritualized and purposeful activity, and most acknowledged its link to sexual pleasure. Pierre MacOrlan, another prolific writer both of novels and of books classified on police lists as sadomasochistic pornography, implicitly claimed the vice was so irresistible and contagious that Sade's manuscripts were as dangerous as poisonous flowers. Other authors repeated this metaphorical equivalence, warning, in fin-de-siécle fashion, about the dangerous impressions made by sensually stimulating material.[11] DuBarry,

9. Jean de Villiot [Hugues Rebell], *Etude sur la flagellation aux points de vue médical et historique* (Paris: Carrington, 1899), 169, 256. New editions of some of Villiot's works have been published recently under his real name. See *Femmes chatiées* (Paris: Mercure de France, 1994) and *Le Fouet à Londres* (Paris: Viviane Hamy, 1992). He died prematurely at the age of 38.

10. Jean de Villiot, *Les Mystères de la maison de la Verveine*, iii; id., *En Virginie: Episode de la guerre de sécession. Précédé d'une étude sur l'esclavage et les punitions corporelles en Amérique* (Paris: Carrington, 1901), 260–61.

11. Pierre MacOrlan [Pierre Dumarchey, pseud.], *Le Masochisme en Amérique; suivi de la Petite marquise de Sade* (Paris: J. Fort, 1910), 208–9; id. [Pierre de Jersange, pseud.], *La Comtesse au fouet* (Paris: Collections des Orties blanches, 1911), 80, 96.

who wrote a multivolume series on sexual "aberrations," claimed that "flagellation is such a common aberration that the majority of prostitutes become tools with which their chance lovers practice it."[12] "Dr. Cabanès," another popularizer of medical texts, claimed that flagellation had existed in all places and times but implied that it had recently increased, citing examples from Emile Zola and the brothers Edmond and Jules de Goncourt.[13] And finally, a "Dr. Samuel" says that while flagellation was known to the ancients, it has become the "ultra-modern vice," practiced with great frequency by all sorts of people.[14]

But it was during the interwar years that most critics and medical men insisted not only on the primacy of "sexual emotion," but repeatedly stressed "the narrow connection between *jouissance* [pleasure] and suffering" in all human beings rather than in a limited number of odd characters.[15] For prewar writers' claims about the diffusion of flagellation throughout the population were tempered by their assertion that flagellates and sado-masochists were finally aberrant people whose pathology doctors had finally defined: Villiot claimed they had "sick minds," DuBarry asserted that they were "degenerates of both sexes" in whom "compulsion was more forceful than reason," Dr. Samuel insisted that they were "not normal" and that the vice was hereditary. And although

12. DuBarry, *Flagellants*, 15.
13. Dr. Cabanès, *La Flagellation dans l'histoire et la littérature* (Clermont: Daix Frères, 1899).
14. Dr. Samuel, *La Flagellation dans les maisons de tolérance* (Paris: Maurice Wandnoel, n.d.), 1.
15. See Malherman, *Le Plaisir dans la souffrance*, trans. Charles Wincker (Paris: A. Quignon, 1929), 300; François Nazier [Henri Drouin], *Trois Entretiens sur la sexualité* (Paris: Editions du Siècle, 1926), 39.

Guénolé used the pretext of flagellation's proliferation to legitimate his work, he nonetheless finally associated the practice mostly with homosexuals (primarily women), with upper-class debauchees, and with prostitutes.[16] But, as "Dr. Apertus" wrote in 1927, books about flagellation had proliferated because "the taste for the whip is no longer found only among mad sadists, but has been tempered and diffused, so that it is now shared by those beings infinitely more evolved and who, conscious of their aberration, are capable of moderating their own desire."[17]

Although this discourse about the increasingly pervasive and fundamental link between sexuality and violence was partly a consequence of the war—one thinks of Freud's 1920 *Beyond the Pleasure Principle*—it also constituted some of the terms within which the war was discussed. For a wide range of commentators, war now became an extension of sexuality and sexuality an extension of the violence intrinsic in warfare, a connection often established by equating war with sadomasochistic sexuality. In 1933, for example, in a prurient book about the history of "eroticism" translated into French that same year, the German Dr. Paul Englisch urged a direct link between the Great War and flagellation: "Whereas before the war of 1914, German pornographers focused on normal sexual relations, in its aftermath, pornography about sexual perversion flourished. Long years in the trenches stirred men's sadistic instincts and their taste for horror."[18]

16. Villiot, *En Virginie,* 261; DuBarry, *Flagellants,* 15; Dr. Samuel, *Flagellation,* 235–38; Guénolé, *Etrange Passion,* 121.
17. Dr. Apertus, *La Flagellation dite passionelle* (Paris: Collection des Orties blanches, 1927), 124.
18. Dr. Paul Englisch, *L'Histoire de l'erotisme en Europe,* French adaptation by Jacques Gorvil (Paris: Aldor, 1933), 244. For an Austrian account of the relationship between the war, "sexual crimes," and pornography, see Franz Exner, *Krieg und Kriminalität in Österreich* (Vienna: Holder-Pichler-

Englisch's remarks need to be set in the context of more generalized myths about modern war, in which violence and the spiritual cleansing of the male body are oddly continuous: violence paradoxically purges the suffering intrinsic in violence. War is a "natural" form of destruction aimed at social regeneration and "the happiness of all," the journalist Paul Gautier argued in 1919. It is a process that repairs "seams in the social fabric" by awakening "moral force and courage": war, which is also a sin, is a form of "punishment, expiation, and suffering," but a "purifying suffering [*douleur purificatrice*]" and hence a sin that also cleanses the social body of sin.[19] Gautier was only reiterating a long romantic tradition in this construction of patriotism as willful self-sacrifice, a tradition repeatedly invoked by journalists and novelists throughout the war's duration. Governments, as historians have demonstrated, likewise propagated the image of the brave soldier whose soul goes to heaven, his spiritual wounds healed by the figurative tears of the nation. War-induced suffering purges the body of sin, and that suffering itself is transcended through national mourning.

But the Great War, with its unprecedented violence and its revelation of weak national nerves, provoked a reassessment of this myth. In 1917, the literary columnist Edmond Haraucourt wrote a report, commissioned by the government, about pornography laws and the effects of "demoralizing" literature and images in a far more critical vein. He argued that the Great War had transformed the willful and noble sacrifice of men's bodies

Tempsky; New Haven, Conn.: Yale University Press for the Carnegie Endowment for International Peace, 1927), 106–10.

19. Paul Gautier, *Leçons morales de la guerre* (Paris: Flammarion, 1919), 9, 13, 135.

into the love of death. In this account, patriotism no longer served to heal wounds, but became a pretext for inflicting more wounds, more eviscerations: "Vers l'amour" now meant "pour la mort." He goes on: "At the end of this long alert, which unleashed violent instincts, we can expect to find those instincts alive and well. . . . We shall continue to kill a great deal after the war." For Haraucourt, pornography instantiates this never-ending cycle of death and destruction evacuated of transcendent meaning, and deprives this myth—whereby the soldier's suffering cleanses the national body of sins—of narrative closure. Before the war, "[pornographers] troubled morality; during the war, they did not respect our mourning, and after the war, they constitute a threat to the motherland." Although he never articulates a clear relationship between the war and pornography, he believes that pornography has become one of the primary vehicles through which the "contagion" of war, the "attraction to death," will be disseminated. Depicting human life as a struggle between love and death, Haraucourt argues that the war has signaled the triumph of death and transformed sexual desire into longing "for death." Pornography both represents and produces a national psyche in which the supreme sacrifice is continuous no longer with the body's cleansing but with its degradation.[20] In his work, pornography displaces the traumatized individual male soldier as the cause and effect of collective moral failure and thus of collective trauma.

Many critics no longer equated self-sacrifice with spiritual cleansing, but with spiritual degradation; the body had become enslaved by its own instincts, or, more spe-

20. Edmond Haraucourt, *La Démoralisation par le livre et par l'image* (Paris: Ollendorff, 1917), 30, 34, 36, 11.

cifically, by a compulsive death drive.[21] The war, in this
view, had turned into a pretext for the satisfaction of
other pleasures. In a 1921 work graced with a preface by
the famous Swiss sexologist Auguste Forel, the highbrow
journalist and amateur historian André Lorulot compared the Great War's "barbarism" to the sadistic pleasures that Spanish inquisitioners had taken in perform-
ing their task. He conjured up predictable anticlerical
images of debauched, perverted priests, but in a later
work he made his real point more explicit. In a book
about German barbarism that is essentially a litany of
anecdotes about flagellation and "sexual perversions," he
considers the question of how punishment could produce
sexual feelings so powerful that men and women "passionately sought them out." Lorulot finally associates
sadomasochism with pathological politics, and specifically with Hitler's rise to power.[22] The writer and occasional pornographer Jean de Mézerette, in a similar and
by then predictable theme, would figure Hitler and his
entourage as effeminate, homosexual, sadomasochistic,
and Jewish (although he deleted all references to Jews in
the 1945 edition).[23]

In the anti-German articles he penned in 1917, Dr. Paul
Voivenel had argued that sadomasochism directed the
German war effort on the grounds that German soldiers
took masochistic pleasure in "waxing the boots of the

21. See, e.g., Louis Dumur's controversial *Nach Paris!* (Paris: Payot,
1919), 231.
22. André Lorulot, *Barbarie allemande et barbarie universelle: Le Livre
rouge des atrocités mondiales* (Paris: L'Idée libre, 1921); *La Flagellation et
les perversions* sexuelles (Paris: L'Idée libre, 1948), 13, 53. For a similar
treatment, see Roland Gagey, *Le Visage sexuel de l'Inquisition* (Paris: Chez
l'auteur, 1932), esp. 312–15.
23. Jean de Mézerette, *Les Amours d'Hitler: Reportage* (Paris: Jean
Mézerette, 1935).

state."[24] Sadomasochism implies the submission of the individual to the state and the collapse of private and public, symbolized by the constrained, even wounded, body, flushed with pleasure in spite of itself, and depicted in the many anecdotes purveyed by André Lorulot and Georges Anquetil. The novelist Louis Dumur's antihero describes an assassination that makes his companions' faces light up with a "pure and evident pleasure" and confesses that the sadistic rape and murder that constitute the center of the novel "disgusted and excited me at the same time."[25]

Moreover, the association between sadomasochism and war was symbolized above all by female sexuality, itself encoded as "pornographic" by the connection established between perversion, pornography, and femininity. Voivenel predictably remarks in an article about the war that most sadistic men have "feminine constitutions."[26] In postwar novels and commentaries, sadomasochism lost the theatrical, restrained, aestheticized voluptousness of late-nineteenth-century erotic rituals, with their props and fetishes. Sadomasochism was embedded less in the cold and calculated violence characteristic of pornographic scenarios, more in the uncontrollable rage associated with the war—the dismemberment of corpses, the meaninglessness of patriotic props in the context of anonymous trench warfare, the stripping of aesthetic form from decidedly naked and therefore degraded bodies. Anquetil likens the public to bloodthirsty, sexually stimulated female spectators at an ancient Roman

24. Paul Voivenel, "À Propos de Sacher Masoch: Les Allemands et le marquis de Sade," *Progrès Medical* 1 (6 January 1917) and 7 (17 February 1917): 5.
25. Dumur, *Nach Paris!* 139, 147.
26. Voivenel, *A Propos de Sacher Masoch*, 6.

arena and denounces "pornographic" novels that repli-
cate this stimulation in readers rendered susceptible by
the war. He denounces Marcello Fabri's *Visage du vice*
(among other novels), in which two women eviscerate
each other and the violence is not, as in earlier accounts
of lesbian sadism, mediated by the contrast between
passion and aristocratic countenance. Rather, it is seemingly transparent, grotesque, atrocious, and aesthetically
unredeemed.[27]

In another 1921 novel, Fabri represents the war as a seductive female vampire who drains male bodies of their
virility, and he notes a correlation between the "thirst for
blood," sexual perversion, and pornography.[28] According
to Fabri, patriotic self-sacrifice is no longer a dignified,
because freely chosen, gesture, but a pleasurable, irresistible, virility-sapping perversion. The popular writer
Charles-Noël Renard also allegorizes the war as a pack of
vampire lesbians whom men find irresistible.[29] In Joseph
Delteil's equally popular novel, *Sur le fleuve amour,* a
sadistic woman who is an expert in the art of flagellation
nearly destroys the spiritual brotherhood between two
soldiers who are in love with her. Their struggle over her
is as grotesque as their parodic resurrection: like the
"unique and indivisible French Republic," the soldiers
are reunited in death, their cadavers floating downstream
together. The woman, again a metaphor for the war, is
both instigator and vehicle of their destruction. Finally, in
his introduction to a work on the pleasures of forbidden

27. Quoted in Georges Anquetil, *Satan conduit le bal* (Paris: Georges-
Anquetil, 1925), 314.
28. Marcello Fabri, *L'Inconnu sur les villes: Roman des foules modernes*
(Paris: J. Povolozky, 1921), 56, 117, 124.
29. Charles-Noël Renard, *Les Androphobes* (St. Etienne: Imprimerie
spéciale de l'édition, 1930), 94–99.

books, Sylvain Bonmariage claims that the "mystique of liberty" that had infused the violence of 1793 was very different from "these four years of the Great War." In the stories that follow this introduction, his character Martienne unleashes and embodies the war's murderous violence.[30]

Critics thus increasingly associated corporeal degradation with the war's unprecedented destruction and emasculation of bodies, and they saw tales of German war atrocities as pedagogical tools for instructing civilians about the horrors of war. In their frequent efforts to portray German militarism as the pathological (because sadomasochistic and emasculating) desire for discipline, they implicitly question the motives of all military discipline. The Germans' sadomasochism implies that patriotic self-sacrifice more generally might have other, more suspect motives. The war, in these accounts, appears to transform *all* soldiers into sexual perverts, permanently contaminating postwar French culture as well. Although the "thirst for blood" has existed in all places and all times, Fabri writes, the soldier of this war has demonstrated an unparalleled desire to "jouir-avant-la-mort." This desire has proved contagious: "no longer content to suck at wounds like a vampire [the people] demand more victims to pollute, and this ignominious spectacle is still not enough to satisfy their senses."[31] Now, Renard writes, in this "feminine" Republic, "all begins and ends in sexual sensation."[32]

30. Joseph Delteil's *Sur le fleuve amour* (Paris: Gallimard, 1933), 122–23; Sylvain Bonmariage, *Les Plaisirs de l'Enfer* (Paris: Raoul Saillard, 1983), 36–37, 177.

31. Marcello Fabri, quoted in Anquetil, *Satan conduit le bal*, 310.

32. Renard, *Androphobes*, 202.

In 1925, in a work entitled *Satan conduit le bal* (Satan
Leads the Dance), Anquetil similarly equates the war
with sadomasochistic sexuality). Trench journalists had
already described the spectacle of dismembered corpses
in macabre detail, but Anquetil implicitly eroticizes such
images by juxtaposing flagellation scenes in brothels with
anecdotes of war atrocities.[33] He transforms the war into
a transnational brothel, another eroticized mise-en-scène
in which the body's private pleasure and pain become
public affairs.

One part of Anquetil's story is narrated by a Monsieur
Hermès, a fortuneteller who can see the future. He takes
public officials to the brothel in order to demonstrate to
them the magnitude of postwar moral degradation and to
persuade them that this is the vision of France he sees in
his crystal ball. When they inevitably protest that such
brothels "have always existed and will always exist," Hermès responds: "[T]hey are no longer the playground of a
few unstable sorts of people. Today you're allowing this
rottenness to spread: don't be surprised by the degenerate
race about which you complain." He then proceeds to
take them into a "house of illusions"—a grand hall—in
which they witness this scene, among others:

> Here, on a horizontal beam, pierced in the middle by a hole
> and supported by two supplementary pillars, lay a nude
> woman, wrists and ankles attached by two leather knots, be-
> ing flagellated by painful blows delivered by a breathless,
> nude man. . . . There, the nude body of another lay, sus-
> pended by the neck, wrists bound . . . to the ceiling by two
> heavy chains. This way all the parts of her poor body were

33. Stephane Audoin-Rouzeau, *Men at War: National Sentiment and
Trench Journalism in France during the First World War* (Providence, R.I.:
Berg, 1992).

better exposed to the strokes of the whip ferociously admin-
istered by a uniformed foreign officer. Her breasts were not
spared: on the contrary, they evidenced the . . . brutality with
which they were being sadistically targeted.

In short, he represents "depraved morality" as an eroticized quest for death whose most privileged embodiment
is sadomasochistic spectacle: the body bound, unclothed,
mutilated, humiliated.[34] Writers who believed that the
war was motivated by perversion rather than patriotism
indict the French government for legitimating the war's
unparalleled, frenzied sadism. The brothel in which this
scene occurs is peopled mostly by (French) government
officials, policemen, and of course, prostitutes. In this
narrative context, the bound women represent wounded,
martyred France (being beaten by a "uniformed foreign
officer") and also symbolize degraded, feminized, and
eroticized postwar culture, a new, "prostituted" France
for whom the pleasure of bondage and the sacrifices of
war have become indistinct. Anquetil and the other critics do not criticize warfare itself, but the effects of this
war and its contamination of postwar French culture, a
disease imagined in terms of the proliferation of sexualized violence.

These accounts call into question the distinction between "normal" sexual instinct and perversion, insofar as
they leave it unclear whether sadomasochistic sexuality is
a natural inclination of human beings freed from social
stigmas (a sign of atavism), or the perverted product of
industrialized warfare. For Lorulot and Anquetil, the war
is merely a vehicle for the acting out of sadomasochistic
pleasure, even as they characterize that pleasure as the

34. Anquetil, *Satan conduit le bal,* 189–90.

pathological product of war. The neo-Malthusian Manuel
Delvadès noted that the male sexual role was itself an
act of war, and implied that the war had unleashed the
"egoism, aggressiveness, cruelty, and domination" proper
to men's sexual instinct, because it had made us aware
that to "snuff out or to give life produces the same thrill
[*frisson*]."[35] In 1918, Voivenel and another doctor, Louis
Huot, sought to explain soldiers' psychology as the ebb
and flow of sexual instinct. At the beginning of the war,
when young European men marched blindly and bravely
off to the front in the name of patriotism, they were like
"rooster[s] hypnotized by sexual instinct."[36] Yet Voivenel and Huot also claim that the war was responsible
for transforming men into machines of destruction, although they do not meditate on the contradiction between the phenomenon of men being transformed both
into machines *and* into animals—or does this oddly
amount to the same thing? Haraucourt similarly argues
that the war both "unleashed violent instincts" *and* produced them.

In perhaps the most dramatic (yet common) illustration of this paradox, debates among medical men about
the effects of war on soldiers suggested that barbaric acts
manifested an "instinct of preservation" in the face of
fear. They transformed barbarism into an expression of
the body's natural quest for survival. The shock of so
much violence, the effect of being "a plaything" of overwhelming forces, produced irrational, unmanly behavior,
which nevertheless had a rational and reassuring expla-

35. Manuel Delvadès, *La Guerre dans l'acte sexuel* (1934; Paris: Pacifisme scientifique, 1936), 13–14.
36. Louis Huot and Paul Voivenel, *La Psychologie du soldat* (Paris: Renaissance du Livre, 1918), 82.

nation. At the same time, doctors presumed that bar-barism—here the male body's instinctive defense against unnatural sensations and feelings of powerlessness—is also psychopathological.[37] Hence the best soldiers (with some exceptions) turned out to be alcoholics and per-verts, because their "impulsiveness," "taste for adven-ture," and "morbid courage" transformed them into he-roic soldiers.[38] Psychopathology is a tragic symptom of war, Dr. René Charpentier argues, and yet the best sol-diers are often psychopaths. He recommends that "in times of war, we not systematically exclude from the army certain men we would reject in peacetime . . . [their] psychopathologies are, at least temporarily, com-patible with national defense."[39]

If psychopathology was compatible with national de-fense, then nationalism—soldiers' willingness to die for their country—no longer always required self-discipline. The soldiers' self-sacrifice was not necessarily an act of supreme self-restraint. This blurry distinction between sexual pleasure and restraint and between compulsion and will made the motives for war so suspect that, in ret-rospect, the Great War no longer constituted a simple quest for national glory. The ambiguity between disci-pline and pleasure, and thus between war and the eroti-cized desire for death, that Haraucourt associates with

37. See Adam Cygielstrejch, "La Psychologie de la panique pendant la guerre," *Annales médico-psychologiques* 7 (April 1916): 172; id., "Séance du 26 Juin 1916: De l'utilisation des indisciplines en temps de guerre," ibid. 7 (October 1916): 526–29.

38. Maurice de Fleury, *L'Angoisse humaine* (Paris: Editions de France, 1918), 225.

39. René Charpentier, review of *La Folie et la guerre, 1914–1918*, by A. Rodiet and A. Fribourg-Blanc, *Annales médico-psychologiques* 1 (Febru-ary 1931): 211.

pornography gradually transformed the meaning of war so dramatically that war no longer described regenerative violence. Many interwar critics thus could not clearly distinguish discipline from pleasure, and they were not certain about whether sadomasochism was a cause or an effect of war (whether it was self-evidently innate or artificially induced); in their efforts to demonize warmongers, they simply reiterated the ambiguity between the pure self-sacrifice of the soldier and the impure gratification afforded by battle. They so completely conflated patriotic self-sacrifice and sadomasochistic desire that they portrayed nationalist impulses as sadmasochistic ones, and rendered the sacred national body indistinct from a profane, contaminated one.

Toward Regeneration

If the war had compromised the distinction between compulsion and will (between a "pornographic" and a pure social body), how was it to be restored? If will was no longer distinct from sadomasochistic pleasure, how were critics to determine the difference between redemptive virility and emasculation, between edifying, educational, and ethical material and the pornographic texts they claimed reiterated the war's violence? All the writers I have discussed are emphatic about the patriotic intent of their works and were certain that their patriotism was self-evident to readers not duped by politicians' lies or emasculated by abnormal desires and perceptions.[40] Their logic had recent precedents: in 1903, for ex-

40. In a recent and compelling essay on the French government's narrative about German soldiers' rape of "enemy" women during the Great War, Ruth Harris argues that "[n]ormally the stuff of pornography, such sadistic visions became an integral aspect of patriotic discourse and, I would argue, a means of projecting a range of anxieties onto an eroticized vision of the mutilated female form." See Harris, "The 'Child of the Bar-

ample, in defense of Emile Zola, Ernest Charles noted that readers' saturation with repulsive texts would regenerate literature.[41] Zola himself, we recall, believed that in order to cleanse the social body, a writer was obliged to expose and describe the causes of its impurity. Louis Dumur's defense against censorship was that his book about the war "told the truth." His editor claimed he had received hundreds of letters protesting the sadistic scene of an aristocratic Frenchwoman being raped by German generals; they accused him of being "a pornographer." In his defense, Dumur claimed that the Germans counted on the silence of thousands of Frenchwomen who refused to speak out from a sense of shame and modesty (*par pudeur*).[42] Dumur did not denounce war but the German people—the book is Dumur's rewriting of the stories told to him by a German captain at a POW camp. His aim was not to depict the horrors of war or to call the concept of women's *pudeur* into question but to demonstrate the reality of the atrocities perpetrated by the Germans. He argued that his admittedly fictional account of the war would restore the French to their senses; the *pudeur* of ashamed women, like the *pudeur* of a nation raped and pillaged, had to be violated in order to be restored.

Similarly, Anquetil, whose book is a 700-page compendium of the most ghastly war atrocities, juxtaposed

---

barian': Rape, Race and Nationalism in France during the First World War," *Past and Present* 141 (November 1993): 188. I am also interested in how exactly pornography became an integral aspect of patriotic discourse, but cannot, obviously, assume the self-evident status of pornography.

41. Ernest Charles, quoted in Albert Eyquem, *De la répression des outrages à la morale publique et aux bonnes mœurs, ou de la pornographie au point de vue historique, juridique, législatif et social* (Paris: Marchal & Billard, 1905), 147.

42. Dumur, *Nach Paris!* 340.

with stories of sexualized violence meant to serve as civil-
ian analogues, asks, "Am I the only one to denounce the
perversion all around us?" He goes on to "cite and resume all the unimaginable series of savageries, of sadism,
of cruelty, and of pederasty . . . during the war," in order
to make them imaginable and hence unimaginable in the
future. As we have seen, Lorulot's and Anquetil's documentary and high moral style compromises the distinction between self-sacrifice and sadomasochism, since
their work often reiterates the sensationalism of novels
replete with sadomasochistic content that have no such
pretensions: their writings detail the body's humiliation,
how it is bound, and where and how deep its wounds are.

Haraucourt also argues that literature that simply repressed what he calls the natural links between sex and
war did not restore discipline, but encouraged degeneration. Books, he argued, should no longer be censored according to abstract formulations of good and evil, but,
rather, according to changing social and cultural mores,
which themselves determine which books "cool" passions. Haraucourt's aim of cooling passions was predictable. But the way he proposed to achieve it—a flexible censorship grounded in loosely defined mores rather
than abstract moral laws—derived from his conviction
that in the Great War, military discipline had heated
rather than cooled passions. Men had been as excited by
death as they were because interdictions (in the form of
overzealous censorship and social taboos) against the
"literature of love" forced writers to focus on "the terri-
tory of death," "and they threw themselves into this ter-
ritory with passion. Fear was the supreme thrill."[43]

---

43. Haracourt, *Démoralisation*, 11.

Much like those authors who sought to neutralize sexuality by expanding the realm of the nonobscene, these commentaries represent perversion (or suggest the lifting of taboos against many erotic works) in order to prevent it, dismembering bodies in order to restore their integrity. Material that tells the truth about the war does not encourage the violent sexuality inherent in human nature, but, oddly, exposes sexual violence in order to restore integral, phallic bodies. The sexuality once indissociable from the degradation of bodies is now indissociable from their redemption. It is perhaps no coincidence that during the interwar years, Sade began to be revered as a moralist who revealed our inhumanity to ourselves. That is, Sade—according to a literary critical tradition initiated by the surrealists and most forcefully expressed by Jean Paulhan—sought to repel his readers in order to show them the error of their ways.[44]

Critics thus reproduced the voyeuristic, sadomasochistic pleasure they denounce but did so in the interest of national and moral regeneration. But how exactly does reiterating and remembering the horrors of war transform degenerate into regenerative violence? How does the graphic dismembering and violation of bodies restore

---

44. This idea that nonpornographic texts redeem by virtue of their pornographic effects—the pleasure that is a component of self-restraint, the compulsion that is a component of willful patriotism—invites some psychoanalytic inquiry into the abject in particular that I cannot undertake here. Freud refers to the link between libido and disgust in his letters to Fliess. See Sigmund Freud, *The Complete Letters of Sigmund Freud to Wilhelm Fliess, 1877–1904,* trans. and ed. Jeffrey Moussaieff Masson (Cambridge, Mass.: Harvard University Press, 1985), 280. And see Jean Paulhan, *Le Marquis de Sade et sa complice* (Brussels: Editions complexes, 1987), 61–62. For this interpretation of the reception of Sade during the interwar years, see Carolyn J. Dean, *The Self and Its Pleasures: Bataille, Lacan, and the History of the Decentered Subject* (Ithaca, N.Y.: Cornell University Press, 1992), 123–99.

their impermeability? And what then marks the difference between these texts, which are nearly indistinguishable from the pornography they denounce, and pornographic ones?

In critics' eyes, this effort to defend explicitly sexual and violent material against charges of pornography was a means of defending the nation against the erosion of its moral fiber.[45] The question of why some pornographic books were deemed pornographic by writers themselves accused of (and who denied) being pornographers is interesting. Anquetil, for example, includes the pseudonymous Balkis in a long chapter euphemistically titled "Nos mœurs d'après les romanciers" (Our Mores According to Novelists). Balkis's "pornographic" work *Personne* (No One, or Someone) is an unnamed young woman's diary, filled mostly with her sadomasochistic sexual experiences and her reflections about them.[46] In one part of the "diary," its author muses: "*Personne* represents me, perhaps, since I have never taken up a single posture [*posture*] but a hundred of them, always leaving open the possibility of others. *Personne*, because, being no one, I am necessarily someone. . . . *Personne*, since, changing form so easily, each form once sketched is but the shadow of a form."[47] The "no one" whose diary might be someone's or anyone's, paradoxically desires "cerebral purification" by humiliating others or being humiliated.[48] Balkis not only

45. This effort often seemed in the eyes of many contemporaries to contribute to that erosion, and that is why some critics accused Dumur of writing pornography.

46. The word *personne* in this context deliberately leaves the identity of its author ambiguous: it refers to "no one," but because it is not in the negative, it might also refer to "someone." Jaqueline Carroy called this ambiguity to my attention.

47. Balkis, *Personne* (Paris: Edgar Malfere, 1922), 188–89.

48. Ibid., 56.

links sexual "postures" to the loss of self-definition but also yokes sexuality to the desire for self-purification; he thus conflates self-loss and purity and compares *"personne's"* pure self-loss to the mentality of a general in the Great War. Leading men into war thus entails the loss of ego proper to patriotic self-sacrifice, but it is so entwined with the sadomasochistic desire for eroticized self-sacrifice that nationalist selflessness takes on the appearance of selfish sexual gratification.

Anquetil denounces this (evidently parodic) desire for self-shattering purification, criticizing *Personne* on the grounds that its author is perverted and sadistic. In his view, the book is pornographic because it is really about the possibilities of self-multiplication and not about self-transcendence. The book depicts sexual violence not to condemn but to revel in it. In the part he chooses to excerpt, *"personne"* takes on a variety of different roles, including Salomé, and becomes "a woman just like all women—no one." "La petite fille" who becomes a woman in the course of the diary "has become a *garçonne*," meaning a nobody, or someone who doesn't know who she is.[49] Like pornography, the discourse about purification is only a pretext for having more sex and enjoying more eroticized violence, much in the same way that the war became a pretext for more stimulation. Anquetil draws our attention to this dissimulation when he singles out *"personne's"* playing the part of Salomé; that is the moment when she most explicitly positions herself as "no one," as an actress capable of playing multiple roles, whose only identity is her assumption of other identities. In another passage, Anquetil condemns a poster inviting Parisians to a "ceremony" in honor of the war dead. The

49. Anquetil, *Satan conduit le bal*, 302.

poster's title, *Monuments aux morts* (Monuments to the Dead), was misleading. In fact, when you read the fine print, it suggested you join a group of partygoers to spend the evening dancing or, rather, two-stepping like soldiers. Anquetil denounces such irreverence. He does not use the incident to condemn immoral youth, however, but rather to denounce a pornographic culture in which young people could conflate exhausting dancing with exhausting combat.[50]

In these passages, it is as if pornography represents the inability to grasp the meaning and consequences of one's actions, and thus the dissolution of the will that differentiates human beings from animals. The "pornographic" poster is not pornographic because of its content, but because it represents youth's inability to distinguish between dancing and combat, between pleasure and duty, and thus its inability to understand the intrinsic meaning of right and wrong. Anquetil treats this confusion as the central meaning of pornography, thereby denying pornography its status as a specific category of texts and images. He uses the term instead to refer to a wide variety of material whose only common attribute, according to him, is it refusal to take a stand, to proclaim its meaning. Thus critics themselves conflated discipline and pleasure, but they also transformed that conflation into the very meaning of pornography; the term "pornography" simultaneously described a state of ethical confusion so widespread that it permeated all of French culture and the specific, abject behavior of sexually degraded bodies moved solely by compulsion. Pornography is thus com-

---

50. Ibid., 31. In fact, Anquetil juxtaposes so-called novels of our times with modern "reality" in order to demonstrate that there is no distinction that can be reliably made.

mensurate with a description of a degraded and abject postwar culture that Anquetil and others expose, denounce, and seek to cleanse.

In the interwar years, writers transformed pornography into an elastic category of meaning and gave it a negative valence. The nonpornographic transcended the purported barbarism and psychopathology of sadomasochism, and the pornographic described a concession to sadomasochistic pleasure symptomatic of and produced by the war and synonymous with fantasies of cultural decline.[51] I do not wish to argue that these writers were pacifists or that they were opposed to nationalist ideology. Rather, their disdain for the material they deemed pornographic and their insistence that their own work was not demonstrates that they used pornography as a metaphor for the sexual contamination of postwar France. That contamination was largely attributed to the Great War and its effects, and by being honest about war's horrors, these writers sought to redeem the sacrifice of the men on the battlefield. In its seeming transparency, their work is indistinguishable from the formal properties these men assign to pornography: its "nakedness," its repudiation of aesthetic form, and its appeal to sadomasochistic pleasure. Again, in their view, nonpornographic literature redeemed the violated male body paradoxically by telling the truth about war, by repeating and remembering the horror of the soldier's experience. But this truth-telling was no simple return to the nationalist fiction of the pure and duty-bound soldier. The soldier's martyrdom is now redemptive because it has become an object-lesson in the futility of this war. Nonpornographic

51. It is significant that this question of whether pornography was a cause or an effect of war remained unresolved.

works infuse meaning into the patently senseless violence of war by telling it like it is and warning us of the consequences of political folly.

Interwar critics thus expanded the nonobscene for the same reasons other literary critics rendered the boundary between literature and pornography increasingly flexible: they sought to cleanse the social body by exposing its wounds. Their particularly ambiguous usage of the pornographic may explain its now extraordinary descriptive breadth to include all things deemed to violate the social body and spectacles of violence in particular. But they also transformed pornography into the metaphorical locale of sadomasochistic violence, the symbol of the nation's "rape" at the hands of its own leaders and of its enemies, its subsequent emasculation and degeneration into a morass of debauched pleasure-seekers who had abandoned the quest for truth. Pornography reiterates the insatiable pleasure apparently inseparable from the sight of spectacularly shattered bodies. It has no intrinsic meaning other than to produce more pleasure, and thus offers no resolution or perspective other than the nihilistic vision of a world dominated by aimless sexual drives.

In seeking to redraw this line between social criticism and pornography, critics believed that they had reinstated the dissipated boundary between the noble discipline of redemptive immolation and the pleasurable discipline of degraded self-sacrifice. But if their quest for truth revealed the inextricability of discipline and pleasure, how could critics account for that pleasure? How could "true" tales of war atrocities produce patriotism without also reproducing the wrong sort of pleasure? As I argued earlier, they fashioned a new male body whose desire was only ever manifest in the commitment to national duty and another "body" of pornography in which the self-shattering and thus degraded pleasures were located. And more: the interwar writers who made these claims and sought to reinstate old boundaries gave birth to a new and astoundingly versatile concept of pornography, while expanding the parameters of the nonpornographic (to the explicitly detailed, "documentary"-like novel or essay): pornography now both described the degradation of all cultural ideals *and* was limited to material deemed to mimic degraded sadomasochistic bodily pleasure. In so doing, they made explicit the mutability that the pornography concept now represented. Pornography was both commensurate with the degradation of the body and it was not; it was a specific body of material and it was any textual or visual symbol that represented the newly mobile (and hence both elusive and omnipresent) lines between once rigidly demarcated bodies, whether private or public or gendered ones. The preceding three chapters have sought to demonstrate how pornography symbolized the eroticized and violently compulsive circulation of disease, effeminacy, and injury from body to body and became a repository of those things that should not circulate. In the section that follows, I focus on how homosexuality also came to symbolize the fluidity between bodies and the marker of that which distinguished them.

4

The Making of Gay Male Sexuality

> The obscure part of morality is that which has
> reference to sexual relationships, and this part is
> not easily expressed in formulas. . . . It is, more-
> over, the fundamental part; when it is known the
> whole psychology of a people is understood.
>
> Georges Sorel, *Reflections on Violence*

In this chapter and the next, I turn to the rhetorical reconstruction of male and female homosexuality. I do so
in order to emphasize the structural similarities in fantasies about pornography and homosexuality, both of
which symbolically violate the social body. Like pornography, homosexuality became a privileged repository of
the war's violence; like pornography, it became a synecdoche of the abject sexuality perceived to be threatening
the integrity of the social body. Pornography and homosexuality do not have the same histories, although they
are entwined by virtue of their social function—as dual,
privileged signs of abjection, as related ways of defining
threats to the social body. They are also diffused throughout that body and yet oddly distinct from it. My purpose
here is not to claim that pornography and homosexuality
are the same thing or are interchangeable categories of
meaning—that is the social effect of the particular set
of discourses that interest me, and thus the *consequence*

of the cultural fantasies I wish to explore. Rather, I assert that they had comparable cultural functions in spite of their differences, and that rhetorically at least, fantasies about both are far more similar than different.

These chapters, like the chapters on pornography, thus focus on discussions about homosexuality rather than on those labeled "homosexual" themselves, except to the extent that gay people with exceptional creativity forged identities within the structure of those fantasies. Moreover, although the legal and political history of homosexuality is conceptually inseparable from fantasies about homosexuals, I focus primarily on the rhetorical construction of those shifting mental visions in order to make this intellectual project manageable. Legal and political history punctuates all discussions of both pornography and homosexuality and is central to the context within which rhetoric about them emerged. But those histories were also formed by the rhetoric I seek to reconstruct. There have been no anti-sodomy laws in France since 1791, but in the legal imagination pornography and homosexuality were so inextricable that antiobscenity law, as we have seen, was used to censor material with homosexual content, as well as to repress homosexual sex acts as violations against decency. Moreover, in the case of female homosexuality, there are no laws and almost no political history to speak of that is not embedded paradoxically in the insistence that lesbianism must be unspeakable, or worse, unknowable. In chapter 5, I suggest that knowledge about lesbians might be sought in fantasies about lesbians' presumed unknowability rather than in legal texts.

The legal history of homosexuality will demonstrate that homosexuality was almost always conflated with "public indecency" or pornography, and will help us understand the consequences of that conflation. Historians have argued that both homosexuality and pornography represent threats to normative, reproductive heterosexuality in a nation anxious about population decline, but such arguments, however valuable, do not help us understand the sorts of ideological and other investments that account for the link between them.[1] As with the chapters on pornography, I move briefly through a discussion of the fin-de-siècle medical and legal status of gay men. That discussion forges the underpinnings of the rhetoric that will later be used and transformed, rather than offering a comprehensive treatment of such discourses on homosexuality during that period. I focus most of the chapter on the interwar elaboration and transformation of the contradictory logic already embedded in late-nineteenth-century constructions of the category "male homosexual."

Homosexuality, Crime, and Secrecy

In the late nineteenth century, French medical commentators generally saw homosexuality as a scourge on a nation suffering from a low birthrate and emasculated by the Prussian army in 1870. As is now well-known, medical men first defined "homosexuality" as a form of selfhood—as a means of identifying and differentiating some people from others—at the end of the century. According to Michel Foucault, the homosexual was invented as part of the more general expansion of demographic surveys, laws, and medical tracts aimed at controlling sexuality in the interests of capitalist and competing secular nation-

---

1. For a synthetic account, see George Mosse, *Nationalism and Sexuality: Respectability and Abnormal Sexuality in Modern Europe* (New York: H. Fertag, 1985). See also secondary works on pornography already cited.

states, which required healthy and productive popula-tions.[2] In this context, same-sex desire threatened repro-ductive heterosexuality, and the idea of a group of people that experts could define as homosexual facilitated sexual regulation.

The concern with sexual deviance intensified at the end of the nineteenth century as efforts by women and working-class men to gain political power intensified. As Martha Hanna argues, women and even bachelors were stigmatized as unpatriotic and selfish as natalists struggled against feminist demands for suffrage and in-sisted that women were repudiating their maternal obli-gations.[3] Hygiene movements aimed at preventing vene-real disease, deviant sexuality, and alcoholism through education flourished.[4] Moreover, as France expanded its empire abroad, nationalism became increasingly synony-mous with racial purity and virility; medical men were called upon to maintain the nation's fitness and superior-ity against impurity and emasculation. The regulation of (homo)sexuality was regarded as an essential part of this campaign, necessary for the preservation of the French "race." Like other forms of sexual "deviance," particu-larly masturbation, critics saw men's homosexual desire as both the cause and symptom of the male body's enervation and hypersensitivity. Using old language com-mon in texts about masturbation, doctors argued that

2. Michel Foucault, *The History of Sexuality,* vol. 1 (New York, Random House, Vintage Books, 1980).

3. Martha Hanna, "Natalism, Homosexuality, and the Controversy over *Corydon,*" in Jeffrey Merrick and Bryant T. Ragan, Jr., eds., *Homosexual-ity in Modern France* (Oxford: Oxford University Press, 1996), 218.

4. On hygiene movements in France, see William H. Schneider, *Qual-ity and Quantity: The Quest for Biological Regeneration in Twentieth-Century France* (Cambridge: Cambridge University Press, 1990).

homosexuality drained the body of vital fluid and left the mind unfocused and distracted and thus incapable of fulfilling its productive and reproductive function in the industrial age.[5] Moreover, homosexuality was antisocial: since the criminal and civil codes defined the family as the basic social unit, homosexuality violated social order and the gender norms that inhered in it. Although homosexuality was not a crime, it was associated with violence and public scandal, and gay men were frequently arrested under Article 330 of the criminal code, which prohibited public indecency.[6]

The legal association of homosexuality with criminality and the medical association of same-sex practices with disease converged in most discussions of homosexuality, especially those about blackmail, which was linked to male prostitution.[7] Already in 1857, Dr. Ambroise Tardieu had published the path-breaking *Etude médico-legale sur les attentats aux mœurs,* which linked a medical concept of homosexuality as disease with another discourse about blackmail, and provided evidence of gay

5. The classic text on masturbation was the Swiss doctor Samuel Tissot's *L'Onanisme, ou Dissertation physique sur les maladies produites par la masturbation* (1760). For discussions of masturbation, see Thomas Laqueur, *Making Sex: Body and Gender from the Greeks to Freud* (Cambridge, Mass.: Harvard University Press, 1990), 227–30; Vernon Rosario, *The Erotic Imagination: French Histories of Perversities* (New York: Oxford University Press, 1997), 13–43.

6. William A. Penniston, "Love and Death in Gay Paris: Homosexuality and Criminality in the 1870s," in Merrick and Ragan, eds., *Homosexuality in Modern France,* 129–30. For a fuller treatment of the legal status of gay men during the Third Republic, especially the early years, see William A. Penniston, "'Pederasts and Others': A Social History of Male Homosexuals in the Early Years of the French Third Republic" (Ph.D diss., University of Rochester, 1997).

7. Penniston, "Love and Death," 130, and id., "'Pederasts,'" 47–57, for a fuller discussion.

men as a source of social disruption, crime, and "corruption." In contrast to female prostitutes, who were, according to the popular writer Léo Taxil, compelled by poverty to enter their profession, male prostitutes are "bandits of the worst kind, who use homosexuality as a means of blackmail, thievery, often assassination."[8] Since there was no legal recognition of male prostitution, or any narrative to legitimate it (as a "necessary evil"), those men who were prostitutes or whom authorities presumed to be were treated as criminals who had violated public decency. Discussions of blackmail accordingly painted a picture of male homosexuality as afflicting either working-class degenerates or upper-class aesthetes with money to spend and reputations to worry about.

Tardieu and other commentators refused to concede, as they would later, that homosexuality was on the rise. Instead, they insisted, there was now rising anxiety about its detrimental effects: "more police surveillance," claimed Dr. Ambroise Tardieu as early as 1857, "more blackmail," coupled with the increased use of homosexuality as a "pretext for assassinations," led to a rising awareness of an old social problem. As Dr. L. Thoinot

8. Dr. Ambroise Tardieu, *Etude médico-legale sur les attentats aux mœurs* (Paris: J. B. Baillière & fils, 1858), 119. Léo Taxil [Gabriel Jogand-Pagès], *La Prostitution contemporaine* (Paris: Librarie populaire, 1884), 9. Tardieu wrote that "after having corrupted the man who had the misfortune to approach [the blackmailers], they suddenly change their tone, jump him from behind and pretend they are policemen." Blackmail follows. The precise meaning of this corruption remains ambiguous, but it clearly refers to the willingness of these men to engage in homosexual sexual practices. In *La Bourgeoisie, le sexe, et l'honneur* (Brussels: Editions complexes, 1984), 82–83, Jean-Paul Aron and Roger Kempf write that Tardieu's work initiated the medical discussion of male homosexuality in France but that that discourse was not organized or coherent until the 1880s.

argued in 1898, "Tardieu's portrait" of the "state of pederasty" in France had not changed in the least.[9] Tardieu
urged his countrymen not to be intimidated by "the
shadow that envelops these facts, the shame and disgust
they inspire," and to begin looking for a solution to the
problem homosexual criminals posed.[10] In 1896, Armand
DuBarry put the problem succinctly: "Pederasty refuses
the light . . . ignoble . . . held in contempt . . . it can only
subsist in the shadows, and requires secrecy."[11] In most
fantasies about homosexuality, homosexuals were furtive operators who, in spite of police surveillance, knew
how to evade the law. Taxil noted that, like "female prostitutes," they are sexually ambiguous and use pseudonyms.[12] Like DuBarry, the writer Pierre Delcourt claimed
that although "these satyrs" always appear on public
thoroughfares, they chose "impasses," covert "angles"
within specific buildings, and public places "apart," where
they could not be seen or heard.[13]

In the late nineteenth century, homosexuality was associated with crime, violence, and furtive criminal elements (in spite of the absence of legal sanctions against
same-sex sexual practices since the French Revolution).
Medical men claimed that criminals were disproportion-
ately homosexual, and "documented" a criminal homosexual subculture of blackmailers and male prostitutes.[14]

9. Tardieu, *Etude médico-legale*, 112–113; Dr. L. Thoinot, *Attentat aux
mœurs et perversions des sens génital* (Paris: Octave Doin, 1898), 295.

10. Ibid., 113.

11. Armand DuBarry, *Les Invertis (Le Vice allemand)* (Paris: Cahmuel,
1896), 154.

12. Taxil, *Prostitution*, 307.

13. Pierre Delcourt, *Le Vice à Paris* (Paris: Librairie française, 1888),
172.

14. Taxil, *Prostitution*, 9. This association of homosexuality and crime
is especially evident in discussions of blackmail. Blackmail became a com-

How then, were these apparently very public and menacing and yet clandestine and slippery men to be identified and restrained? Tardieu insisted that *medical* men join the police to shed light on homosexual subcultures, and several other commentators followed suit. DuBarry wrote that we must not "hide our heads in the sand." [15] In his preface to the pseudo "Dr." Marc-André Raffalovich's study of male homosexuality, the famous and very real Dr. Alexandre Lacassagne declared that doctors who had shied away from the topic out of timidity and the fear of being accused of writing pornography were, intentionally or not, shirking their professional and moral obligations.[16] DuBarry warned that if we refuse to see the danger we simply "abandon ourselves to [it]." [17]

Such comments echo the newly emerging emphasis on prevention and education instead of repression as the solution to perceived moral problems. The French medical discussion about homosexuality reflected confidence that homosexuals could be identified by expert eyes, and that the protection of "normal" society required intensive discussion of the matter. According to the historians Jean-Paul Aron, Roger Kemp, and Robert Nye, although discussions about homosexuality and criminality flourished, male homosexuality did not become a current

---

mon crime in the nineteenth century as a person's virtuous personal life became increasingly perceived as a sign of his public trustworthiness.

15. DuBarry, *Invertis*, 8.

16. Dr. Marc-André Raffalovich, *Uranisme et unisexualité: Etude sur différentes manifestations de l'instinct sexuel* (Paris: Masson, 1896), 15. As Rosario, *Erotic Imagination*, 100–101, notes, Raffalovich was a sometime poet and not a doctor; he was not French, but a Russian Jew. French doctors marginalized him and his views. Rosario also argues that Raffolavich was the first to introduce in France the concept of homosexuality as a form of same-sex attraction that did not rely on a model of gender inversion.

17. DuBarry, *Invertis*, 8.

topic of interest in French medical circles until the 1880s, when the investment in protecting the nation from perceived emasculation was at its peak.[18] Until roughly 1900, the dominant explanation of male homosexuality, proposed by the German homosexual lawyer and classicist Karl Heinrich Ulrichs in the 1860s, was that homosexual men had a "woman's soul in a man's body." Ulrichs defined male homosexuality as an inborn trait located in the brain (and in his later work, in the testicles). The Berlin psychiatrist Karl Westphal dubbed this phenomenon "sexual inversion" and defined it as a psychopathological condition.[19] Vernon Rosario argues that Jean-Martin Charcot and Valentin Magnan first defined "French" inversion in 1882 by linking the concept of the degenerate male hysteric to the elite "pederast" (boy lover), whose inversion had always been perceived as the consequence of sexual boredom. Rosario, following Nye, also notes that French medical men constructed inversion as a variant of fetishism—as an obsession with an inappropriate love object. In spite of these important differences between France and Germany, the model of "gender inversion" still supplied an important, if not the only, framework for understanding same-sex desire.[20]

Homosexuals were also identifiable, of course, because gay men were arrested and harassed on a regular basis

18. Aron and Kempf, *Bourgeoisie*, 82–83. Robert Nye, *Masculinity and Male Codes of Honor in Modern France* (Oxford: Oxford University Press, 1993), 114–15.

19. This view of male homosexuality, later mirrored by that of female homosexuality, was widely influential throughout Europe. See Gert Hekma, "A History of Sexology: Social and Historical Aspects of Sexuality," in Jan Bremmer, ed., *From Sappho to de Sade: Moments in the History of Sexuality* (New York: Routledge, 1989), 176–77; Karl Westphal, "Die conträre Sexualempfindung," *Archiv für Psychiatrie und Nervenkrankheiten* 2.1 (August 1869): 73–108.

20. Rosario, *Erotic Imagination*, 85–86.

for public indecency. Since the late eighteenth century, Paris had had a large homosexual subculture and known locales for social and sexual encounters, which police targeted, especially during times of political instability, such as the early years of the Third Republic.[21] But on another level, French doctors believed so-called criminal elements were recognizable because they saw homosexuals as fundamentally effeminate, classifiable freaks of nature—hermaphrodites, uranists, inverts, unisexuals, and so forth. These terms were invented, borrowed from other national contexts ("uranist" and "invert," for example, originated in Germany), and generally used interchangeably and often incoherently.[22] Doctors divided homosexuals into congenital and acquired (usually uranists and pederasts, respectively) types, the former conforming to a physiological deformation, the latter to a consciously chosen desire for more varied sexual thrills. Robert Nye claims that in France—to the extent there was any coherent paradigm explaining homosexual difference—doctors were wedded to the idea that homosexuality was a form of libidinal weakness. Moreover, the French tended to attribute homosexual desire to anatomical anomalies rather than psychic states, even when they insisted the anomaly was "acquired"—that is, consciously chosen or the product of circumstances like gender-segregated environments.[23]

Most frequently the homosexual's clandestinity was figured as a facet of his effeminacy. Taxil categorizes

21. Penniston, "Love and Death," 130.
22. Thus far I have been using "gay" and "homosexuality" to describe gay men. Most commentators, however, used one of these other terms, and I use them to distinguish between the specific context of nineteenth-century and interwar France and my own commentary about that context.
23. Nye, *Masculinity and Male Codes of Honor,* 104.

"pederasts" according to different levels of effeminacy, and claims that even those men who show no signs of outward femininity bear it somehow, imperceptibly, within. He calls such men "les honteuses."[24] Ambroise Tardieu noted that you cannot always tell who is and is not a pederast, but that they usually have "curled hair, powdered skin, accentuate their waists, wear jewels, perfume."[25] Dr. Emile Laurent insisted that "bisexed" persons, as he called them, could not be soldiers or marry because they were impotent and tended to be over-weight. "The individuals I have just described," he wrote, "are, in physical terms, hardly men at all."[26] While con-ceding that some inverts were manly in appearance, Dr. L. Thoinot said many were vain and gossipy.[27]

Doctors thus remained confident that homosexuality could not ultimately keep itself hidden: the underworld is always detected before it is too late. Most accounts depict homosexuality as a secret that always reveals itself, like a shadow cast by the body. Moreover, to the extent same-sex desire is an "unregulated impulse that torments," an "obsessive idea" provoked either by masturbation or sex-ual exhaustion, it ultimately cannot control its own ex-pression. Inverts "lie for the pleasure of lying," without, as Dr. Raffalovich assures us, "even knowing it."[28] Be-cause the revelation occurs in spite of the homosexual, his self-exposure can never be interpreted as a manly coming-to-terms. His sexual secret is the source of his weakness—his susceptibility to temptation, his insatia-

24. Taxil, *Prostitution*, 284–85.
25. Tardieu, *Etude médico-legale*, 130.
26. Dr. Emile Laurent, *Les Bisexués* (Paris: Georges Carré, 1894), 109–10, 181.
27. Thoinot, *Attentats aux mœurs*, 307.
28. Dubarry, *Invertis*, 157; Raffalovich, *Uranisme*, 115–16.

ble need for sexual variety, his inability to tell right from wrong. The homosexual, like the deviant woman with whom he was equated, emblematized the lack of self-control and judicious altruism required of the good citizen, and thus violated the social body. As Jean-Paul Aron and Roger Kempf have written, the nineteenth-century bourgeois body was, by definition, "inviolable," and homosexuality described a "network of fantasies" about the body's permeability.[29] Homosexuality, blinded finally by its "egotism" and intractability, is incompatible with the social contract on which civilization is based.[30] Homosexuality was thus an abuse of power in an ideally democratic regime predicated on the transparency of all of its male citizens. Until the interwar years, this power remained, at least in fantasy, checked by self-styled experts who knew homosexuals when they saw them, as well as by the fundamental inability of homosexuals to keep their secret to themselves.

But the presumption that homosexual men were weak—the tendency to perceive them as pale imitations of men—does not explain, however, why doctors so often believed inverts' putative furtiveness was a source of

29. Aron and Kempf, *Bourgeoisie,* 264.

30. Fin-de-siècle critics worried about the prevalence of homosexuality among artists, among whom it was traditionally seen as both an aesthetics and a sexual practice. The association between homosexuality and the aesthetics of moral ruin has been well documented in both England and France. This association between homosexuality and the decadent literary tradition, in the eyes of some, meant that homosexuality existed only "for its own sake," narcissistic and sterile. "[I]n its blind pursuit of sensual joy, homosexuality is only an aestheticized form of egotism"that threatens the "judicious altruism" on which civilization is based, Louis Estève wrote in his preface to Willy [Henri Gauthier-Villars], *Le Troisième Sexe* (Paris: Paris Editions, 1927), 21. On decadence and homosexuality, see Mario Praz, *The Romantic Agony* (Oxford: Oxford University Press, 1933), 392–94.

social danger, especially when police clearly used their power to arrest those men perceived to menace the public. In all these discussions, the invert's source of weakness is also paradoxically the source of his strength. After all, homosexuals may be shadowy and therefore easily intimidated figures, but they also "shadow" other men. Delcourt's instructions are telling: he claimed homosexuals were easily rebuffed and humiliated, and yet swelled with pride at having rebuffed them, as if he had slain a dragon rather than swatted an insect. For all their seeming confidence, these experts and critics do not seem at all comfortable with their ability to contain perverts: remember that homosexual men's activity may be secretive but it is still in "public," and although they are shadowy and insignificant, like predatory beasts, they prey upon the innocent. Similarly, the homosexual's secrecy was also the source of his control—of his ability to bend the law in his own financial interests, his ability to strike fear into the hearts of passers-by, his ability to subject any young man to his will. Homosexuality represented secrecy conceived of as shame and powerlessness, and secrecy understood as the power to destroy moral order.

After the war, these anxieties about secrecy became more and more pronounced: homosexuals were simultaneously now less ashamed and less covert, but even harder to detect; they sought to increase their numbers more brazenly than ever, but they were strangely difficult to locate. I use discussions about homosexuality's perceived menace to demonstrate that, like pornography, critics defined homosexuality as increasingly protean, increasingly resistant to conceptual clarity. In so doing, however, they forged a new distinction between heterosexuals and homosexuals that, like the distinctions between pornography and literature and pornography and patriotism, defined the parameters of fully developed manhood in new terms.[31]

Homosexuality and War

By the interwar years, the number of books about (and by) male homosexuals increased dramatically. Most were written for popular consumption and had large print runs. Attacks on homosexuality after the war were inseparable from images of humiliated, violated male bodies that haunted interwar thought and politics and constituted the backdrop for the increasingly voluminous attacks on liberal democracy from both the Left and the Right. Both the syndicalist Georges Sorel (1857–1922) and the fascist Georges Valois (1878–1945) held liberal

---

31. Here I draw on Eve Sedgwick's concept of homosexuality as both "minoritizing" and "universalizing"—specific to a minority of people and potentially inherent in all of us. On another note regarding a more fluid concept of homosexuality, historians often argue that gay men, like Jews, were perceived as sterile, effeminate, and "foreign." But these analyses neglect powerful other accounts of homophobia, which rely not on theories of homosexual difference (gay men's putative effeminacy, sterility, and difference), but on their similarities to other men. Psychiatrists and lawyers have explained gay-bashers' motives in terms of their need to differentiate themselves from the victim. "Homosexual panic," a diagnostic category invented in 1920 in the United States to explain why a man would assault another man he perceived to be gay, presumes that the assailant's motive was fear that he, like his victim, might be homosexual. This category formed the basis of some assailants' legal defenses beginning in the 1950s. See Robert Bagnall et al., "Burdens on Gay Litigants and Bias in the Court System: Homosexual Panic, Child Custody, and Anonymous Parties," *Harvard Civil Rights–Civil Liberties Law Review* 19 (Summer 1984): 499. In her now famous book, *Epistemology of the Closet* (Berkeley and Los Angeles: University of California Press, 1990), Eve Kosofsky Sedgwick argues that homosexual panic manifests "intense male homosocial desire as at once the most compulsory and the most prohibited of social bonds" (ibid., 187). That is, the compulsive identification of men with other men is always haunted by a powerful taboo against that identification. Sedgwick's theoretical foundation is Freud's concept of paranoia—(the straight) man's unconscious traversal and denial of the psychic and sexual boundary between men.

democracy responsible for France's Pyrrhic victory in World War I and the dissolution of bodies and souls that accompanied it.[32] Historians have long claimed that the war's unmet promise to regenerate and virilize the nation gave new impetus to anti-democratic forces. Except for gender historians, however, they have rarely focused on the important formation of male sexuality after the war; yet sexuality, and homosexuality in particular, was one of the most pervasive metaphors used to discuss that conflagration.[33] The writer Victor Margueritte, author of the infamous and "morally questionable" 1922 bestseller *La Garçonne,* defended his intentions by declaring that he only sought to use the heroine's sexual "frenzy" as a metaphor for the war and for the "promiscuous" transactions of the businessmen who profited from it.[34] Commentators frequently linked war and sexuality, and most often, as we have already seen, the war's violence was located metaphorically in so-called deviant bodies and particularly in homosexual ones.

It is never clear in these works whether homosexuality was the cause or symptom of the war (again echoing the similarly confusing status of pornography), but in every instance, homosexuality reenacts the trauma of war as the experience of spectacularly degraded manhood. In Michel DuCoglay's interwar novel about sailors, *Sous le Col Bleu,* for example, homosexual advances are meta-

32. See Zeev Sternhell, *Ni droite ni gauche: L'Idéologie fasciste en France* (Paris: Seuil, 1983), 92–105; 107–13.

33. For France, the best account is Mary Louise Roberts, *Civilization without Sexes: Reconstructing Gender in Postwar France, 1917–1927* (Chicago: University of Chicago Press, 1994). Roberts, however, is concerned primarily with cultural responses to changing gender roles and discusses sexuality within that context.

34. Victor Margueritte, "Pourquoi j'ai écrit *La Garçonne* et *Ton Corps est à toi,*" *Grand Guignol* 40 (Winter 1927–28): 265–66.

phors for the war's cruelty. The sailor Jean is drawn into a homosexual's bed by a ruse as cunning as the propaganda politicians used to lure young soldiers onto the battlefield. Jean is horrified, his dignity and faith in humankind destroyed.[35] Georges Anquetil deftly relates a scene out of Maxim Gorky's account of Russian women being tortured to interwar homosexuality. The passage from Gorky, he argues, is not only an "allegorical image of persecution and torture" but a reference to real violence witnessed by the Russian writer.[36] Anquetil goes on to conflate the spectacle of publicly "flaunted" homosexuality with the spectacle of the war, which, he says, confused "love and death" and caused people to "forget their souls." He compares the sexual excitement produced by public fighting in ancient Rome with the stimulation produced by the Great War, manifested not only, we recall, in women's bloodthirstiness, but now also in the spectacle of dancing pederasts. He links all the decadent periods in history to an increase in sexual violence, of which homosexuality is emblematic. The consequences are dire: homosexuality leads to contempt for war veterans and to the loss of bodily integrity specific to violent sexual pleasure.[37]

Alarmed critics linked increased homosexual activity to the perceived emasculation of young men by a humiliating and unjust war, for which elite politicians and businessmen were so often held responsible.[38] DuCoglay ar-

---

35. In the novel, the failed coup by right-wing groups at the Place de la Concorde on 6 February 1934 is called "a day of beauty" and homosexuals represent moral and national decline (Michel DuCoglay, *Sous le Col Bleu* [Paris: Raoul Saillard, 1938], 172).

36. Anquetil, *Satan conduit le bal*, 20.

37. Ibid., 20, 33.

38. See, e.g., George Mosse, *Fallen Soldiers: Reshaping the Memory of the World Wars* (Oxford: Oxford University Press, 1990), 69.

gues that homosexuality is but one tool of hypocritical and powerful men of the elite, who "kill the souls" of young men and in so doing, "kill the man of tomorrow." [39] He also claims that the "hard-hearted" businessmen and politicians who had corrupted or degraded young soldiers were homosexual, thus characteristically linking the corruption of the established order—the "old men" of the Third Republic—to homosexuality. Charles-Etienne, author of a series of interwar pulp novels, similarly conflates homosexuality with the corruption of those politicians who had sent young men to war. He attributes his hero's sexual problems (homosexual inclinations, gender ambiguity) to a childhood rape by an expansive bestial woman who is transmogrified first into a "masculine woman painter who wore a monocle," and then into an implicitly homosexual Dreyfusard. [40] For his part, Anquetil insists that military penitentiaries had become "hotbeds of demoralization," in which homosexual couples formed, and asserts that the war itself encouraged officers to take abominable liberties with their subordinates. He links the war to "sadism, cruelty, and pederasty" and blames the government for allowing such practices to continue or to have occurred without investigation. [41]

These and other accounts rhetorically linked the war to homosexuality. They also inadvertently claimed that

39. Michel DuCoglay, *Chez les mauvais garçons (choses vues)* (Paris: Raoul Saillard, 1938), 203–4.

40. Charles-Etienne, *Le Bal des folles* (Paris: Curio, 1930), 72.

41. Anquetil, *Satan conduit le bal*, 269. In Radclyffe Hall's classic novel *The Well of Loneliness*, which is framed by the war. gay men in a Paris "haunt" constitute a "miserable army," "battered remnants of men whom their fellow men had at last stamped under; who, despised of the world, must despise themselves beyond all hope, it seemed, of salvation" (1928; reprint, New York: Avon Books, 1981, 387).

the war revealed all men's susceptibility to homosexuality. After the war, homosexuality no longer represented a secret, contained, and identifiable threat to national sovereignty manifest most commonly in upper-class effetes and working-class thieves. It was now located everywhere and in everyone, in all milieux, and yet was more elusive than ever. Since the war, Anquetil asserted in 1925, "Saphism and pederasty display themselves in public places . . . and penetrate austere and closely guarded dwellings of yesteryear's bourgeoisie."[42] The war, another writer declared, permitted "homosexuality [to] shred the poetic veil in which the delicate bards of antiquity had shrouded it."[43] In another 1938 text of the "eye-witness" genre, Michel DuCoglay now predictably insists that the only way to rid Paris of this "scourge" on society is to "know" these men: "But how to obtain this impossible result [elimination], if we reject these hoodlums without knowing them?[44] And, he continues, shedding "light is the first and the best form of repression." The proof: Paris police prefect Monsieur Chiappe drove homosexuals from public places simply by "putting up lights in somber areas."[45] But this "light" is necessary because, "since the war," in contrast to nineteenth-century perceptions, "pederasts flourish in all milieux, and there are more of them than ever."[46]

Was this alarm justified? Certainly gay men and gay self-expression *were* more visible. For much of this anxiety derived from the publication of the first homosexual

42. Anquetil, *Satan conduit le bal,* 25.
43. Saint-Alban, "Chronique des mœurs," *Mercure de France* 105 (1 August 1928): 674.
44. DuCoglay, *Chez les mauvais garçons,* 17–18.
45. Ibid., 117, 155.
46. Ibid., 134.

French revue, *Inversions,* in November 1924. It was seized by the police in December, only to reappear under a new name—*L'Amitié*—in 1925, and was finally condemned to silence under the 1882 anti-pornography law (since homosexual sexual practices had been legal since the French Revolution). The disappearance of the revue did not quell Anquetil's anxiety, for Marcel Proust openly wrote of homosexuality in *A la recherche du temps perdu*—specifically in the volume published in 1921 entitled *Sodome et Gomorrhe,* and André Gide leant "pederasty" the prestige of his name in his 1924 work *Corydon.*

A flurry of writing both exploited and denounced the apparent pervasiveness of homosexuality. Colette's infamous ex-husband Willy (Henri Gauthier-Villars) wrote a voyeuristic account of "homosexual life" in Paris.[47] The literary critic Louis Estève's preface to Willy's *Le Troisième Sexe* calls attention to the "dangerous democratization of homosexuality."[48] Another literary critic, François Porché, wrote that when Proust won the Goncourt Prize in 1919, literary elites no longer "relegated [homosexuality] to the basement of the library and officially recognized [it]"; homosexuality "set up shop in the very heart of the City of Books, in the most beautiful sections of town." Porché also argued that it was now necessary to move beyond the nineteenth-century medical and police focus on "the professional uranist"—the blackmail and thief. "Everyday, hidden uranism . . . is never talked about . . . as if it did not exist."[49]

Porché's sentiments were echoed over and over again: DuCoglay wrote that "the homosexual is everywhere; in

47. Willy, *Troisième Sexe,* 205.
48. Ibid., 11.
49. François Porché, *L'Amour qui n'ose pas dire son nom* (Paris: Grasset, 1927), 10, 47.

the smallest village there is one who seeks another. . . . The evil is invisible, but it exists."[50] André Lorulot claimed that "pederasty has made extraordinary strides in France since the war. It is one of the fruits of general decadence. Homosexuality marches hand in hand with . . . all current aberrations."[51] Charles-Louis Vignon bemoaned the fact that "prostitutes today . . . do not have the same . . . power [as in the past]." For "we need them to counter the extension of pederasty and saphism."[52] In a letter to the anarchist Ernest Armand, one Frenchman wrote that "homosexuals now parade their tendencies around in public and can be found everywhere."[53] Finally, in a survey about the influence of homosexuality taken by the upscale literary journal *Les Marges*, one critic wrote that the interwar years marked a transition from a "literature of homosexuals" to a "homosexual literature."[54] In so doing, he reconceived clear authorial identities (a literature *of* homosexuals) as fluid ones that compromised the boundaries between the works of homosexual and heterosexual writers. If the "literature of homosexuals" distorted reality, now the existence of "homosexual literature" suggested that that distortion had become a permanent dimension of all postwar social relations.

Prevalent opinion on homosexuality manifested this fear of contagion in public discussions whose tenor was

50. DuCoglay, *Chez les mauvais garçons*, 215.

51. André Lorulot, *La Véritable Education sexuelle* (1926; reprint, Paris: L'Idée libre, 1945), 404.

52. Charles-Louis Vignon, *Histoire du sexe* (Paris: Pierre Garn, 1935), 61.

53. Letter from C. de Saint-Hélène to Ernest Armand in *La Camaraderie amoureuse* (Paris: Edition de l'en-dehors, 1930), 27.

54. *Les Marges* (March–April 1926). Reissued in *Cahiers Gai Kitsch Camp* 19 (Paris, 1993): 57.

determined primarily by journalists, self-styled social critics, some highbrow literary critics, and popularizers of medical theories. "Serious" medical men certainly wrote about homosexuality—indeed the psychiatrist *cum* psychoanalyst Alexander Hesnard proclaimed that "homosexuality is the obsession of our contemporary literature"—but they remained attached to organic explanations of a phenomenon that they believed had psychopathological consequences.[55] Although French psychoanalysts were not so biologically oriented, their theories were crude and reductive; they presumed that overbearing mothers produced gay sons. More sophisticated (if equally problematic) theories remained the province of doctors in other nations. Perhaps the most significant difference between pre- and postwar medical discourse was that most doctors no longer insisted so vehemently on the invert's feminine appearance; now they were more inclined to view homosexuality as a physiological problem that was not usually visible.[56]

55. A. Hesnard, "Psychologie de l'homosexualité masculine," *Evolution psychiatrique* 1 (October 1929): 47.

56. Pierre Humbert, *Homosexualité et psychopathies: Etude clinique* (Paris: G. Doin, 1935), links male homosexuality to problems of glandular secretions. Rogues de Fursac's classic *Manuel de psychiatrie* (Paris: Felix Alcan, 1917) does not have an entry for homosexuality, but one for "Anomalies de nature" attributes "l'inversion sexuelle ou homosexualité (uranisme chez l'homme, tribadisme ou saphisme chez la femme)" to discordance between physical and psychical sex (Krafft-Ebing's classic 1886 account of gender inversion), claiming that "complete" sexual inversion, meaning exclusive desire for same-sex partners, is "always congenital" (397, 401–2). Paul Ladame, "Inversion sexuelle et pathologie mentale" *Bulletin de l'Académie de médecine* 70 (21 October 1917): 226–29, classifies homosexuals as "degenerates." Dr. Witry, "Lettre de deux prêtres homosexuels. Guérisons après fièvre typhoide. Homosexualité et traumatisme," *Annales médico-psychologiques* 1 (May 1929): 398–419, attributes homosexuality to a blunt trauma to the head. C. I. Parnon, "Phénomenes d'inversion sexuelle ou d'intersexualité psychique et somatique, en rapport avec des altérations de la région infundibulo-hypophysaire," ibid. 2 (June 1931): 91–93, links homosexuality to cerebral dysfunction caused by

Thus after the war, homosexuality—as it was constructed and understood by self-styled experts and writers who most shaped public opinion—no longer remained in the shadows, confined to certain milieux and types of persons. While gay men were more visible, the narratives about that visibility were simply incommensurate with their presence: those narratives, after all, told fantastic tales in which in which all literature was "infected" by homosexuality, in which homosexual men appeared on every street corner, and in which all men were potentially homosexual. On the one hand, commentators stressed anew the danger represented by the visibly "virile" pederast, as if to render visible his difference. On the other hand, social critics conceived of homosexuals as less obviously effeminate, less clearly distinct from manly men, and therefore less visible.[57] In their struggle to control the meaning of the gay visibility (much of which they had themselves had produced), they insisted on the specific

---

traumas to the head. Numerous other articles of this sort similarly link homosexuality to somatic and psychic dysfunction with a somatic cause, especially blows to the head. The titles generally speak for themselves: e.g., René Allendy, "Sentiment d'infériorité, homosexualité, et complex de castration," *Revue française de Psychanalyse* 3 (1927): 505–48. René Laforgue, "La Pratique psychanalytique," ibid. 2 (1928): 239–304, identifies homosexuals as one of the principal "morbid types" one encounters in psychoanalytic practice. They are effeminate, have weak fathers, masturbate a lot, and tend to be impotent. (Hesnard, Allendy, and Laforgue were among the founders of French psychoanalysis). Finally, for a work that proposes castration as a cure for homosexuality, see Hector Ghilini, *Le Secret du Dr. Voronoff* (Paris: Eugene Fasquell, 1926), which seeks a way around the Penal Code's preclusion of castration even if a man should consent to his own mutilation.

57. As Rosario, *Erotic Imagination*, 77, notes, the threat posed by the homosexual was not effeminacy per se but his travesty of gender roles and traversal of class divisions. In *Gay New York: Gender, Urban Culture, and the Making of the Gay Male World, 1890–1940* (New York: Basic Books, 1994), 346, George Chauncey observes that there was a blurring of lines between effeminate and manly men, but still insists on the increased rigidity of sexual boundaries as its consequence.

danger of the pederast, the invert "by choice," as well as on the infectiousness (and hence the potential homosexuality of all men) of this choice.

Before the war, doctors compared homosexuality to the compulsive, irresistible impulse characteristic of deviant women, most dangerously manifested in "pederasts" who chose rather than were born with their vice. In 1909, Dr. Riolan had vehemently denounced pederasts, claiming that they had "an insatiable sexual appetite" and engaged in unnatural sexual practices "by choice." Congenital inverts were timid and most often educated, distinguished, even married men with "irreproachable reputations," while pederasts retained "a masculine mentality and virile tastes, often tainted by violence, vulgarity, or sadism." [58] A defender of homosexuals and a homosexual himself, the pseudo-doctor Marc Raffalovich, a Russian Jewish immigrant, distinguished between manly inverts and feminized perverts: "born" (congenital) inverts were masculine men, as upstanding as the next fellow, whereas perverts become inverts due to their attraction to "vice, or [because of their] impotence, their vanity, love of money, by imitation, or by cowardice or fear or simply by the desire to take advantage of someone who might prove useful." While he gave "inversion" a positive meaning, he did so only by linking the invert-pervert dichotomy to a gendered one: "the more a unisexual [invert] has moral values, the less effeminate he is." [59] After the war, all sorts of critics believed pederasts were

58. Dr. Riolan, *Pédérastie et homosexualité* (Paris: Librairie artistique et médicale, 1927), 6–7, 130. See also Max des Vignons, *Frédi à l'école: Le Roman d'un inverti* (Paris: Librairie artistique, 1929), who argues that congenital homosexuals are recognizable because they are timid when boys.

59. Raffalovich, *Uranisme*, 15, 16.

more numerous than "congenital" inverts and specifically emphasized the danger of pederasty. Dr. Henri Drouin, a venereal disease expert, wrote an essay on sexual inversion under the pseudonym François Nazier in which he argued that desire "against nature" is felt most acutely in those persons with a taste for luxury and excess.[60]

Both François Porché and the critic Marcel Réja insisted that most inverts are "occasional ones," not born ones.[61] Réja argued less sympathetically than Riolan that all the emphasis on "born inverts" had a misplaced apologetic effect: the idea that inversion was "in nature" encouraged others to treat gay men "no longer as repugnant monsters, but as people like others."[62] The pulp novelist Charles-Etienne attributed the downfall of most of his characters to the irresistible temptation homosexuality exerts, that "secret fire of vice" from which one character wishes to flee: "[H]e horrified and tempted me at the same time" (recall the novelist Louis Dumur's account of his attraction to and repulsion by war atrocities). Later, the hero predictably "succumbs" to the "abominable desire that he conjured within me."[63] In another novel, a man disgusted by his piano teacher's homosexuality finds himself "brutally possessed by the teacher's will" in spite of his repugnance. He becomes an invert—by choice.[64]

But how does one "choose" a compulsion? Or how can an irresistible impulse be represented as a choice of the conscious will? Critics' constructed homosexuality para-

60. Henri Drouin [Dr. François Nazier, pseud.], *L'Anti-Corydon: Essai sur l'inversion sexuelle* (Paris: Editions du Siècle, 1924), 98–100.

61. Marcel Réja, "La Révolte des hannetons," *Mercure de France* 13 (1 March 1928): 334.

62. Ibid., 334.

63. Charles-Etienne, *Bal des folles*, 42–43; 59.

64. Charles-Etienne and Odette Dulac, *Les Désexués: Roman des mœurs* (Paris: Curio, 1924), 40.

doxically as a force that was simultaneously irresistible (potentially inherent in all men) and the tendency of some abnormal, criminal class of men who willingly engaged in morally repugnant behavior.[65] Although, as Eve Sedgwick has famously argued, this paradox was implicit in nineteenth-century accounts of homosexuality, it never became explicit, because medical men were confident of their ability to distinguish homosexuals from other men by reference to their effeminacy, however imperceptible. The new emphasis on the "occasional" invert manifested anxiety about commentators' inability to delineate homosexuals so clearly because they could not precisely locate the source of their difference from other men.

Another prominent theme commentators used to locate the gay man's difference was the homosexual's "proselytizing," which, like religious fervor, compelled him to impose his choice on other men. The novelist DuCoglay portrays a Christmas Eve party in 1935 and a New Year's Eve ball in 1936 (these balls were common events) at which "hundreds" of homosexuals (*tantes*) gather to carouse.[66] The "danger of homosexuality," he writes, "rests first and foremost, perhaps uniquely, in *proselytizing* [emphasis in text]; I find deplorable these expeditions in which the microbe is spread in peaceful cities or villages." DuCoglay describes this highly visible and yet invisible (how, after all, does this "microbe" spread, why, and to whom?) presence in the bodies of gay men in public parks:

65. See Sedgwick, *Epistemology of the Closet*, ch. 2, and throughout the book.
66. *Tante* was standard slang for a homosexual man.

Rarely do the police seize the *corpus delicti* [the body of the crime]; nevertheless the "crime" enters into the "body" accompanied by a certain fear, which constitutes a supplemental thrill [*jouissance*]. And all these forms are mute, lugubriously mute; one might say void of all substance, of all life. One could deny that the body is emptied of its substance, but it is certain that these bodies extended on the ground are really in seventh heaven . . . from which they descend, their sighs muffled, amplified by darkness.[67]

In this extraordinary scene, these very public bodies, extended alongside one another as if they were corpses, are imagined as living dead,[68] inhabited by a "crime"— a microbe? They are substanceless, translucent and yet opaque, their "sighs" marking their presence. The "crime"—same-sex desire—moves mysteriously and quietly in and out of bodies that are images of the crime itself: impossible to grasp, ominous, they mock the police, from whose grasp they slip the moment they are captured. In this celestial setting, the homosexual body, oddly, is evacuated of any criminal agency even as the so-called crime migrates from body to body. The crime to which these men are compelled is visible, even audible, and yet it is entirely elusive.

Homosexual men were everywhere, no longer hidden, and yet they eluded identification. Increased "light" was necessary not only because critics perceived inverts as more difficult to recognize, but, paradoxically, because

67. DuCoglay, *Chez les mauvais garçons,* 175.
68. "Now someone whom I had never seen before came out of the shadows toward me. It looked like a mummy or a zombie . . . something walking after it had been put to death," James Baldwin writes in *Giovanni's Room* (New York: Laurel Press, 1956), 54. Set in Paris after the war, like part of Radclyffe Hall's *Well of Loneliness,* Baldwin's novel extends the metaphor of the homosexual as living corpse by means of conventional tropes associating gay men with death, artifice, nausea, and asphyxiation.

the more visible they were, the harder it was to see them—as if they did not reveal themselves when they were most "out"—in public, on street corners, and so on. François Porché claimed that the more "uranists repudiated the shame attached to their behavior, the more they discovered an unprecedented, provocative . . . pleasure . . . infused with fear, in making themselves even more visible."[69] Réja located this "moral contagion" in an "immense sect . . . with its own emblems and its own secret language," in which the "deviation of the instinct becomes . . . a reformed religion."[70] He also claimed that homosexuals were an "erotic sect" constituting a "monstrous octopus" that extended its tentacles throughout Paris.[71]

The judge who condemned the publishers of *Inversions* noted in his decision that it was his duty to protect the public from a magazine that had become "a vehicle through which homosexuals of all countries network, and thus constitutes active propaganda on behalf on pederasty." By virtue of its "lure," it served to "recruit" pederasts from the ranks of the normal.[72] Finally, Georges Anquetil noted that "since the war, pederasty has made extraordinary progress," and has been transplanted by means of moral contagion from Berlin to Paris. These "special propagandists," however, are hard to find without a guide. Ever enterprising, Anquetil finds a friend to take him to a bar "from which emanates a nauseating smell" and within which he finds an entirely clandestine world "behind a curtain."[73]

69. Porché, *Amour*, 69.
70. Ibid., 12.
71. Réja, *Révolte*, 324, 326.
72. *Recueil des Gazettes des Tribunaux*, 27 October 1926.
73. Anquetil, *Satan conduit le bal*, 255–56.

Here homosexuality was spread by moral contagion, whose origins were located in proselytizing fervor that is at once a compulsion and a conscious strategy of expansion. Homosexuality is a disease whose origins were finally located in a secret community of men whom no one could locate, even as this community "brutally possessed" the wills and inhabited the bodies of millions, whether by rendering them morally or physically sick. Anquetil left the bar nauseated by a smell whose origin is the homosexual body, which, oddly, emits no special odor in public. Moreover, this proselytizing fervor itself originated in the "thrill" of proclaiming one's homosexuality. But, to recall Porché, this thrill was oddly inseparable from another masochistic "thrill" (*jouissance*) that accompanies such proclamations. The joy of self-exposure was thus inextricable from a darker, masochistic, and inexplicable desire to be exposed, as if one were not finally the agent of one's own exposure, but, as DuCoglay envisioned it, compelled by a "crime" that took possession of the body.[74]

These allusions to homosexuals' participation in secret communities with dark collective souls echoed an old fantasy, born of the French Revolution, about monasteries and convents. Liberal thinkers depicted those institutions as hotbeds of same-sex activity lacking the transparency required for adherence to the social contract and hence as secret sects devoid of social responsibility. This concept resurfaced in nineteenth-century accounts of homosexuality, recalling its association with the dark underworld of crime. Now again, gay men were the high apostles of a secret society whose power is everywhere

74. Porché, *Amour,* 228–29. Note the striking resemblance to the vertiginous image of pornography.

but cannot be held to account. They are consequently
threats to the openness of democratic order in which
each man must be accountable for his actions, in which
secrecy itself constitutes an abuse of power. The more visible it became, the more secret, inaccessible, and protean
homosexuality was imagined to be.[75]

Heterosexuals, according to Réja, should consider
themselves in a state of "legitimate defense in the name of
the inalienable right of majorities." Homosexuality, he
said, "attracts snobs."[76] André Lorulot insists that men
choose to be homosexual because "they are snobs, are
vain, because they want to seem stylish, or to attract at-

75. In the most general terms, homosexuality threatened the fundamental principles of democratic manliness—self-exposure, self-explana-
tion, transparency. Since the late eighteenth century in England, Germany, France, and the United States, as George Mosse has argued, the
"corruption of the purity and chastity of manhood stood for the sickness
and dissolution of society," and one important sign of a man's purity and
chastity was his transparency: "[A] man may be considered in the light of
a placard, hung up on the wall to be read." In the early nineteenth century,
the American Samuel Stanhope Smith wrote in praise of the "people":
"There is not an emotion or thought which passes through the mind . . .
that does not paint some image of itself on the fine and delicate lines of the
countenance." And in 1789 the Frenchman Jérome Pétion de Villeneuve
claimed that the free man's "joy is pure . . . his feelings gentle and good;
these inner sentiments manifest themselves in the perfect development of
his body." The ideal male body, in whose image social order was forged,
reconciled dynamism (virility) and order (virility restrained by form): the
body's virile interior was consubstantial with its exterior form, so that its
virility was expressed paradoxically through its self-restraint, and the soul
was revealed by the body. George L. Mosse, *The Image of Man: The Creation of Modern Masculinity* (Oxford: Oxford University Press, 1996),
7; Smith quoted in Gordon Wood, "Conspiracy and the Paranoid Style,"
422 n. 54. Wood also points out that this concept of transparency under-
girded the pseudo-science of physiognomy in Europe and North America.
Villeneuve quoted in Antoine de Baecque, *Le Corps de l'histoire: Métaphores et politique, 1770–1800* (Paris: Calmann-Lévy, 1993), 174; Mosse,
Image of Man, 52.

76. Réja, *Révolte*, 339–40, 326–27.
77. Lorulot, *Véritable Education*, 404.

tention."[77] Homosexuals, one fictional character says, most admire Napoleon, St. Vincent de Paul, and the marquis de Sade, men who possessed an "incommensurable egoism," incompatible with democracy, and "love their fellow men" out of a thirst for life that is inseparable from a desire for pleasure (*jouissance*). Homosexuality was thus associated with anti-democratic forces—authoritarianism, the Church, and aristocracy—at the moment it was itself being "democratized," and hence also, in other discourses, associated by right-wing forces with Jewishness and socialism.[78] The "legitimate defense" of heterosexuals entailed a contradictory fantasy about a small minority of snobs who sought to widen their circle, who had, for no explicable reason other than their contempt for normalcy and desire for distinction, declared war on normal citizens and thus on France herself.

Homosexuals looked and acted like other men. They were homosexual because they were virile and homosexual because they were not virile enough; they were compelled by their desires and they chose them. They were everywhere and yet could never be located, and all men were so susceptible to their beckoning that homosexuals steadily increased their numbers. In making this sort of argument, commentators legitimated the necessity for some sort of "defense" against homosexuals but also compromised the distinction between homosexuals and other men. If homosexuals were virtually indistinguishable from other men, if the boundaries between "normal"

---

78. Charles-Etienne, *La Bouche fardeé* (Paris: Curio, 1926), p. 90. Of course, these three anti-democratic institutions were often invoked by decadent writers and artists in order to celebrate the mystical excesses of the putatively sadomasochistic Catholic spirit. Homosexuality had been equated with these forces since the late nineteenth century. On the fin-de-siècle, see Praz, *Romantic Agony*.

citizens and homosexuals were so porous, what sort of men were not homosexual?

In order to purify the national body by containing and eliminating homosexuals, writers oddly wrote them into every imaginable script and glimpsed them behind every curtain. Suddenly homosexuals were everywhere, and yet the light was no longer adequate to expose them, transforming them into a more pervasive and ominous presence. Homosexuality now escaped not only the confines of a dangerous, shady underworld, but eluded detection. Critics at once forged an image of gay male bodies as malleable forms with no interior—and hence capable, like Satan, of taking on any identity—and as "interiors" with no form, microbes that traveled freely in quest of a body in which to reside.[79] Journalists, social critics, and doctors took gay men's visibility as a sign of the invisible circulation of homosexuality from body to body. This same fantasmic proliferation thus made homosexuals so difficult to locate and the boundary be-

---

79. Homosexuality thus required more and more commentary and study because it represented the absence of any correlation between form and content and causes and effects, on which reliable knowledge depended. This perpetual need for more "light" thus intensified, as Michel Foucault has argued in relation to sexuality more generally—as if homosexuals were but a pretext for the expansion of regulatory power. In other words, according to Foucault, knowledge about homosexuals is part of the expansion of a larger disciplinary apparatus whose origins can never be known. But oddly, the production of homosexuality in the account I have just offered is an allegory for the production of power as Foucault defines it: an increasingly visible body of material whose origins remain elusive; a form that mutates but whose mutation remains inexplicable except by tautological reference to the fact of its mutation (i.e., "power" creates homosexuals because it requires them for its own expansion—but what force is motivating the expansion?); a force that inhabits and shapes bodies for reasons that remain mysterious. But to the extent that homosexuality, if we follow Foucault's logic, is intrinsically unknowable, neither its history nor the history of heterosexuality can be accounted for.

tween homosexuality and heterosexuality so fluid that
national purification could no longer take the form of the
repression or the restraint of a clearly identifiable homosexual body or same-sex desire. In their unconscious,
paradoxical efforts to restore national integrity through
the proliferation of fantasies about homosexuality, interwar social critics rendered the national, presumably heterosexual body indistinct from a boundaryless homosexual one.

Gay Men and Gay Identity

The gay male discourse about homosexuality in this period was multidimensional and complex. Jean Cocteau
and Marcel Proust, among others less well known, made
no special plea for tolerance for homosexuals, but offered
a rich and often ironic assessment of homosexuality in
their work. Cocteau was generally fascinated by the power
of sexual pleasure, and Proust, according to some (and
as he was interpreted by most commentators in his
own time) equated homosexuality with sexual inversion.
André Gide rejected Proust's work on such grounds: he
claimed it "stigmatized uranism." [80] But, as recent criticism has suggested, Proust's work cannot be reduced to
such simple formulas. When Gide sent him a copy of his
own *Corydon,* a plea for tolerance which I discuss below,
Proust confirmed his homosexuality and remarked with
typical irony and acuity that because Baudelaire had so
successfully ventriloquized a lesbian voice, he should be
included in the "Société des Tantes." Proust also noted
in a letter to Gide that "the enemies of homosexuality will

80. André Gide, quoted in Emily S. Apter, *André Gide and the Codes of
Homotextuality* (Saratoga, Calif.: Anma Libri, 1987), 138.

be revolted by the scenes I shall depict" in *Sodome et Gomorrhe*, "and the others will not be any more pleased at seeing their ideal of virility presented as the consequence of a feminine temperament."[81] Proust thus made no apologies and accurately predicted the responses of both critics and other gay men to his work.

In this discussion, however, I focus on gay men who engaged explicitly and without irony in a discourse on the politics of homosexuality, those who demanded inclusion on their own terms. Their fantasies about homosexuality and those of Cocteau or Proust (and no doubt countless others) were not the same. But these men made the first public case for homosexual equality in France, and for that reason I make them my focus. In other words, how did a vocal minority of gay men clamoring for respect conceptualize their sexuality? I argue that many of these gay men sought to renew and regenerate virility by forging a more visible, forceful, and positive gay identity. Most of this sort of discussion about homosexuality among male homosexuals began with Gide's decision to publish his defense of pederasty, *Corydon*, for a general public (it had been circulated among a small group of friends in 1911).[82] Gide's invocation of Socratic dialogue

81. See ibid., 138, for Proust on Baudelaire (paraphrased here). Proust on *Sodome et Gomorrhe* is quoted by J. E. Rivers, "The Myth and Science of Homosexuality in *A la recherche du temps perdu*," in Elaine Marks and George Stambolian, eds., *Homosexualities and French Literature* (Ithaca, N.Y.: Cornell University Press, 1979), 267. Proust's narrative voice can hardly be reduced to "the banal thematization [of sexual inversion]," Eve Sedgwick writes, because, even when portraying homosexuals as effeminate, his work always "displays, even as it uncontrollably *transmits*, sheer representational anxiety" about such deceptively uncomplicated depictions (*Epistemology of the Closet*, 216–17). On Cocteau, see René Galand, "Cocteau's Sexual Equation," in Marks and Stambolian, eds., *Homosexualities*, 279–94. Recall that *tante* (auntie) was slang for male homosexual.
82. André Gide, *Corydon* (Paris: Nouvelle revue française, 1924). This work was first published in an anonymous limited edition in Bruges in

and an ancient Greek text to legitimate pederasty conformed to a long aesthetic and scholarly tradition (primarily in England and Germany). Since the early nineteenth century, gay male academics and writers turned to
the "virile" homoerotic friendships explicitly depicted in
ancient Greek texts for affirmation. But during and after the war, as Martha Hanna argues, neoclassicism also
found exuberant adherents in republican intellectual culture. Republicans used its emphasis on rationality to pit
classical France against barbaric Germany. Hence this
"return" to a classical tradition was part of the political
valorization of Frenchness not confined to gay men, and
cut across traditional political divides. Gide's work must
also be placed, as Hanna insists, in this context.[83]

These men not surprisingly turned Gide into a hero.
They were also acolytes of the Swiss-born Camille Spiess,
who wrote in French, was well known in these circles (he
was at the center of much discussion), and celebrated a
"new man." Gide became a communist, and Spiess was
clearly sympathetic to fascism; this gay discourse derived its politics from a broad, symbolic repudiation of

---

1911, reissued in 1920, and published under Gide's name only in 1924. See
Patrick Pollard, *André Gide: Homosexual Moralist* (New Haven, Conn.: Yale
University Press, 1991), ch. 1, "The Chronology of *Corydon*." On Gide's
sexual politics more generally, see, among others, Apter, *André Gide;* Lucille Cairns, "Gide's *Corydon:* The Politics of Sexuality and Sexual Politics," *Modern Language Review* 91.3 (July 1996): 582–96; and Jonathan
Dollimore, *Sexual Dissidence* (New York: Oxford University Press, 1993),
esp. 2–17.

83. Hanna, "Natalism, Homosexuality, and the Controversy over *Corydon*," 210–11. This fascination with ancient Greece on the part of gay male
scholars is part of a long tradition in Victorian England and in Germany—the famous art historian Johannes Winckelmann is a prominent
example. On the Victorians, see Linda Dowling, *Hellenism and Homosexuality in Victorian Oxford* (Ithaca, N.Y.: Cornell University Press, 1994).
See also Robert Aldrich, *The Seduction of the Mediterranean: Writing Art,
and Homosexual Fantasy* (London: Routledge, 1993).

femininity rather than a commitment to a specific ideology. Zeev Sternhell has argued controversially that French fascism derived from a complex metamorphosis of left-wing thought. But his passing revelation that regardless of their location on the Left or Right, all the thinkers and activists he discusses were equally committed to different versions of revitalized virility is accurate: these gay men were no exception.[84] The journal *Inversions* often reiterated the anti-Semitic and misogynist rhetoric associated with Spiess, even though its name seems to belie such associations. Its contributors often denounced homosexuality in favor of "pederasty." In seeking to give pederasty a positive valence, many gay contributors to the journal, as well as Gide and Spiess, distinguished it from homosexuality, which they associated with effeminacy. In so doing, they invoked the "hellenistic" ethos of Oxford University, in which tutorials between student and teacher emphasized the "spiritual procreancy" celebrated in Plato's *Symposium* and encouraged a noble love devoid (at Oxford, not in Greece) of bodily pleasures.[85] At the same time, all these men but Spiess—and then somewhat disingenuously—saw no contradiction between what Oscar Wilde called the nexus of "intellectual enthusiasm and the physical passion of love."[86] Their celebration of ped-

84. I am not suggesting that Sternhell's controversial assertion that fascism has its roots in alienated Marxism is correct but the myriad documents he cites on both the Left and the Right attest to the centrality of virility in rhetoric about nation-building. For a recent synthesis of debates about French fascism, see Robert Soucy, *French Fascism: The Second Wave, 1933–1939* (New Haven, Conn.: Yale University Press, 1995), 1–25, who takes issue with Sternell. See also Sternhell, *Ni droite ni gauche.*
85. See Dowling, *Hellenism and Homosexuality,* esp. 32–66.
86. Oscar Wilde quoted in ibid., 124. Camille Spiess's defenders claimed that he was "married to a woman who detested pederasts." Aside from the oddity of this defense, the vast majority of Spiess's critics believed him to be disingenuous. See Camille Spiess, *Ceux qui l'attaquent et ceux qui le comprennent: Opinions diverses et commentaires suivis d'une étude de*

erasty was full of joy and desire rather than the joy-tinged agony Linda Dowling claims tortured the Oxonian John Symonds as he sought to reconcile "spiritual procreancy" with his "physical passion."[87]

In his work on *Pédérastie et homosexualité*, Spiess argued that unschooled critics—he refers to a neo-Malthusian journal entitled *La Vie intime*—used the word "pederasty" in a derogatory sense to mean acquired homosexuality.[88] But, he argued, "to confound homosexuality with pederasty is to confound sexuality with the philosophical, anti-Semitic, inspired heroism of the real poet formed by God." Spiess claimed he wanted to "offer an apologia for pederasty using an appeal to Love, Plato, and [Walt] Whitman," and by opposing Christianity to "Aryan platonism." "Women's only purpose," he continued, is to "give birth to virile men."[89]

In the same vein, Louis Estève wrote that women's beauty was corporeal, while men's bodies exhibited that "purity of form" that had so enamored the Greeks. With the "androgyne," he claimed, "the character of the race is reborn without seams" and manifests the "incorruptible paternity of Platonic love." Greek love was not necessarily a perversion; rather, it was "the original representation of the virile cult of heroism and passionate friendship." Moreover, the "white Aryan is not as lascivious as men of color. He is as repulsed by normal copulation as

C. Spiess sur A. Gide et le problème de l'inversion sexuelle (Paris: Annales d'Hermétisme, 1930), 45.

87. Dowling, *Hellenism and Homosexuality*, 88. Dowling points out that this contradiction between idealized Platonic love as it was represented at Oxford and homosexual men's physical desire became untenable as Walter Pater, John Symonds, and Oscar Wilde grew older.

88. Camille Spiess, *Pédérastie et homosexualité* (Paris: H. Daragon, 1917), 11–12.

89. Ibid., 15, 23–24, 34.

by the abjection represented by sodomy." And in perhaps the most powerful reinterpretation of homophobic discourse, Estève argued that narcissism had nothing to do with blindness and everything to do with civilization, culture, and intellect. By "embracing his own reflection in the image of the adolescent," the pederast's thought is "fertilized," made fecund, as if pederasty defined not same-sex desire but, as Estève called it, the "cerebralization of the sexual instinct."[90]

Réja called Spiess's point of view "mystical," and Drouin claimed that Gide's views constituted a pretty gloss on a bestial desire.[91] As noted, Gide, Spiess, and others like them did not represent the only available gay reading of homosexuality. But theirs was provocative, because they insisted overtly that same-sex physical passion could be redeemed if properly restrained and channeled, whereas Proust, for example, implicitly repudiated such ideas. These gay men evoked simultaneously rage and contempt, not because they parodied normative masculinity, but because they defined pederasty in the same (although never clearly articulated) terms as others had historically celebrated manhood. They defined it in the name of restoring the real warrior capable of defending his nation, and, in so doing, they transformed pederasty into a paradoxically disinterested desire in which the innately manly man, immune to sexual corruption and hence to the self-

90. Louis Estéve, *L'Enigme de l'androgyne* (Paris: Monde moderne, 1927), 61, 109, 72, 38. See also his series of articles on "L'Amour romantique et ses aberrations dans notre littérature" in *Bon Plaisir* (June 1922 through April 1923). Estève is the same critic who denounces homosexuality in his preface to Willy's *Le Troisième Sexe*. The two positions are consistent because he disdained homosexual desire that served no redemptive purpose, the sort of desire all critics denounced as a symptom of postwar moral decline.

91. Réja, *Révolte*, 331; Nazier, *Anti-Corydon*, 110.

interest associated with the bestiality of instinct, reinvigorates the world. This political and cultural mission suggests that the celebration of pederasty was not about an alternative conception of male sexuality but about the restoration of a redemptive male sexuality. This vocal minority of gay men were thus no different from those critics who assailed homosexuality as the cause of moral decline. The recovery of this virile sexuality promised the restoration of (different versions of) moral order based on the purging of the base corporeality associated, above all, with women, femininity, and, in one variation, "racially inferior elements" more generally. They thus celebrated a male sexuality whose defining features were its transcendence and transparency.

Marcel Réja and Drouin denounced this celebration of the marriage between virility and "poetry" when it was advocated by gay men who first proclaimed their equality to "normal" men in the interwar period. Drouin insisted that Gide would never convince anyone that pederasty was purer than heterosexual love. Réja, one of the only commentators even to use "heterosexuality" as a descriptive term, tellingly conflated it with "French civilization."[92] When he argued that heterosexuals defend themselves in the name of the "rights of majorities," he transformed male heterosexuality into the symbolic bond between the nation and its necessarily disinterested defenders. For him, the heterosexual, unlike the homosexual, seemingly had no desires or interests to protect ex-

---

92. Réja, *Révolte*, 331. In *The Invention of Heterosexuality* (New York: Dutton, 1995), 66, Jonathan Katz notes that even Freud only uses some version of the term "heterosexual" twenty-nine times in all 24 volumes of the *Standard Edition*. Katz rightly notes that although heterosexuality was being disciplined and defined, it was never seen as a "problem," or as nonnormative, and so was rarely discussed *as* heterosexuality.

cept those of the majority, meaning "France" herself. Heterosexual men had no need to proclaim their identity; they had nothing to hide and were not (at least in theory) "snobs." Many French thinkers, including Réja and Drouin, made a connection between fascism and homosexuality because fascism provided an example of the sort of *interested* virility that proclaimed itself too loudly. The male body ceased to be an impermeable and healthy symbol of vigor when Robert Brasillach, a French fascist collaborator, proclaimed enthusiastically that the "nighttime ceremonies" of Nazi rallies turned politics into "poetry."[93] In the torch-lit night, those virile bodies became suspiciously porous and passive, soft as poetry, enthralled by the siren song of a man to whom they were absolutely submissive. Jean-Paul Sartre implicitly insisted that French fascists were effeminate: in fascist writings, he claimed, "One can pick out . . . curious metaphors that present the relations of France and Germany under the aspect of a sexual union, where France plays the role of the woman."[94] Most important, Sartre

93. Brasillach quoted in Sternhell, *Ni droite ni gauche*, 271.
94. Jean-Paul Sartre, "Qu'est-ce qu'un collaborateur?" in *Situations*, vol. 3 (Paris: Gallimard, 1949), 58. Alice Yaeger Kaplan discusses his essay, among others, in *Reproductions of Banality: Fascism, Literature, and French Intellectual Life* (Minneapolis: University of Minnesota Press, 1986), 13–20. For a recent set of literary-theoretical essays that touch on homophobia and fascism, see Melanie Hawthorne and Richard J. Golsan, *Gender and Fascism in Modern France* (Hanover, N.H.: University Press of New England, 1997). Regardless of their anti-feminist and homophobic rhetoric and policy, fascists have been rhetorically constructed as homosexuals in popular culture and in the highbrow writings of men like Sartre and Theodor Adorno. Obviously, this does not mean that fascists are never homosexual—the SA leader Ernst Röhm, slain on Hitler's orders in 1934, was well known to prefer men. Rather, it means that in mainstream and even high intellectual representation, fascists are generally perceived as repressed homosexuals, and that this representation should be investigated. See Andrew Hewitt, *Political Inversions: Homosexuality, Fascism, and the Modernist Imaginary* (Stanford, Calif.: Stanford University Press, 1996).

attributed fascists' "virility" to an impure and interested pleasure associated both with homosexuality and female sexuality more generally.

Conclusion

In interwar France, calls to repress homosexuality in order to restore moral order paradoxically took the form of proliferating fantasies about homosexuals. As this chapter argues, these fantasies developed as part of an effort to preserve national integrity by metaphorically locating the war's unprecedented and inescapable violence in degraded and unrestrained male homosexuality. Yet such fantasies also undermined the nation, because they implicated all men's sexuality in the nation's moral ruin: that is, the nation could only by preserved to the extent that homosexuality was seen as pervasive and legitimated the increased surveillance of all men. Most historians identify this development as a process through which the boundary between homosexuality and heterosexuality became more and more rigid.[95] Such accounts are true—

---

95. Drawing on medical literature and images of visible gay male subcultures, bourgeois cultural elites believed homosexual behavior was a form of gender transgression; they thus imposed formal and informal sanctions against homosexuality to regulate perceived *gender* deviations, in the process solidifying medicalized sexual identities in new and more popular forms. George Chauncey notes that in response to a "crisis" of masculinity whose social consequences were increasingly dramatic, New York City police harassed "obviously" gay men and forced drag balls from Times Square in the 1930s. Allan Berubé demonstrates how witch hunts against homosexuals in the U.S. Army became increasingly draconian after 1953, when the Cold War intensified fears about gender deviants. Martha Hanna argues that in interwar France, natalists believed that eliminating homosexuality would preserve normative families and help increase the birthrate. Finally, women's historians have long argued that during the interwar years in both the United States and western Europe, lesbianism—and by extension any form of female friendship—became increasingly suspect and stigmatized as women challenged conventional gender roles. Chauncey, *Gay New York*, 305–54; Allan Berubé, *Coming Out Under Fire: The History of Gay Men and Women in World War Two* (New

homosexuality was increasingly perceived as a secret repository of contamination that had to be identified and regulated whatever the cost. But they generally do not view homosexuality simultaneously as a repository of contamination and as diffused throughout the social body. For if homosexuality is diffused throughout the social body, it cannot be so neatly divided from heterosexuality. Critics thus rendered homosexuality, like pornography, continuous with the social body even as they marked its "otherness."

In conclusion, I wish to speculate briefly about the importance of this interpretation of homosexuality in understanding recent meanings attributed to heterosexuality and homosexuality. Until the interwar years, manliness presumed heterosexuality, and when the word "heterosexual" was mentioned, medical men used it to designate either straight or bisexual desire. But during and after the war, these critics conceived of homosexuality as so elastic, so contaminating, and so fluid that it was no longer possible to imagine the divisions between hetero- and homosexuality as those between repressed, sanctified, normal manhood and irrepressible, ignoble effeminacy. Although heterosexual intercourse remained and remains the privileged symbol of sexuality, interwar critics paradoxically purified the "act" of its sexuality by rendering it coextensive with the nation and with civilization itself. For the first time, heterosexuality did not only describe a desire best repressed and regulated within the confines of marriage. Most self-identified "heterosexual" writers now implicitly reinstated the division between homo- and heterosexuality using the same terms

York: Plume, 1990), 260–72; Hanna, "Natalism, Homosexuality and the Controversy over *Corydon*," 202–24.

a minority of gay men employed to define the "purity" of homosexuality: heterosexuality oddly transcended sexuality, and for non-gay writers, homosexuality became a synecdoche for sexuality. This does not mean that the identification of heterosexuality with first-class manhood precluded the recognition of or discussion about heterosexuality as a form of desire. Rather, heterosexuality described *both* a desire and a form of privileged manhood that oddly transcended desire. Homosexuality was thus not conceptually parallel to heterosexuality because it described a form of manhood always reducible to sexual acts, always imagined as the menacing, contaminating, and yet elusive agent of destruction against which "heterosexuals," now peculiarly synonymous with good citizens and France herself, must mobilize.

That homosexuality was a form of disease-bearing but identifiable and confinable humanity is a legacy of the nineteenth century. That homosexuality was a contagious and contaminating symbol of sexuality from which no man was immune was a postwar invention that generated heterosexual identity as a multidimensional, rhetorically significant form of "being" that had never existed as such before. Moreover, the currently bizarre division of homosexual personhood into sexual "acts" and the declaration (or nondeclaration) of "identity" prevalent in current French discussions about homosexuality and the "closet" (as well as in recent debates about the entry of gays into the U.S. military), must also be a legacy of these cultural fantasies.[96] In those debates,

96. In the United States, the legal terms for identity and acts are speech and conduct. For France, see the articles in "Same Sex, Different Text: Gay and Lesbian Writing in French," *Yale French Studies* 90 (1996). The compulsion in France to keep homosexuality "private," and the logic that homosexuals will be accepted as long as they do not declare their homosexuality, dramatically enforces the reduction of the gay person to his or her

sexual acts are always impure and unspeakable, and identity is defended as the right to define and express oneself, as if the two were practically separable. In this context, homosexual sexuality must always be soiled, contagious, and contaminating, irreconcilable with any form of respectable humanity and certainly not with citizenship. Since the late nineteenth century, this much had changed: now male heterosexuality within or outside of marriage is one of the important rhetorical grounds of citizenship, and homosexuality is respectable only to the extent that it is not soiled by sexuality.[97] Heterosexual identity now essentially defines a man as both sexually prolific and (rhetorically) desexualized, and homosexual identity describes a man whose respectability is dependent on his celibacy, and whose sexuality cannot finally be redeemed by reference to the nation or the family. "Homosexuals" must now thus carry the enormous political and social burden of this recently constructed fissure between their sexual acts and their identities. "Heterosexuals" carry other burdens. But these sufferings, including painful questions about worthiness or normalcy, derive from the presumption that they are complicated, multidimensional people.

---

acts and renders the notion of a purified homosexuality virtually unthinkable. Declarations of identity in this context constitute a demand for publicity that, as in the United States, is inseparable from gay people's refusal to be reduced to their sexuality, and yet also produces a bizarre bifurcation of sexual acts and self-identity. In the context of heterosexuality, identity is always presumed to be multidimensional and never reducible to sexuality alone; that is, heterosexuals don't leave their sexual preferences behind closed doors, even though they may leave their sex lives there.

97. The same applies to heterosexual women, but in more complicated ways, since female heterosexuality also implies some form of subordination to men. I deal with the question of female heterosexuality via the path of lesbianism in chapter 5.

5

The Making of Lesbian Sexuality

Should we, like Diogenes the cynic, roam the
forum, lamp in hand, looking for a lesbian?
Anne Garréta, "In Light of Invisibility" (1996)

Postwar French cultural commentators bemoaned the
increasing visibility of urban male homosexual subcultures. They argued that gay men should be more discrete
and not "flaunt" their preferences, and journalists de-
cried men's snobbery, their sense of superiority, their
cliquishness and allegedly ostentatious tendencies. Discussion about male homosexuality proliferated. But the
literature concerned with female homosexuality was just
as voluminous—and perhaps more so, because it was included in an increasingly vast pornographic repertoire.
As I argued in chapter 4, efforts to repress male homosexuality did not only generate fantasies about their increased visibility but also produced fantasies of homosexuality's irresistibility; commentators believed there
was a potentially gay man in every apparently straight
one, transforming homosexuality into an omnipresent but
invisible enemy. This logic, moreover, mimicked fearful

Epigraph: Anne Garréta, "In Light of Invisibility," *Yale French Studies*
90 (1996): 208.

fantasies about pornography as equally omnipresent and invisible.

In what follows, I shall argue that although the para-doxical—indeed paranoid—structure of fantasies about pornography and male homosexuality applied to inter-war female homosexuality as well, we should make an important distinction between men and women. Fantasies about the omnipresence of both male and female homosexuals surfaced for closely related reasons, including natalist anxieties, fears about national "emascula-tion," and feminist questions about gender roles, all of which I discuss in greater depth below. Those fantasies accented gay men's visibility, and although critics also perceived lesbians everywhere, they were, it seems, never visible *enough*.[1]

1. This interpretation of lesbianism was common in a wide variety of texts and was perhaps best put by Freud: "Homosexuality in women, which is certainly not less common than in men, although much less glaring, has not only been ignored by law, but has also been neglected by psy-choanalytic research." See "The Psychogenesis of a Case of Homosexual-ity in a Woman," in Sigmund Freud, *Sexuality and the Psychology of Love* (New York: Collier, 1963), 133. Havelock Ellis, who believed homosexual-ity was a benign natural variation, also claimed that "inversion" was "less easy to detect in women." See Ellis, *Studies in the Psychology of Sex*, vol 2: *Sexual Inversion* (Philadelphia, F. A. Davis, 1904), 121. There is now a vo-luminous if eclectic body of work about lesbians, mostly by literary theo-rists. On the interwar period in France, there is an article on working-class lesbians (which tends to be concerned with fantasies about them) by Francesa Canadé-Sautman in Jeffrey Merrick and Bryant T. Ragan, eds., *Homosexuality in Modern France* (Oxford: Oxford University Press, 1996), 177–201. See also Christine Bard, *Les Garçonnes: Modes et fantasmes des années folles* (Paris: Flammarion, 1998). For the nineteenth century, see work by Victoria Thompson in ibid., 102–27; Nicole Albert, "Sappho Mythified, Sappho Mystified, or the Metamorphoses of Sappho in Fin-de-Siècle France," in Rommel Mendès-Leite and Pierre Olivier de Bus-scher, eds., *Gay Studies from the French Cultures: Voices from France, Bel-gium, Brazil, Canada and the Netherlands* (New York: Haworth Press, 1993), 87–104.

Of course right-wing nationalists and Republicans alike denounced "mannish" women and often implicitly conflated feminism and lesbianism, using the latter "aberration" to discredit feminist ideas as well. I do not mean to underplay this narrative, pervasive at the end of the nineteenth century and used to shame sexually and politically dissident women during the interwar period. In this chapter, I wish merely to shift the emphasis from one discourse to a less obvious and perhaps less evidently stigmatizing but equally pervasive one: in the French postwar cultural imagination, lesbian sexuality refused to show itself.

I mean to argue here that the important critical focus on self-identified lesbians, increasingly visible lesbian subcultures, bars, and clubs does not address the significant investment that interwar critics had in rendering lesbians literally or metaphorically invisible. By neglecting this important discourse, other arguments, however inadvertently, imply that lesbian invisibility is the product of benign neglect: the French, in Vernon Rosario's recent words, "had become inured to the pornographic spectacle of tribadic couples . . . and to the fantasmatic titillation of sapphic lovers in nineteenth-century literature." And, "male inverts, on the other hand, were quite threatening." Although Rosario also claims that Frenchmen did not *want* to know about lesbians, he does not elaborate sufficiently. For how is the desire not to know related to the oversaturation proper to the state of being "inured" to a particular set of representations? Rosario is certainly not alone in his construction of gay men as more "threatening": I use his words here because his recent work promises to explore the French erotic imagination and for the most part does so quite eloquently. His dismissal of lesbians in this fashion (while trying not to dismiss them) is thus odd and yet sadly predictable, for the fascinating question—why did Frenchmen *not* want to know—remains unanswered.[2]

Nevertheless, in contrast to these and other claims of lesbians' unthreatening status, and drawing on a century-old fantasy of aristocratic lesbian sects, a vast array of interwar novelists and cultural critics imagined that lesbians were omnipresent and yet impossible to detect. Remember that interwar discourses about male homosexual visibility proved the dialectical point of departure for drawing a more rigid line of demarcation between gay and straight men *and* produced an increasingly porous boundary between them. During the same period, narratives about lesbian *invisibility*, I argue, similarly demarcated lesbian identity *and* construed lesbians as less and less distinct from other women. In so doing, critics wanted to expose the dangers of female sexuality (and therefore of female *hetero*sexuality too) for which the lesbian, often unidentified and unidentifiable, was a privileged emblem. Thus lesbian invisibility was not just a symptom of cultural negligence but the product of a cultural obsession with female sexuality expressed dramati-

---

2. Vernon Rosario, *The Erotic Imagination: French Histories of Perversity* (Oxford: Oxford University Press, 1997), 108–9, borrows Eve Sedgwick's neologism "un-knowing" to suggest that medical men's more limited treatment of lesbianism was the product of willful ignorance. Rosario devotes an entire chapter to male homosexuality but barely two pages to explaining why he has not felt compelled to discuss lesbians (because the medical men did not). Jean-Paul Aron and Roger Kempf mention lesbianism in *La Bourgeoisie, le sexe, et l'honneur* (Brussels: Editions complexes, 1984), 91, but they claim that nineteenth-century writers manifested a more "indulgent" attitude toward lesbians than they did toward gay men. They are careful, however, to place this indulgence in the context of the male bourgeoisie's need to dominate women more generally.

cally in interwar French cultural commentary. The reality that lesbians were present in every walk of life but, from critics' perspective, difficult to identify, became part of an elaborate fantasy about the secretive, elusive nature of the lesbian. Moreover, that fantasy also formed the parameters within which some self-described lesbians forged an alternative language for their own sexuality.[3]

Female Gender Deviance

In the late nineteenth century, political and cultural commentary demonized lesbianism in the context of the low birthrate and feminist challenges to normative heterosexuality. In the vast secondary literature on French feminism, there is only marginal discussion of lesbianism, and on lesbianism itself there exists very little.[4] Nevertheless, as with pornography and male homosexuality, literary and medical narratives emphasized the sterility both of nonprocreative and same-sex desire and the threat that they posed to the size and health of the population. In the context of fears about "depopulation" after the French defeat in the Franco-Prussian war and

3. I use the term "lesbian" to designate an always culturally and historically specific identity formation rather than a fixed entity. This should be clear from my historicization of both male and female homosexuality. Finally, as I have suggested, the invisible lesbian tends to be a "feminine" one. Lisa Duggan notes that this feminine lesbian became a "figure of instability and betrayal" because she moved between men and women. As I argue, I believe she is figured that way also because she cannot be tied to clear gender norms. Duggan notes that she disappears at the turn of the century (in the United States), inasmuch as most critics focused on the masculine lesbian. In France, both narratives were equally powerful. Lisa Duggan, "Theory in Practice: The Theory Wars, or Who's Afraid of Judith Butler," *Journal of Women's History* 10 (Spring 1998): 17.

4. For the most comprehensive treatment available, see Marie-Jo Bonnet, *Les Relations amoureuses entre les femmes* (Paris: Odile Jacob, 1995).

women's demand for suffrage, feminists and women more generally had to defend themselves against charges of skirting national duty by repudiating motherhood: at their shrillest, legislators accused women of treason to their "race." After 1870, the social control of women's bodies became essential to a nation menaced by a sluggish birthrate, and both the proto-fascist Right and the revolutionary socialist Left used natalist anxieties in different ways to attack both republican feminists and republicanism more generally, so that republicans themselves resisted feminist demands and were often among feminists' most virulent opponents.

Critics of all political stripes sought to undermine feminist demands by equating them with sexual perversion and deviant womanhood. The great French author Barbey d'Aurevilly denounced women writers as "bas-bleus" [bluestockings], an appellation reiterated over and over by anti-feminists and associated with women who, like "Sappho—the first bluestocking, [imitate] men naively or perversely."[5] Republican feminists sought to discredit such charges by distancing feminism from the taint of sexual subversion. In 1891, Maria Desraimes denounced "masculine" women who repudiated sexual difference: "I would like women to remain women," she wrote. "I am an enemy of all these ugly fashions . . . that make us into hybrid beings and God knows, into those neutral and shady [*louches*] intermediaries between man and woman."[6] Most historians concur that with few excep-

5. Albert Cim, quoted in Albert, "Sappho Mythified," 99. Translation slighly modified.

6. Quoted in Christine Bard, *Les Filles de Marianne: Histoire des féminismes, 1914–1940* (Paris: Fayard, 1994), 204. See also the synopsis in Anne-Louise Shapiro, *Breaking the Codes: Female Criminality in Fin-de-Siècle Paris* (Stanford, Calif.: Stanford University Press, 1996), 192–200.

tions, French feminists adhered to a politics of "equality in difference." Karen Offen terms this insistence on sexual difference within the framework of equality the foundation of a specifically French "relational feminism" that deemphasized individual rights and argued for women's equality in the context of the family—in their capacities as wives and especially as mothers.[7] This argument was not unique to France or to the late nineteenth century, but in France, where natalist anxieties were preeminent, "relational feminism" predominated, and feminists defended their agenda by insisting vociferously on the virtues of gender conformity.[8]

7. On "relational feminism," see Karen Offen, "Feminism, Antifeminism, and National Family Politics in Early Third Republic France," in Marilyn J. Boxer and Jean H. Quaertet, eds., *Connecting Spheres: Women in the Western World, 1500 to the Present* (Oxford: Oxford University Press, 1987), 179.

8. Both Mary Wollstonecraft and Olympe de Gouges argued (in 1792 and 1791, respectively) that women could only be worthy companions and mothers if they were granted equality. Both (although this argument was more pronounced in Anglo-American feminism) argue that women are intrinsically more virtuous than men and that if given the suffrage, they will necessarily cleanse public life of corruption. This argument was made primarily by bourgeois feminists, but socialist men and women also used such moral arguments in their own, anti-capitalist and sometimes profeminist interests. On this, see Joan Scott, *Gender and the Politics of History* (New York: Columbia University Press, 1988). For synthetic accounts of French feminism, see in particular, Claire Goldberg Moses, *French Feminism in the Nineteenth Century* (Albany, N.Y.: SUNY Press, 1984); Steven Hause with Anne Kenney, *Women's Suffrage and Social Politics in Third Republic France* (Princeton, N.J.: Princeton University Press, 1984); Bard, *Filles de Marianne;* Joan Scott, *Only Paradoxes to Offer: French Feminists and the Rights of Man* (Cambridge, Mass.: Harvard University Press, 1996). For a comparative approach, see Olive Banks, *Faces of Feminism: A Study of Feminism as a Social Movement* (New York: St. Martin's Press, 1981). Both Moses and Bard insist on the significant role French feminists played in pushing for reform in the face of republican opposition, and warn against downplaying their activity in light of the generally fierce resistance to and slow pace of feminist reform in France.

In 1908, the nationalist critic Théodore Joran condemned feminism as a "sapphic peril":

> Feminism began as an obsession with equality and then became an apology for bestial instinct. It emits the . . . odor of depravity. Didn't one of our most shameless feminists, a certain Renée Vivien, transform herself, in a series of bad poems that women compose [*riment*] in desperate moments, into the modern priestess of "lesbian love"? This Sappho always mixed her feminist declarations with her "lyricism."[9]

The link Joran forged between feminism and bestial instinct by way of lesbianism does not only equate feminists with masculinity and thus with gender deviance or the gender inversion model of homosexuality prevalent in the late nineteenth century. Instead, the allusion to lesbianism helps Jordan paint feminists as depraved, debauched, perverted *women* whose sexuality he links to the rhythm of bad poetry unrestrained by proper form. And even as he associates weak form with the unrestrained sexuality of lesbians, he links it to femininity more generally: Vivien's poetry is not only bad because she is a lesbian and a feminist, but because *women* utter her verses, *women* find comfort in them. Like the lofty intellectual who sneers at women's romance novels and silly rhymes, Jordan sneered at Vivien's poetry because he believed it was too womanly.

Although it would be erroneous to read too much into one statement, Jordan's views were echoed by the voluminous literary production about lesbians, as well as by nineteenth-century medical and other narratives. As with male homosexuality, lesbianism became extremely topical in the fin-de-siècle as natalist anxieties provoked more

9. Quoted in Bard, *Filles de Marianne*, 179.

and more discussion. As Mario Praz wrote in his classic account of late nineteenth century literature: "Of all the monsters which pullulate in the fiction of this period, Lesbians are among the most popular."[10] In literature from the Greeks until this time, lascivious "tribades," as female lovers were called in ancient Greece, were most often comedic or parodic figures, sexually insatiable women who could not provide their prey the "complete" joys of phallic conquest.[11] Nineteenth-century lesbians, by contrast, were truly sinister, and, like inverted men, warranted medical classification as inverts for the first time.[12] Although an exhaustive study of either literary or medical texts from the nineteenth-century is beyond the scope of this account, suffice it to say that works from Charles Baudelaire's "Femmes damnées" of 1857 to

10. Mario Praz, *The Romantic Agony* (Oxford: Oxford University Press, 1933), 346. "The progressive aestheticiziation of female homosexuality culminated in a fiction of Sappho as the alter ego of the male decadent outsider," Joan DeJean notes in *Fictions of Sappho, 1546–1937* (Chicago: University of Chicago Press, 1989), 265.

11. Elaine Marks, "Lesbian Intertextuality," in id. and George Stambolian, eds., *Homosexualities and French Literature* (Ithaca, N.Y.: Cornell University Press, 1979), 353–77.

12. Michel Foucault argues in *The History of Sexuality*, vol. 1: *An Introduction* (New York: Random House, Vintage Books, 1980), that the homosexual was invented in the late nineteenth century as a specific type of person with a specific character. According to him, homosexuals now formed a discrete group that could be surveyed, interrogated, and regulated by the state. The establishment and extension of this "scopic regime"—a legal and medical disciplinary apparatus that sought to make homosexuals visible by defining precisely who they were, how they behaved and originated—is undeniable, and yet that regime works very differently when lesbians rather than gay men are its subjects. Most of the contemporary medical literature in France, Gemany, and England concerns itself primarily with male homosexuality and "masculine" women. One of the most elaborate discussions of the lesbian is Ellis's *Sexual Inversion* (see n. 2 above). As already noted, in the sexological literature, women's homosexuality was seen as far less visible and more difficult to detect than men's, and this necessarily led to different conceptualizations of desire.

Emile Zola's 1880 novel *Nana* associated lesbians, not only with sterility and artifice, but with atavistic, depraved femininity.[13] Both works associate lesbianism with sterility and prostitution, as did scores of lesser-known novels, including Catulle Mendès's *Méphistophéla* (1890) and Adolphe Belot's 1870 bestseller, *Mademoiselle Giraud, ma femme*. In one of several surveys of this literature, Nicole Albert argues that after the mid nineteenth-century, the image of Sappho was transformed from that of a dignified, heterosexual if manly poet into that of a sexually depraved lesbian, sometimes cast as a prostitute, sometimes as an ugly and undesirable poetess, now stripped of nobility. In most of these novels about Sappho (as well as those in which she does not figure), lesbianism is either associated with upper-class women seeking stimulation of already overwrought nerves or with the depravity of oversexed working-class women, especially prostitutes, whom Dr. Alexandre Parent-Duchâtelet had associated with lesbians in his comprehensive 1836 work on prostitution.[14]

Medical and other narratives mirrored this correspondence between lesbianism and sexual voraciousness and depravity, and identified lesbians in these terms.[15] For our purposes, it is worth exploring briefly how nineteenth-century medical and pseudo-medical discussions of lesbians differed from discussions of male homosexuals'

13. "[T]he comic, lascivious tribade lives on in the demonic corrupter, but in general [from the modern period on] the imitation of the male is less pronounced than the affirmation of incomprehensible femininity," Elaine Marks notes ("Lesbian Intertextuality," 361).

14. Alexandre Parent-Duchâtelet, *De la prostitution dans la ville de Paris* (Paris: Baillère, 1836).

15. For further discussion, see Bram Dijkstra, *Idols of Perversity: Fantasies of Feminine Evil in Fin-de-Siècle Culture* (New York: Oxford University Press, 1986), 145–59; DeJean, *Fictions of Sappho*, 245–99.

perversity. Doctors used the same categories to explain female and male inverts: some were congenital (i.e., hereditary), some "acquired" the vice in the context of same-sex environments or expressed it as a facet of their own perversity. Some inverts were thus motivated by innate "perversion," and some were merely the bearers of "perversity" acquired in the course of a depraved and debauched life. As with men, medical commentators associated "real" gender inversion (a man's soul in a woman's body) with congenital inverts and attributed "acquired" inversion mostly to the willful expression of vice—the sort of inversion almost always associated with the upper classes and with "pederasty."

Robert Nye contends that in nineteenth-century France, male inversion was seen as an inferior form of heterosexual love rather than an equally powerful desire directed at the "wrong love object." That is, as I have sought to illustrate in chapter 4, homosexual men were imagined as weak, timid, lacking, and hence feminine beings. Nye does note that the "weakness" of homosexual men's desire was paradoxically linked to the strength of desire itself, because weak men were more susceptible than strong ones to inappropriate temptation.[16] Gender inversion expressed the extraordinary irresistibility and power of desire for lesbians as well. But in lesbians, inversion was not linked to weakness; rather, it reiterated received ideas about the power and insatiability of female desire. Female inversion was, moreover, most often associated with "vice" and moral turpitude.

Thus, while lesbian desire conceived as gender (and hence conceived as congenital) inversion pervaded medi-

16. Robert Nye, *Masculinity and Male Codes of Honor in Modern France.* (Oxford: Oxford University Press, 1993), 114–15.

cal and literary discourses, lesbian desire understood in terms of hyperbolic femininity was equally prevalent. Dr. L. Thoinot conceded in 1898 that real female inverts were tomboyish when young, and warned that although the great sexologist Richard von Krafft-Ebing included only eight lesbians in forty-four cases of inversion, we should not conclude that lesbianism is infrequent. But nor, he insisted, should we judge its frequency on the basis of the "tribadism" "now so common," because tribadism was motivated by vice. As far as he could tell, it was impossible to know exactly how many real female inverts there were: he was sure only that most of the lesbian activity then so common was not the consequence of hereditary disposition but of debauchery among women. And, Thoinot continued (in marked contrast to discussion of male homosexuality), lesbian lovers bring the same passion to their love as normal women.[17] Similarly, the Swiss sexologist Auguste Forel mentioned lesbians' masculinity oddly in terms of what he believed was most womanly about women. In a fantasy remarkable because at that time so unremarkable, he wrote that: "the intensity of tribades' excesses surpasses that of male inverts. One orgasm succeeds another, night and day, nearly without interruption."[18] Although he claimed that "nymphomani-

17. Dr. L. Thoinot, *Attentat aux mœurs et perversions du sens génital* (Paris: Octave Doin, 1898), 348, 318.

18. This reference to intense passion among homosexual men and women was part of a larger discussion of the extreme jealousy purportedly proper to lesbian and gay relationships. Jealousy emasculates gay men, because they are always in a state of uncontrolled emotion (as opposed to the momentary loss of reason that might account for a "normal" man murdering his lover in a fit of jealous rage). In women, extreme jealousy is an extreme expression of normal femininity, since jealousy is supposed to be a "feminine" trait, expressed most frequently and uncontrollably by women prisoners, prostitutes, and lesbians. At the same time, and confusingly, these women are also coded as masculine, because they are subjects rather than objects of desire.

acal inverts" were fairly rare, he conceded that all "female inversion" expressed the "very nature of the . . . sexual appetites of women."[19]

The writer and sometime pseudo-sexologist Léo Taxil also asserted that lesbian passion was frenzied rather than romantic. Quoting Alexandre Parent-Duchâtelet's multivolume work on prostitutes (1836), he repeats that "tribades have fallen into the most extreme degree of vice of which a human being is capable," and associates this unspeakable depravity with unrestrained sexuality as well as with masculinity. The illustration of "tribades" that adorns the book (and which authorities sought to censor) shows two women vying for the attention of another seated in their midst. The women are dressed in seductive attire meant to place them in a brothel. "Jealousy between women given to the vice of sapphism often occasions quarrels and sometimes veritable duels," the caption notes. In these duels, the "most frequently employed weapon is the hairpin," an absolutely ruthless, if feminine—messy, prolonged, and painful—means of destruction.[20] In two related, novelistic accounts with pseudo-scientific pretensions, similar links between lesbianism and female perversity prevail. In his preface to *La Dernière Journée de Sappho* (1901), the ex-Inspector General of Historical Monuments Gabriel Faure asked: "What was Sappho? She was not a sick woman [a congenital invert] since she first loved a man, since we know she was married and had a daughter . . . since she died for

19. Auguste Forel, *La Question sexuelle exposée aux sdultes cultivés* (Paris: Steinheil, 1906), 275–76. Consistent with the congenital/acquired division, Forel also claimed the pure invert felt that she was a man and took up men's clothing and habits (278). That is, he took both positions— that a lesbian was manly and the womanliest woman—at once.

20. Leo Taxil [Gabriel Jogand-Pagès], *La Prostitution contemporaine* (Paris: Librairie populaire, 1884), 174–75.

Phaon. She didn't [practice 'sapphism'] for money or out of need. It seems that she epitomized the perverse woman." And, in another 1906 account, the writer Adrienne Saint-Agen emphasized the difficulty of distinguishing between the lesbian, and hence manly, invert and all other women: "Sappho is [easily] revived in every woman."[21]

Doctors' emphasis on "acquired" inversion in women helps to deconstruct Jordan's linking "sapphism" to bestial instinct and to understand the threat of lesbianism not only in terms of gender inversion (the manly woman), but as the fear of femininity and all that was attributed to it. Indeed, Nicole Albert, like Elaine Marks, notes that after 1880, the name Sappho began to mark not only same-sex desire but all perversion among women.[22] That is, gender inversion explained the origins of female homosexuality (the lesbian is sexually active and hence manly) and yet provided an internally inconsistent explanation: for the lesbian is sexually active and hence also acting out the immoral sexual excessiveness that characterizes unrestrained femininity. The lesbian is at once a man in a woman's body and an atavistic, depraved woman. She is no longer only the slightly comical lascivious tribade who can never have the real phallus, but is a sinister harbinger of castration. In their construction of the lesbian, then, late-nineteenth-century medical and literary men so completely blurred the medical and moral categories of illness and vice that the medical origins of illness could be found only in the moral unraveling of the female self. Or, to put it differ-

21. Both quoted in Albert, "Sappho Mythified," 93, 95. Translation modified.
22. Ibid., 97.

ently, the model of gender inversion could not distinguish between so-called manly lesbians and other women because it was not fully consistent with the theory in which the lesbian had a man's soul. Whereas the homosexual man's susceptibility to pleasure extends the theory of male inversion because it expresses his emasculation, the lesbian was *both* a manly woman and the womanliest woman. But this implicitly fluid construction of the lesbian, like the equally paradoxical construction of gay men as simultaneously threatening and unthreatening, did not render lesbians difficult to identify in the late nineteenth century. For medical men and writers, lesbians were manly women or abnormally womanly women located in specific milieux. After the war, however, mirroring their anxieties about gay men, experts' increasingly associated lesbianism with the dissolution of gender boundaries that that appeared to characterize all postwar women, and in so doing blurred the lines between lesbians and other women.

Interwar Lesbianism

I cannot fully explain here this nineteenth-century construction of and obsession with lesbian sexuality. The threat posed by lesbianism was something more than gender inversion and something more than a reversion to images of lascivious women who were but pale imitations of men (although it drew on those images). Novelists, writers in all genres, and medical (and pseudo-medical) men not only perceived increasing numbers of lesbians but used them as privileged symbols of eroding gender boundaries at the end of the century. The war hardly provoked the concern with lesbians or invented the sorts of discourses that circulated about them, but the interwar period deepened that concern and reshaped those discourses in many significant ways: most important, the representation of lesbian sexuality unraveled conventional gender distinctions because it could not be figured clearly as active or passive desire. Older images reappeared but were also refashioned in the interwar context of a backlash against feminism and as new symbols of women's sexual "liberation" took center stage.

The war necessitated that women take over men's jobs, earn higher salaries and thus achieve some measure of social and economic autonomy. Many wartime gains were lost as demobilization required that men return to their jobs, women did not receive the right to vote, and French legislators passed the most draconian anti-abortion and anti-contraception laws in Western Europe in 1920. Victor Margueritte's *La Garçonne*, we recall, became a best-seller in 1922 and sanctioned the name with which the new icon of postwar womanhood was dubbed. With her bobbed hair, loose clothing, cigarettes, and cars, the "garçonne" emblematized women's new mobility and assertiveness. Although Margueritte's fictional heroine realizes the error of her ways and becomes a model of bourgeois feminine virtue, the book nevertheless occasioned an attack on postwar moral decline which the book's heroine embodied. The fictional garçonne's bisexuality and the real garçonne's "unfeminine" attire symbolized the war's erosion of sexual difference—she was, after all, the product of an upheaval that had emasculated men and allowed women to take their place.[23] The gar-

---

23. See Mary Louise Roberts, *Civilization without Sexes: Reconstructing Gender in Postwar France, 1917–1927* (Chicago: University of Chicago Press, 1994), 63–87. There are numerous historical accounts of women's economic and social position after the war. For a recent summary, see Françoise Thébaud, "The Great War and the Triumph of Sexual Divisions," in id., ed., *A History of Women: Toward a Cultural Identity in the Twentieth*

çonne's apparent defiance of proper gender roles provoked Dr. Pierre Vachet to insist that "since the war, female couples have become more and more numerous."[24]
Since the advent of the garçonne, "many works [now]
celebrate lesbianism," the social critic François Jean-
Desthieux remarked.[25] A 1923 debate at the literary
Club du Faubourg about "Notre-Dame de Lesbos" not
only indicated the increasing level of concern about
lesbianism but gave the feminist Marguerite Guépet a
forum in which to denounce the garçonne: she was
"unnatural and rotten" and emerged out of a "questionable milieu."[26] Yet such virulent denunciations clarified
what was really at stake in the perception that lesbianism
was now so pervasive: one alarmed critic wrote that men
could no longer tell the difference between honest and
deviant women, since now all women "smoke, drink . . .
drive cars."[27] And Marise Querlin wrote that the increased frequency of lesbianism meant that it was more

Century (Cambridge, Mass.: Harvard University Press, 1994), 21–75. Most
historians concur that the interwar period represented a backlash against
feminist reform, although this view has been somewhat nuanced by arguments that women made more socioeconomic gains than previously understood. Such gains did not, however, alter the cultural image of femininity. See Siân Reynolds, *France Between the Wars: Gender and Politics*
(New York: Routledge, 1996). For expressions of interwar men's anxiety
about women in the literature of the period, see Sandra Gilbert and Susan
Gubar, *No Man's Land: The Place of Women Writers in the Twentieth Century* (New Haven, Conn.: Yale University Press, 1988).

24. Dr. Pierre Vachet, *L'Inquiétude sexuelle* (Paris: Grasset, 1927), 156.
25. François Jean-Desthieux, *Femmes damnées* (Paris: Ophrys Gap,
1937), 127.
26. Quoted in Bard, *Filles de Marianne*, 197. I should note that *Notre
Dame de Lesbos* was the title of novel by the writer Charles-Etienne about
which we shall have occasion to speak. I presume the title of the debate
was derived from that of the novel.
27. Léon Bizard, *La Vie des filles* (Paris: Grasset, 1934), 45.

and more difficult to determine with any precision who was normal and who was not.[28]

Most narratives about lesbians were obsessed with describing their activities, and sorting them out from other women. Many critics attributed the "cause" of lesbianism to men's "sexual selfishness" or to men's "deception" of faithful, trustworthy women.[29] Moreover, they explained the lesbian's sexual fury by claiming that women who did not engage in heterosexual sex were incomplete and had to compensate for that lack.[30] But in spite of this expressed confidence about lesbians' inferiority as well as this certainty about the causes and effects of their deviation, the clearly demarcated line between lesbians and other women was apparently no longer so clear; for a wide range of commentary began to focus instead on lesbians' invisibility with the aim of clarifying that demarcation. As Jean de Mézerette put it in 1939, "Pederasts flaunt themselves, flagellants hide no longer, drugs can be easily found; but young women who love women have an irritating tendency to dissimulate their tastes. Nevertheless, it [lesbianism] is, I believe, a pervasive practice in France."[31] In Willy's *Le Troisième Sexe*, in Charles-Louis Royer's *Le Club des damnés*, in Georges Anquetil's *Satan conduit le bal* and in Charles-Étienne's novelistic series

---

28. Quoted in Albert, "Sappho Mythified," 9.

29. See, among others, Jean-Desthieux, *Femmes damnées*, 89; J. Lauris, *Les Amies perverses* (Paris: F. Schmid, 1933), a novel that tells a tale of lesbians who become lesbians for want of decent men and when finally ravished and "completed" become heterosexual; Maryse Choisy, *L'Amour dans les prisons: Reportage* (Paris: Montaigne, 1930), 144–45; and the anonymous *Caresses . . . ou les mémoires intimes de Jacqueline de R.* (Paris: Couvre Feu, 1933), 93.

30. Dr. Caufeynon [Jean de Fauconney], *Les Vices féminins* (Paris: Librairie artistique, 1928), 33–34, 61.

31. G. de Charonsay [Jean de Mézerette], *Orgies galantes et scènes saphiques* (Paris: Editions du Vert-Logis, 1939), 42.

about the homosexual underworld—and these works hardly exhaust the list—lesbians are located metaphorically behind or underneath the visually accessible urban landscape, and often blend into that landscape. You remember Anquetil's claim that both pederasts *and* lesbians have penetrated public life and even "austere bourgeois dwellings."

Lesbians were everywhere, and commentators of all varieties sought to ferret them out. Drawing on nineteenth-century themes in which lesbians were located predictably in aristocratic circles and among working-class women (specifically prostitutes), one medical book obsessively discussed methods for detecting women who desired women. The author claimed that wealthy lesbians, always accompanied by poodles, walk discretely on the Champs-Élysées in quest of other women. When their eyes meet, "each performs a rapid motion of the tongue and lips; this is the conventional sign, adopted by tribades to signify, 'I am on the lookout for a woman.'"[32] Jean de Fauconney, another scientific popularizer, wrote twenty books about sexuality under the pseudonym "Dr. Caufeynon" for the Bibliothèque populaire, many of which were translated into English and Spanish. He insisted that since "sapphic" practices were masturbatory, lesbians might be found rubbing themselves against the table where they smoothed linen or profiting from the movement of the sewing machine. When he inquires about the practices of women in textile factories, the foreman claims that such behavior is so common that he no longer pays attention.[33] Finally, nearly every book

32. Jacobus X (Augustin Cabanès), *Crossways of Sex: A Study in Eroto-Pathology*, translator from the French not noted (New York: American Anthropological Society, 1934), 329.
33. Caufeynon, *Vices*, 40–41, 49.

about lesbians drew on the old theme in which prostitutes, weary of men and of "common" pleasures, are
notorious tribades. Lesbianism was rampant in women's
prisons, and female criminals were "recruited primarily
among prostitutes," the literary celebrity Maryse Choisy
asserted.[34]

Lesbians move surreptitiously through public space or
are almost always (unlike gay men) behind closed doors;
either lesbianism is the irresistible vice even "normal"
women succumb to when protected by the anonymity of
sex clubs or it is practiced like a religion whose shrines
look like any other house on the block. Many of the discussions about lesbians or the semi-pornographic texts
offering a glimpse behind those doors drew on a famous
fantasy first articulated by Pidansat de Mairobert in 1784
about the "Secte des Anandrynes"—a secret lesbian sect
reserved for aristocrats, including Marie-Antoinette.[35]
In keeping both with late-eighteenth- and nineteenth-
century references to that fantasy, the highbrow literary
critic Octave Uzanne identified the Secte des Anandrynes
in 1921 as the origin of underground lesbian communities.[36] In an anonymous 1933 pornographic work, the
heroine meets a "Maréchale B" who promises to introduce her into the sect, and a critical text published the
same year invoked its rituals.[37]

34. Choisy, *Amour dans les prisons,* 162. For a fuller account of Maryse
Choisy, see her "Dames seules," *Le Rire,* 21 May 1932, reprinted with an introduction by Nicole Albert, *Cahier Gai Kitsch Camp* 23 (1993): 25–47.

35. Pidansat de Mairobert, *La Secte des anandrynes: Confession de Mlle
Sapho* (1784; Paris: Bibliothèque des curieux, 1920). I thank Pierre Saint-
Amand for the precise reference.

36. Octave Uzanne, "Du Saphisme en Poésie," *Les Marges* 20 (15 March
1921): 132.

37. *Caresses,* 173–76. See also Otto Flake, *Le Marquis de Sade,* trans.
Pierre Klossowski (Paris: Grasset, 1933), 125.

Most books did not invoke the sect directly, but used images of secret chambers and clubs to describe the world lesbians putatively inhabited. Although these spaces retain their aristocratic trappings, many interwar narratives effectively democratize them. In keeping with interwar fantasies about the bourgeois garçonne, aristocrats and prostitutes gradually ceased to be the privileged repositories of lesbian desire; all women were now as likely to enjoy lesbian affairs. As Willy noted in 1927, "this once noble vice" had been "dangerously democratized."[38] Private clubs, masked balls, and mirrored rooms are the most common tropes in interwar works about lesbians, suggesting not only lesbians' secrecy (and hence the works "unmasking" or revelatory purpose) but, ultimately, their impenetrability. As Jean de Mézerette put it: "We are thus in the heart of the lesbian milieu; I assure you, however, that it is the hardest milieu to discover in Paris."[39]

Who, then, are lesbians? The constant use of voyeurism in many narratives produces lesbianism as a form of eroticized, accessible, and yet ultimately impenetrable secrecy. In "the most modern countries, it is not rare for lesbians to belong to clubs," according to the pseudo-professor Malherman. Like Mézerette, he suggests that such clubs are so impenetrable that their activities can only be observed by men disguised as women; a costumed man joins one of these groups on a yacht, where he watches their orgies and flagellation parties.[40] In *Le Club des damnés*, female same-sex desire characterizes

38. Willy [Henri Gauthier-Villars], *Le Troisième Sexe* (Paris: Paris Editions, 1927).
39. Charonsay, *Orgies galantes*, 42.
40. Malherman, *Le Plaisir dans la souffrance*, trans. Charles Wincker (Paris: A. Quignon, 1929), 57.

all the Baudelairian "damned" who frequent the underworld; the hero's companion, lured away from him by
other women, behaves like a *"femme damnée,* acting in
spite of herself, as if in the grip of an insatiable, torment-
ing fever."[41] Moreover, most of the women in the club
are sadomasochists "attracted by violence more than by
caresses," and sadomasochism precedes and is often a
condition of their "fall" into that feverish, "damned" state
of being.

The male spectator at such clubs thus learns the secret
of lesbians, as if their preference for women is far more
mysterious, far more in need of explanation, than men's
sexual preference for other men. The secret that lesbians
are perverts ruled by insatiable desire is both reassuring
and alarming. Voyeurism permits the fantasized containment of lesbianism in metaphorical spaces and offers the
spectator conceptual clarity and knowledge. At the same
time, such fantasies mark themselves as fantasies because these secret clubs can never be found (the reader is
always told that their location cannot be revealed) and
lesbians cannot be positively identified outside of them.[42]

41. Charles-Louis Royer, *Le Club des damnés* (Paris: Editions de
France), 159.
42. Charonsay's (i.e., Jean de Mézerette's) *Orgies galantes et scènes
saphiques* states quite frankly that the vignettes of lesbian activities in
brothels of which it is made up are "illusions" created for spectators. Readers cannot "see" directly, and mirrors mediate what is seen such that the
voyeur can never be sure of what he is seeing. In this way the book plays
upon the trope of homosexual narcissism, but here it is not the woman
adoring herself in the mirror but the man who cannot know if what he sees
are lesbians or his own projections: "No matter which social class one addresses, in chic bars or poor ones . . . all these houses of pleasure, these
houses of joy . . . are only temples of illusion! And don't we owe what is
happiest in love to illusion?" (ibid., 200). Charonsay's account is thus a banal tale of the self-deception proper to loving. But in spite of its banality,
the novel dramatizes men's necessarily illusory images of all women, and
significantly uses lesbians to make its point.

At the beginning of Charles-Étienne's novel *Notre-Dame de Lesbos,* for example, the hero Julien attends a costume ball. Upset by the number of homosexuals in attendance, he writes a nasty article about the "third sex." After it is published, he learns to his surprise that he has alienated many friends whose homosexuality he had not suspected. Moreover, he eventually learns that the woman he loves is a lesbian, and the rest of the novel is devoted to her life and his struggle to know her. She sends him her intimate journals, and the more he reads, the more mysterious and illegible she proves to be. In the end, her lesbianism destroys her, but it nevertheless represents an irresistible drive toward self destruction that remains beyond comprehension. Her desire is contained only by her death and prolonged in Julien's tormented fantasies.

In this and many other of Charles-Étienne's novels, the author characterizes interwar French society in terms of the contagion, debauchery, and duplicity he associates with female homosexuality: not only are bourgeois women unable to resist the advances of other women, not only does their sexuality prove beyond containment; the boundaries between the lesbian and other women prove to be porous and the difference between perverted women and other women cannot be clearly articulated. In most interwar writing with (homo)sexual themes, the French social body had not simply been contaminated by ever more numerous lesbians; the line between the degenerate lesbian body and the normal woman's body could not be clearly drawn.

Toward Containment

Commentators thus presumed that female homosexuality was both pervasive and unmarked; in so doing, they raised the suspicion that any woman might be a lesbian. Although the pseudonymous Dr. Alibert approvingly quoted another expert on the art of recognizing lesbians—"generally they wear dresses exactly similar, they have the same jewels, and they say they are sisters"—he also insisted that "taking into account the ease with which they [women] trample upon all conventions, it must be admitted that the majority have a predisposition to vice."[43] More significantly, however, Alibert insisted that all women are potentially lesbians and warns husbands that sapphism is so contagious they ought not to expose their wives to "known" lesbians for fear of producing "committed sapphists."[44] Dr. Caufeynon used the same language to argue that most women may become lesbians because the moral laws implicit in social organization made by men are wholly incompatible with women's nature.[45] Regardless of cultural norms [woman] cannot help herself: "Education, role models, nothing works because an unwholesome curiosity dominates her. . . . "The proof: man's superior self-restraint and modesty. Just look, he exclaimed, at "the ease with which women permit themselves to be visited by male doctors and at the resistance men put up to the idea of being examined by a woman doctor."[46] The lesbian, then, is no longer an identifiable (if implicitly fluid) creature as outlined in nineteenth-century literary and medical narratives: instead, she cannot be clearly distinguished from any other woman.

Medical men used a model of gender deviance to make the very distinctions between normal and perverted

43. Dr. Alibert, *Tribadism and Saphism* (Paris: New Edition, 1921), 21, 14.
44. Ibid., 39–40.
45. Caufeynon, *Vices*, 29, 30–33.
46. Ibid., 29.

women they also claimed were not feasible. To repeat: since the late nineteenth century and into the post-war period, French medical men drew distinctions between congenital ("innate") and acquired lesbianism (or between "tribades" and "sapphics," respectively) made elsewhere in the United States and Europe. In so doing, they linked congenital homosexuality to gender deviance—to "masculine" behavior and dress—and acquired homosexuality to "vice"—the momentary impulses of otherwise normal "feminine" women. The "real" lesbian was masculine, and most doctors did not believe the "feminine" woman's lesbianism was a choice; instead, they conceived it as a predictable if unfortunate reaction to male betrayal and egotism. At the same time, doctors and writers did not sustain this model of gender deviance, a theoretical impasse that, I have suggested, became more pronounced after the war. Increasingly in the interwar years, they did not draw clear distinctions they claimed existed between the devouring, congenital, masculine tribade and the devoured, acquired, feminine sapphist.

Although tribades are cold and calculating—this is especially true in interwar flagellation pornography, in which lesbian flagellants are a predominant feature—their desire for pleasure is so excessive it manifests itself even in extremes of pain. The pseudo-scientific popularizer Pierre Guénolé claimed that "only lesbians enjoy spankings."[47] Indeed, their desire is so insatiable self-annihilation alone can relieve their torment. Hence,

---

47. Pierre Guénolé, *L'Etrange Passion: La Flagellation dans les mœurs d'aujourd'hui* (Paris: Office central de Librairie, 1904), 125–26. Guénolé also tries to distinguish between normal women and lesbians by claiming that lesbians were from an exceptional milieu, but this distinction is not particularly persuasive (121).

according to the writer Sylvain Bonmariage, the lesbian is a "cold-hearted," "self-involved egotist" whose pleasure nevertheless "devours her soul, her senses, and her flesh. . . ."[48] Professor Malherman argued that lesbians take a particular pleasure in hurting others, but that they find the greatest pleasure in their own sexual degradation. He cited Victor Marguerrite's *La Garçonne* to make his point, claiming that the main character, who slept with both men and women, derived pleasure from her humiliation in lesbian relations.[49] In almost all of Charles-Etienne's novels, lesbianism is signaled by or associated with flagellation. In *Notre-Dame de Lesbos,* for example, the main character plays a game of "Mère Fouttard" with a friend at an early age and grows up to be a lesbian.[50] According to Maryse Choisy, lesbians are known for their "tyranny," but this masculine imperiousness is inseparable from the unrestrained emotion characteristic of female insatiability.[51] "Dr." L. R. Dupuy claimed lesbians liked to flagellate men because they harbored tremendous rage against them.[52] Cesare Lombroso's tribade who threatens to tear her lover's entrails out is no different from Marcello Fabri's sapphist who eviscerates her partner.[53]

48. Sylvain Bonmariage, *Les Plaisirs de l'Enfer* (Paris: Raoul Saillard, 1938), 226.

49. Malherman, *Plaisir dans la souffrance*, 57, 65, 68.

50. Charles-Etienne, *Notre-Dame de Lesbos: Roman de mœurs* (Paris: Curio, 1924), 15; id., *Les Désexués: Roman des mœurs* (Paris: Curio, 1924), 125.

51. Choisy, *Amour dans les prisons*, 164; see also Henri Drouin, *Femmes damnées* (Paris: La Vulgarisation scientifique, 1945), 63.

52. Dr. L. R. Dupuy, *The Strangest Voluptuousness: The Taste for Lascivious Corrections* (Paris: Medical Library, n.d.), 19–20, which claims to be translated from the French; the quality of the writing is so poor that this may be true.

53. Lombroso quoted in Alibert, *Tribadism*, 28; Fabri quoted in Anquetil, *Satan conduit le bal*, 314.

The doctors and writers who insisted on the lesbian's gender deviance also suggested that she confounds gender, that she represents the intrinsic volatility of a female sexuality that is always both active and passive, agent and victim, contaminated and contaminating. As was implicit in late-nineteenth-century constructions of lesbianism, she is visibly perverted womanhood and yet her body is the hidden, fantasmic repository of the dangerous, annihilating, and undomesticated sexuality within all women—the normal woman's uncanny double. In this way they depicted lesbians as the secret agents of the social contamination explicitly associated with the moral ruin of postwar France.[54] The containment of the fantasized dangers of female sexuality depended on the fantasy of lesbian invisibility that made all women suspect and yet sustained the illusion of a specific group of women against whom society might mobilize and from whom society required protection. Thus, the boundaries between normal and perverted women were sustained even as all women were subject to more intense regulation.

Renée Vivien and Lesbian "Identity"

This construction of lesbian invisibility also offers a context within which to understand some interwar women's own narratives about same-sex sexuality. Colette's famous and complex portrait of lesbianism in *Le Pur et l'impur* (first published in 1932 as *Ces Plaisirs*), remains the standard account of lesbianism during this period, and, to date, most literary histories of lesbianism in Paris focus primarily on Anglo-American expatriates, most of whom came of age at the end of the nineteenth century.[55]

54. Bonmariage, *Plaisirs de l'Enfer*, 36–37.
55. Shari Benstock, *Women of the Left Bank: Paris, 1900–1940* (Austin: University of Texas Press, 1986).

Colette's book was acclaimed some two decades ago by feminist literary critics because, unlike other narratives, Colette presumed not only the possibility of female sexual selfhood but of lesbian sexual subjectivity as well. Nevertheless, Colette, the author of the "Claudine" novels, *Gigi,* and many others, often represents same-sex love as a surrogate for maternal love. Her portrait of lesbianism is breathtakingly condescending; lesbian love is either sweetly maternal or infused by passion derived from tension between masculinity and femininity. In other words, Colette could imagine lesbian sexuality independently of men, but only in a very limited fashion. As Elisabeth Ladenson notes, *The Pure and the Impure* represents male homosexuality as the purest and most passionate meeting of bodies and souls, while both heterosexuality and lesbianism are fraught, destined to suffer from too much difference or too much sameness, the latter unmitigated by the power of "truly" male passion.[56]

Most other contemporary French lesbians with whom we are familiar participated in various avant-garde circles, such as the filmmaker Germaine Dulac and the photographer Claude Cahun, among others, but their voices, with few exceptions, have yet to be discussed in any real depth. As in chapter 4, I am interested in one set of voices

56. Sidonie-Gabrielle Colette, *Ces Plaisirs* (Paris: J. Ferenczi & fils, 1932). While noting Colette's ambivalence toward and stereotyping of lesbians, Elaine Marks nevertheless calls her a "foremother" of a distinctly lesbian literary tradition because at least she admits the possibility, as noted, of lesbian sexual subjectivity. Elisabeth Ladenson remarks that *The Pure and the Impure* is now treated as central to Colette's oeuvre. She is far more critical of Colette's view of lesbianism and focuses less on her status as foremother than on the author's absent presence in the text and, by implication, the unstable relation between a book and its author. Colette, she seems to indicate, cannot and should not be read in order to understand or evaluate the term "lesbian." See "Colette for Export Only," *Yale French Studies* 90 (1996): 25–46.

who sought *explicitly* to articulate some form of lesbian subjectivity. I present the work of these elite women writers, not as a monolithic or predominant narrative about lesbianism, but as a demonstration of the paradoxically productive if problematic and coercive power of lesbian invisibility.

Unlike gay men, these women did not rally behind a figure who made a specific political argument for a broad public (itself perhaps symptomatic both of the stigmatization of "public" women and of lesbian invisibility as I am defining it here). They sought sustenance instead from the life and work of the lesbian expatriate poet Renée Vivien (Pauline Tarn), who starved herself to death in 1909, having barely passed thirty, and was a lightning rod for discussions about lesbianism and feminism (recall Theodore Joran's 1908 comment) from the end of the nineteenth century through the interwar period.[57] By reading Vivien differently from their contemporaries, these women transformed the dominant and negative construction of lesbians' elusiveness into an affirmative valuation of lesbian sexuality. Repudiating tropes of maternity and masculinity, they replicated in positive terms the cultural fantasy of an intrinsically volatile, elusive, annihilating sexuality. In their homages to Vivien, they reiterated the nonreferentiality of lesbian sexuality already implicit in dominant cultural narratives (critics' difficulty tying lesbianism to conventional gender distinctions), but did so to create a multidimensional rather than reductive image of same-sex love: love that defied gender norms even as it drew on them for its expression;

---

57. Marie-Jo Bonnet, *Les Relations amoureuses entre les femmes* (Paris: Odile Jacob, 1995), 256, the only extant history of lesbianism in France, calls Vivien the "precursor of the women's liberation movement."

that refused to hide itself even as it repudiated the principle of absolute revelation; love located simultaneously within and outside the parameters of medical taxonomies; love that paradoxically proclaimed itself through its own erasure. This love, in contrast to other lesbian interpretations of Vivien's own, romanticized the poet's voice in a very specific manner.

Vivien was English but adopted a French pen name, wrote in French, and enjoyed enormous success during her lifetime. She was briefly the lover of the wealthy American Natalie Barney, whose Paris salon was a famous gathering place for elite lesbians and gay men, among others. Together, Vivien and Barney formed a literary group dubbed "Sapho 1900" in 1951 by the writer André Billy. They transformed Sappho into a cult figure in order to challenge the fin-de-siècle degradation of the great poet.[58] Although Vivien was primarily a poet, she also wrote some prose and some essays, most of which were autobiographical and traced love affairs that ended badly, including the one with Barney. She was also an astute and very funny critic of straight male dominance, noting in one text that she found heterosexuality utterly incomprehensible, and in another parodying normative institutions—the family, the Church, and so on.[59] An entire portion of Colette's book is devoted to an affectionately negative characterization of Vivien (Vivien's poetry is overrated, she lisps, she nails her windows shut and is absurdly secretive). The best-known lesbian portrait of Vivien other than Colette's is Natalie Barney's. Like Co-

58. For details, see DeJean, *Fictions of Sappho,* 285–86; Karla Jay, *The Amazon and the Page: Natalie Clifford Barney and Renée Vivien* (Bloomington: Indiana University Press, 1988).
59. Renée Vivien, *Une Femme m'apparut* (1904; reprint, Paris: Desforges, 1977); id., *L'Album de Sylvestre* (Paris: E. Sansot, 1908).

lette, she remembered the poet sadly and a bit cynically, and like her, she acknowledged but treated her lesbianism matter-of-factly, as but one component of a life not well lived. Although Vivien's writing was of high quality, Barney writes, she "sought glory (but because she despaired of love), as well as religion, in the doubt of surviving otherwise. Weak, she allowed herself to go to the assurances of the highest bidder, and to all those long-term 'investments' from which she anticipated profits and bliss."[60]

Other French male (and some female) writers repudiated Vivien's lesbianism—either by denying it outright or claiming that her homosexual reveries constituted nothing more than a *poetic* identification with her heroine Sappho. Some writers had already sought to revise nineteenth-century fantasies about Sappho's lesbianism in order to save her poetry from the taint of perversion. In their accounts, they transformed the image of Sappho as a depraved poetess into another image of a noble poet and mother, a chaste woman so wounded by Phaon's betrayal that she leapt tragically off the cliff at Leucade.[61] Other writers similarly sought to rescue Vivien by distancing her from lesbianism. Jean-Desthieux claimed that Vivien was being glorified *because* she was a lesbian. But, he argued, her poetry was unrelated to "real" lesbianism

60. Natalie Clifford Barney, *Adventures of the Mind*, trans. John Spalding Gatton (New York: New York University Press, 1992), 188. Barney also claims that Vivien converted to Catholicism because of her mysticism, but is deeply ironic about it: "Jesus Christ has seduced more women than Don Juan" (190).

61. See J. M. F. Bascoul, *La Chaste Sappho des Lesbos et le mouvement féministe à Athènes au IVème siècle av. J.C.* (Paris: Weltner, 1911); Jean Larnac and Robert Salmon, *Sappho* (Paris: Rieder, 1934); Anne Minvielle, *Sappho la Lesbienne* (Paris: Eugène Figuière, 1923); Edouard Romilly, *Sappho, la passionnante, la passionnée* (Paris: Eugène Figuière, 1931).

and represented instead her attachment to Sappho, her "imaginary lover." She was narcissistic and thus fashioned all her lyrical lovers after the ancient Greek poet, whom she wanted to be. In short, Vivien "succeeded simply in giving a modern soul and a woman's body to the genius of Narcissus."[62]

In 1905, Charles Maurras's famous essay on "Feminine Romanticism" claimed Vivien's sapphism was "pure passion embedded in the most intelligent perversity," and did not dispute her lesbianism but her talent: her "imitations" of Baudelaire and Verlaine were "too ardent, too passionate," marking her womanhood.[63] In 1930, Yves-Gerard Le Dantec repudiated Maurras's view, claiming that Vivien was a great poet because she was chaste. She was too "sincere and chaste to be a woman of vice," and her sapphism, like Sappho's own, was indissociable from chastity and misandry—Vivien was too smart to follow Sappho down the road her heroine had traveled with Phaon.[64] Finally, both the symbolist writer Laurent Tailhade and the author André Germain insisted that her identification with Sappho was an identification born of "wounded idealism." Vivien was like a "phantom," and her love was not of the flesh but the soul.[65]

Vivien's male admirers thus mostly idealized the martyrdom they attributed to her life and to her deathbed conversion to Catholicism. Vivien, chaste and pure, died for a love that cannot be named, a love so passionate in its

62. Jean-Desthieux, *Femmes damnées*, 55, 58.

63. Charles Maurras, *Le Romantisme féminin* (1905; Paris: Cité des livres, 1926), 48, 10.

64. Yves-Gérard Le Dantec, *Renée Vivien: Femme damnée, femme sauvée* (Aix-en-Provence: Editions du Feu, 1930), 48–49, 56, 190.

65. André Germain, *Renée Vivien* (Paris: G. Crès, 1917), 51; Laurent Tailhade, *La Médaille qui s'efface* (Paris: G. Crès, 1924), 243.

longing for purity and transcendence that it could only be fulfilled in death.[66] Many women writers also insisted somewhat differently that Vivien's sexuality was so refined it could not be satiated in this world. As Henriette Willette wrote, "shadow was her friend," as if Vivien's desire for closed, stifling spaces and her discretion were continuous with purity rather than with impurity.[67] But in the writings of Henriette Willette and others, Vivien is the agent of her own destruction, not because lesbian sexuality is intrinsically impure, but because it is pure, too "chaste" in its passion, too passionately chaste.[68] This concept of chastity was quite different from that employed by the mostly male-authored texts surveyed. Many female would-be writers, who used pseudonyms and were almost entirely unknown except among a small literary circle, wrote reviews of and homages to Vivien. Sometimes these homages took the form of fiction or poetry, sometimes of more straightforward analysis. Even marginalized positions within these already marginal texts

66. DeJean, *Fictions of Sappho,* 283–84, claims that Vivien's critics read her identification with Sappho too literally as narcissism and quite rightly invokes Jean-Desthieux's *Femmes damnées* to make her point. The majority of Vivien's critics would agree with DeJean that her "repetitive fictions of Sappho are not about becoming Sappho but about a double redefinition: of sapphism as the poetic infinite, an (always impossible) union with Sappho." Vivien's female admirers adhere to this reading and depart from her mostly male fans because, as DeJean also claims (although she doesn't address these women), "sapphism [is] the desire, incessantly emitted by Sappho across the ages, for the ideal beloved girl . . . who will give up without a murmur, in a 'sob' of love, father family, and homeland for the muse of Mytilene." Most interesting for our purposes is how other writers articulate lesbian sexuality through the vehicle of Vivien's lyric voice.

67. Henriette Willette, *Le Livre d'Or de Renée Viven* (Paris: Livre d'Or, 1927), 21.

68. Salma Zakia Galiléah, "Renée Vivien," *Les Muses: Revue féminine* (1910): 11, 18.

differed from the dominant readings offered by Germain, Maurras, and others. Héra Mirtel, for example, argued that Vivien identified with Sappho because she identified with women's resistance to men's repression of women's glory. In her account, Vivien's celebration of Sappho is a form of "universal revolt by women excluded from the male Trinity [Father, Son, Holy Ghost]." In this version, Vivien would have been a lover of men had not men insisted on their supremacy. Vivien's poetry was thus born of anger and rebellion and embraces life and the future— that is why, Mirtel tells us, she converted to Catholicism on her deathbed. Vivien is not a betrayed, fragile soul but a woman who waged war in lyric form against patriarchal power structures and sought everlasting life in another world.[69]

Other texts also interpreted Vivien as a feminist, but not at the expense of her lesbianism. At the same time, they depart from Colette's and Barney's far less romanticized view of Vivien's homosexuality. Traversing these different works was the consensus that Vivien celebrated "languorous feminine passion." "Always with the same fugue, the same violence, the same sincerity, the exquisite poet asserts her vibrant passion, source of the most wonderful joys and the most horrible suffering." "Her delicate and voluptuous art" celebrates "all the splendors of feminine love."[70] But here this sincerity and passion, often figured as chastity, expresses same-sex desire rather than repudiating it: Vivien's otherwordly quest was not aimed at transcending the flesh but at finding a passion capable

69. Héra Mirtel, "Renée Vivien," *La Vie moderne: Journal des lettres et des artistes* 31 (July, 1910), n.p.

70. Camille Lemercier d'Erm, reviews of *L'Album de Sylvestre* and *Sillages*, by Renée Vivien, *Argonautes* 9 (1908): 26; ibid. 10 (1909): 28.

of satiating her longing, one she had been denied. "The almost unreal grace of women's love, light, immaterial caresses, suited her sensibility better than the rough embrace that enslaves," Willette says, in words inspired by Baudelaire's famous poem "Femmes damnées." "For Renée Vivien, virginity did not exclude voluptuousness. She was delicately sensual. Her passion was not a vulgar passion."[71] Or, as "Gêllo," a poet who imitated Vivien's own use of mock Greek names, wrote: "We wish to immortalize the gentle virility of this first kiss, which brightens your agonizing solitude."[72]

For Willette and others then, Vivien's purity in no way excluded sexual love. Nor was Vivien obsessed with death because she was too pure and chaste for this world, a connection drawn by many writers. Instead, these women made it their task to keep Vivien's memory alive as a way of celebrating same-sex desire: they saw her death, not as the consequence of some desire to transcend creaturely status, but as the inevitable toll taken by a heartless world in which same-sex passions were mocked and scorned. "Gêllo" revised famous portraits of heterosexual love, so that Antoine Watteau's lovers go to Lesbos instead of Cythera and Ophelia falls in love with a woman rather than Hamlet; she noted further that "exiled loves" will have their moment "only when the timorous bourgeoisie close their doors."[73] Rita del Noiram wrote that Vivien's poetry infused the bodies of others with her own desire and the courage to express it. In a poem dedicated to

71. Willette, *Livre d'Or,* 25, 27.
72. Gêllo, *Harmonies et Poèmes* (Paris: Albert Messin, 1926), 21.
73. Ibid., 54–55, 59–65, 45. Gêllo is not referring specifically to Vivien, although she is in the same literary circle and makes several explicit and implicit references to the poet.

Vivien, Noiram casts herself as the lover of Sappho, insisting that her desire will "flourish always."[74] Camille Arnot wrote to Vivien: "Your sleep is eternal, O Muse; but your verse will immortalize you and consecrate your glory."[75] This poetic identification with Vivien inspired a series of lyrics devoted to celebrating female same-sex desire and to chastising patriarchal power structures perceived to be responsible for the suffering of all women, from Sappho to Vivien.

It would be simple to interpret this work as the predictable musings of acolytes, imitations of Baudelaire (Maurras's point), or even as verses that reiterate conventional images of femininity (its purity, its "delicacy"—in short, its apparently less "brutal" sexuality). But these readings of Vivien are a long way from other, dominant characterizations and deserve attention on that ground alone. Who was right or not about the "real" Vivien is irrelevant; most important, these specific women who cherished Vivien fashioned visions of their own sexuality after prevalent constructions of female same-sex desire as intrinsically elusive, unlike Colette and Barney. The relationship between these figurations of lesbian desire and the dominant rhetoric of lesbian invisibility is homologous: both discourses employ the fluidity of the lesbian who cannot be pinned down or identified either to regulate female desire, or in the case of Vivien's acolytes, to escape regulation. Most of Vivien's female admirers used dominant discourses about lesbian elusiveness to figure a presence so immaterial it was never in danger of being

74. Rita del Noiram, *Des accords sur le luth* (Saint Raphael: Des Tablettes, 1920), n.p.
75. Camille Arnot, *Des Violettes pour Renée Vivien* (Paris: Sansot, 1910), 6.

erased. They fetishized Vivien's death, it would seem, as a means of staying alive—hence the love of concealment in their work, their invocation of an ethereal and highly eroticized body whose sensuality is omnipresent and yet intangible. Willette: "Renée Vivien! I loved Renée Vivien. I love a dead woman! From the beyond she breathes blessed inspiration into me; I was filled with her. She inhaled me; I went to her. And, since they were so dear to her, I brought her the pale flowers that she so piously sang." ("De l'au-délà elle m'enveloppait d'un souffle béni; j'en étais impregnée. Elle m'aspirait, j'allais à elle. Et je lui apportais, puisqu'elles lui etaient chères, les fleurs pales qu'elle avait si pieusement chantées.") The same sort of invocation of Vivien occurs in a poem by "Milhyris": "My dream alone has known your languor and your eyes, the astonishing gold, the lightness of your . . . hair. And I did not feel your frail hand on my forehead, placing itself there for a moment, like a fluttering wing."[76]

Again, this is certainly not the only or the predominant form of self-representation lesbians employed during the interwar period. But this celebration of Vivien, however normatively "feminine" it may seem, demonstrates clearly how those representations are shaped by discourses about the dissolution of gender boundaries: in different ways, these women refashioned cultural fantasies implicit in one important construction of lesbianism since the late nineteenth century, in which lesbians cannot really be bound to a stable gender identity. Those women conceived of an eroticism that could not be effaced, because, like the difference between honest and deviant women, and between womanly and manly ones, it

76. Milhyris, *La Douceur ancienne* (Paris: Caravelle, 1931), 67.

could not be definitively located: "Renée Vivien's love is a divinely spiritual love, which derives its sensuality only from the purest and most untraceable subtleties [*raffinements*]."[77]

If one version of gay male personhood defined itself in relation to ideal heterosexual manliness—as its analog— does lesbian personhood define itself in relation to ideal heterosexual womanliness? Evidently not, and therein lies the important difference between the construction of lesbian identity and its cultural effects and the invention of gay male selfhood. The women who identified with Vivien clearly repudiated normative womanhood, since they viewed it as a state of slavery. We have seen how the most conservative among them, Héra Mirtel, still saw in Vivien a voice raised against patriarchal oppression, and most of the writers cited referred to men as persecutors who sought to deny Vivien her dreams. And unlike accounts of lesbianism as gender inversion, these particular writers celebrated, not virility, but "gentle virility" and, in so doing, reproduced the gender impasse in which lesbianism was embedded: it was both devouring and devoured, manly and womanly, active and passive. They did not celebrate either sexual purity or impurity; they did not insist that their sexuality was pure by embracing pure womanhood. Unlike the gay men who sought to give gay male sexuality an affirmative meaning without challenging normative manliness, these woman invented a personhood that could not be imagined only in relation to either manliness or womanliness. And unlike the male writers who upheld Vivien as a model of ideally

77. Galiléah, "Renée Vivien," 10.

chaste womanhood and ridiculed her poetry, they transformed Vivien into a martyr for the cause of a sexual desire whose name they yoked at once to purity and impurity. That is, by defining female same-sex desire in terms
of Vivien's self-sacrifice, they redefined the impurity conventionally attributed to lesbianism in terms of a purity
that paradoxically retained its sensuality and "virility" by
virtue of being so very "gentle."

In short, they made lesbian sexuality visible, but only
by insisting on its indecipherability, much as critical
commentary had done. Though they affirmed rather than
stigmatized that sexuality by rendering it opaque, that
affirmation was clearly problematic because it asserted
selfhood only in its erasure, and was sometimes difficult
to distinguish (even though I insist it must be) from cele-
brations of normative womanhood.[78] Gay male visibility,

78. Judith Butler uses the term "resignification" to define the way in
which minority groups take on and appropriate dominant cultural terms
and identities and change them in the process (often subversively embracing their "perversion"). Hence a manly lesbian is not a woman acting
like a man, but a transformation of the idea of what a woman is altogether
that subverts both normative gender roles and the dichotomous logic that
underlies them. In our framework, the theoretical challenge must be to
understand how the emphasis on lesbian invisibility is linked to a particular historical context. Butler presumes that resignification produces cultural change, but never explains how it does so in a historically specific
way. Since resignification involves a subversive challenge to cultural ideals
of gender that is not generally accessible and often looks like something
(e.g., manliness) it is not, Butler is hard-pressed, as several critics have already noted, to explain why the process of resignification challenges any-
thing at all. See Leo Bersani's trenchant criticism in *Homos* (Cambridge,
Mass.: Harvard University Press, 1995), 36–51. Butler's initial response to
much early criticism, in *Bodies That Matter: On the Discursive Limits of
Sex* (New York: Routledge, 1993), clarified some concepts whose misread-
ing facilitated reductive interpretations of her work (e.g., the meaning of
social construction), but she never really addresses this other very fundamental criticism. See Judith Bulter, *Gender Trouble: Feminism and the*

as I have argued, was compelled in large part not only by visible gay men but by the fantasy that gay men were lurking, invisible, behind every corner. In this context, visibility was as much a form of regulation as it was a form of self-assertion on the part of gay men who chose to mark themselves as gay. But in the case of lesbians, *invisibility* was a form of regulation and, paradoxically, an opaque form of self-definition by women who chose to live as lesbians. In other words, the limits intrinsic in this particular construction of lesbian desire's opacity reveal the limits intrinsic in marginalized groups' ability to mobilize dominant rhetoric in their own interests.

Conclusion

The absence of visible lesbians (when they were presumed to be everywhere) emblematized a world in which things were not necessarily what they appeared to be and in which women in particular might have something to hide. In this way, the discourse about lesbians was and is also always a discourse about all women. Critics conceived gay male sexuality simultaneously as too visible and too invisible, but in the powerful narrative I have just reconstructed, they deprived lesbian sexuality of any concrete referent except its own invisibility. This tautology marks the specificity of some fantasies about lesbians. This tautology thus often situates lesbians beyond the long arm of the law, and may explain why laws tend not to target lesbians even as they are constantly being surveyed, discovered, scrutinized, and transformed into objects of anxiety. That logic may also explain why lesbian desire is generally perceived to be more malleable than

---

Subversion of Identity (New York: Routledge, 1990); id., *Bodies That Matter*, esp. 1–55.

gay male sexuality, since it is so often conceived as omnipresent but impossible to identify as such, and since it
is often perceived to be embedded in acts rather than in
clearly demarcated identities.[79]

I do not wish to reduce a series of different and complex historical moments to one narrative. As I noted, I use
this particular narrative around Vivien to demonstrate
the coercive as well as productive potential of fantasies
about lesbians' invisibility. Thus invisibility may often be
a form of persecution, one that is not benign and takes
many different guises that account for very different
forms of oppression. I do not, therefore, wish to suggest
that lesbian desire is subversive because epistemologi-
cally slippery, but rather, to insist that that very slipperi-
ness furnished and still furnishes an occasion both for
identity fashioning *and* a form of persecution far less benign than would seem to be the case. The insistence on
lesbians' invisibility made the quest to find them all the
more urgent and sustained the idea that there were lesbians who could be identified. In this way, critics drew a
distinction between lesbians and other women, and thus
sought to give lesbian identity ontological stability. In
this context, lesbianism remained the repository of the
dangerous female sexuality that any woman could now
be accused of harboring in spite of herself. The lesbian
body, like the gay male body and the "body" of pornography, was equally elastic and omnipresent and equally
specific and abject.

But to what end? The distinction between heterosexual men and women depended on the stability of he-

79. For a reading of this fluidity in the context of Freud's own work
on female homosexuality and in psychoanalytic terms, see Diana Fuss,
Identification Papers (New York: Routledge, 1995).

terosexual manliness. As historians have frequently argued, the ideology of sexual difference, invented in its modern form during the Enlightenment, defined women as biologically different from men and used that difference to legitimate women's inferior social status in a variety of contexts.[80] Gay men during our period challenged the stability and seeming ahistoricity of that difference because they sought to claim manliness for themselves, challenging the idea that they were necessarily, "naturally," unmanly. Some lesbians challenged that stability in a less evident but equally dramatic fashion: drawing, like gay men, on dominant discourses, they fashioned an opaque identity that was difficult to imagine in relation to either manliness or womanliness.

As I have argued, interwar commentators of all sorts constructed lesbians as opaque or invisible because they had great difficulty anchoring lesbians in a clearly gendered (manly or womanly) and hence clearly sexualized (desiring of whom and by whom?) identity. Although it served as a pretext to regulate all women's sexuality, this construction of lesbians' invisibility mirrored the critic's own oddly present and yet absent sexuality. His voyeuristic gaze, his persistent quest to ferret out the lesbian, might be interpreted as a source of pleasure that manifests itself as a form of regulation, of expurgating pleasure and controlling its excesses. How else can we explain

---

80. This argument appears in a vast array of scholarly (primarily feminist) works, and has been recently and provocatively formulated by Scott, *Only Paradoxes to Offer;* Geneviève Fraisse, *Reason's Muse: Sexual Difference and the Rise of Democracy,* trans. Jane Marie Todd (Chicago: University of Chicago Press, 1994); Thomas Laqueur, *Making Sex: Body and Gender from the Greeks to Freud* (Cambridge, Mass.: Harvard University Press, 1990); and Carole Pateman, *The Sexual Contract* (Stanford, Calif.: Stanford University Press, 1988). These works have inspired numerous studies.

the extraordinary power of these narratives and their volume, as well as their enormous weight compared to a noisier narrative about lesbians' manliness? That Renée Vivien's followers took up this narrative to forge an alternative personhood is further testimony to its power. Moreover, this concept of lesbian invisibility is still so potent that in 1994 the French lesbian writer Anne Garréta described it this way: "Since [in France, the category lesbian] exists, but negatively, it prevents anyone from trying to identify herself with the category. Perfect dissuasion. We will tell you positively: the category . . . does not exist. [But] if you identify or are identified there, in the locus of this category . . . you run into trouble." [81] This chapter has sought to understand why a category that presumably exists can never be found, and moreover, why being identified in a category that is not supposed to exist can get one into so much trouble.

81. Anne Garréta and Josyane Savigneau, "A Conversation," *Yale French Studies* 90 (1996): 221.

Epilogue

Interwar critics were clearly obsessed with the dissolution of the body's metaphorical boundaries, a dissolution symbolized above all by pornography and homosexuality. In an old interview, Michel Foucault said that we were now interested in the marquis de Sade's "pornographic" work because it prefigures the more recent historical "dissociation of the ego" in which sexuality comes to signify the dissolution of the social body, the "orgiastic" nature of contemporary sexual pleasures.[1] Foucault must be more or less on the mark, for historians and others have recently traced a long tradition that links pathological sexuality and pathological (antiliberal) politics, most recently discussed in the context of the French revolutionaries' use of Marie-Antoinette's sexualized body to stigmatize the French monarchy.[2] The phantasmatically

1. Michel Foucault, *Foucault Live (Interviews, 1966–84)*, trans. John Johnston (New York: Semiotext(e): 1989), 83–84.
2. See esp. Lynn Hunt, *The Family Romance of the French Revolution;* Sarah Maza, *Private Lives and Public Affairs: The Causes Célèbres of Pre-*

eroticized, incestuous, promiscuous, and dissimulating body of the queen became a metaphor for political corruption of the ancien régime, and she was put on trial for sexual crimes that allegorized political ones. More recently, democratic thinkers as brilliant as Theodor Adorno and as important as Arthur Schlesinger have yoked sexuality and politics in the same vein.[3] Why, for example, do they equate homosexuality with the feminized, porous, and intrinsically eroticized "body" of the fascist or totalitarian state? The equation is particularly egregious because these are the same states that ruthlessly persecuted sexual deviance, including homosexuals and pornographers, in order to present themselves as regenerated, virile national bodies.

This book asks how sexual deviance became associated with the violation of the social body in the context of French liberal democracy under pressure. It shows how, during the interwar period, the commensurability of metaphorical bodily violation and "deviant" sexuality radically transformed the construction of the sexual drive itself: after the war the sexual drive was no longer opposed to culture (or domesticated by it), but itself an expression of highly civilized human beings. Critics defined the new integral body in paradoxical terms: sexuality both springs from and is transcended by patriotic disci-

---

revolutionary France (Berkeley and Los Angeles: University of California Press, 1993).

3. Theodor Adorno, *Minima Moralia* (London: Verso, 1974), 46. "[T]he tough guys are the true effeminates," Adorno said, speaking of Nazism; he linked effeminacy to homosexuality, reiterating the shibboleth that fascists are latent homosexuals. Arthur M. Schlesinger, Jr., *The Vital Center: The Politics of Freedom* (1949; reprint, New York: Da Capo Press, 1988), 53, 85, 141. On homophobia in the Frankfurt School, see Andrew Hewitt, *Political Inversions: Homosexuality, Fascism, and the Modernist Imaginary* (Stanford, Calif.: Stanford University Press, 1996).

pline; its sexual liberation is conceived oddly as continuous with its Frenchness. This curiously bloodless figure, born of so much bloodshed, does not express the transcendence of the natural body; it signals the seemingly impossible continuity of the natural and spiritual bodies. Moreover, this transformation in the concept of the sexual drive explains why, for example, "enlightened" democratic critics who advocated sexual liberation believed quite oddly that liberating sexual pleasures would lead to the abolition of pornography and homosexuality. It explains why sexual pleasure is supposed to be a good thing but consumers of pornography are deemed to have repressed theirs, or they would not need pornography. It might, then, explain why sexual liberation always means the liberation to engage in socially acceptable heterosexuality.

Sexual liberation was thus a means of regulating and sustaining the social body's integrity. We cannot account for this paradoxical solution to the problem posed by self-dissolution after the war by reference to the pros and cons of liberal thought or solely in social histories of pornography and homosexuality. Instead, the historical interpretation of fantasies about the body explains why some fantasies emerged more forcefully than others, and why, most important, the perceived attraction to self-shattering pleasures could no longer merely be repressed. For this odd reconstruction of the sexual drive rendered normal and deviant bodies distinct by producing a new line between civilized and noncivilized people that simply did not and could not rely only on narratives about the efficacy of repression. Moreover, this odd disembodiment of the body's sexual drive operated also as a means of sustaining a clear ideological boundary between a pure and an impure social body. But perhaps pornography

and homosexuality mark the social body's fluidity in spite
of all efforts to render it impermeable. Fantasies about
pornography and homosexuality lay bare a historically
specific image of the body before it is endowed with citizenship, and thus expose the grounds for exclusion from
the national community. At the same time, those fantasies reveal that that pre-political body is not clearly distinct from the social body and thus can never be fully
excluded. But in what ways have we inherited these fantasies and how do they operate? For a short answer
meant to inspire more questions than propose answers,
I turn briefly to the work of two compassionate liberal
thinkers, both of whom seek to understand legitimate
and illegitimate forms of state violence by reference to
the intrinsic dignity of the human body.

Elaine Scarry argues that martyrs are martyrs because
they refuse to bend to a law by which they cannot abide
no matter what the cost in physical suffering, thereby
transmitting the force of their beliefs through their
bodily pain. Torture, prisons, war, capital punishment—
these forms of state-sanctioned violence—exist because
the body is a privileged vehicle for the consolidation of
ideological power, as well as the vehicle by which that
power (as martyrdom demonstrates) may be challenged.
Painfully extracted confession or subtle coercion empties
the body of its intrinsic dignity and stamps it with the "in-
signia of power." No matter how peripheral it may seem
in any given regime, physical pain, suffered willingly or
unwillingly, is central to the maintenance of normative
belief systems.

But Scarry cannot at the same time conceive of a person who would willingly give up the right to "his own
person," her own body, without compensation: the social
contract as she conceives it ensures that in exchange for

some of my freedom I can expect to live in peace with others. She more easily imagines human beings who desire to torture and coerce other people, but interprets this desire, too, not as willful but often as the product of ideological fictions or rationalized bureaucracies in which the perpetrator is distanced from the crime he perpetrates.[4] Or, as she implicitly insists, human beings do not perpetrate violence unless they cannot recognize it as violence, unless ideological fictions have so dehumanized the victim and so thoroughly shaped the mind of the perpetrator that he believes he is acting in the name of the law. Scarry claims that "the act of disclaiming is as essential to the power [of the state] as is the act of claiming. It of course assists the torturer in practical ways. He first inflicts pain, then objectifies pain, then denies the pain—

4. Even Hannah Arendt, whose liberal credentials are complicated, argued that mass murder in Nazi Germany was carried out by a formalized bureaucracy whose purpose was the eradication of Jews but might have been the delivery of grain; see her *Eichmann in Jerusalem: A Report on the Banality of Evil* (New York: Viking, 1957). Arendt's emphasis on bureaucratic structures and implicit and infamous criticism of their victims itself derives less from a liberal humanist inability to conceive willingly inflicted violence than from her discomfort with vulnerable bodies. Her glorification of the polis at the expense of women and slaves, her highly idiosyncratic and often brilliant reading of the French Revolution, and her admiration of Rosa Luxemburg all bespeak an ambivalence about human weakness. Arendt likes human beings particularly tough in the face of suffering. That ambivalence inadvertently flattens out the differences between murderers and victims. Her famous analysis of Eichmann does not only transform his murderousness into banality in the context of an often persuasive Heideggerian critique of the "social"; she also manifests patronizing contempt for a petty bourgeois failure of a man. Gerschom Scholem and others have famously criticized the Eichmann book because of its leveling of perpetrators and victims but paid less attention to this dimension of her work. This dimension might help us understand the more general cultural discomfort with violated bodies, which is my point in bringing her up. From this point of view, I find the recent resurrection of Arendt by feminist political theorists interesting but ultimately difficult to understand.

and only this final act of self-blinding permits the shift back to the first step, the inflicting of still more pain, for to allow the reality of the other's suffering to enter his own consciousness would immediately compel him to stop the torture."[5] The late Robert Cover argued in a pathbreaking essay that judges dispense pain and death, but that they do so in the name of enforcing the law, its formal procedures masking the violence implicit in the very idea of "enforcement."[6] Cover implicitly acknowledges that incarceration is not precisely the same thing as torture, but nevertheless wishes to make a more general point: "A legal world is built only to the extent that there are commitments that place bodies on the line." The law, he goes on, "is transformed into a violent deed despite general resistance to such deeds."[7] Inhibitions on doing violence to others make law possible at the same time that the law is infused with and imposed through violence.

Cover continues:

Furthermore, almost all people are fascinated and attracted by violence, even though they are at the same time repelled by it. Finally, and most important for our purposes, in almost all people social cues may be overcome or suppress the re-

5. Elaine Scarry, *The Body in Pain: The Making and Unmaking of the World* (Oxford: Oxford University Press, 1985), 57.

6. Robert Cover, "Violence and the Word," in Martha Minow, Michael Ryan, and Austin Sarat, eds., *Narrative, Violence, and the Law: The Essays of Robert Cover* (Ann Arbor: University of Michigan Press, 1992). See also Jacques Derrida's essay "Force of Law: The 'Mystical Foundation of Authority,'" in *Deconstruction and the Possibility of Justice*, special issue of the *Cardozo Law Review* 11 (July–August, 1990), esp. 924–30. This special issue is devoted to a more general discussion of this paradox. The authors generally ask about the consequences of the assertion that desire or violence is intrinsic in the structure of the law, although the essays traverse metaphysics and social policy.

7. Cover, *Violence and the Word*, 208, 219.

vulsion to violence under certain circumstances. These limi-
tations do not deny the force of inhibitions against violence.
Indeed, both together create the conditions without which
law would either be unnecessary or impossible. Were the in-
hibition against violence perfect, law would be unnecessary;
were it not capable of being overcome through social signals,
law would not be possible.[8]

And then, in a revealing footnote, he writes that there
are some people who have "varying cultural responses to
linking pain and sexuality," and goes on to define these
people primarily as deviants having "a deeper sadomasochistic attraction to pain or violence," an attraction
whose universality may be "in dispute."[9] But if the attraction to violence is universal, as he claims, and if the
law is defined as the tension between the prohibition and
expression of violence, why is sexual deviance a "deeper"
form of violence? Deeper than what?[10] What is the origin
of that fascination with violence that afflicts "almost all
people" if it is not rooted in corporeal desire, sexual or
otherwise?

Sexual deviance here represents the deeper, dangerous
violence beyond the law, even as our susceptibility to prohibition and punishment is, according to Cover, at the
heart of the law and makes it tick, is even its dirty secret. How to have it both ways? That is, in Cover's logic,
the law depends for its own operations on this deeper violence, and yet that violence is not only masked or inhib-
ited but impossible to interpret at all. The interpretative

8. Ibid., 218–19.
9. Ibid., 218.
10. See Dominick LaCapra, "Violence, Justice, and the Force of Law,"
Cardozo Law Review 11 (July–August, 1990): 1071–73. Here, in the context
of deconstruction, LaCapra addresses the "riskiness" of theorizing violence in the form of aporia.

community founded on violence it both represses and requires thus pushes this violence out of its interpretative framework and relegates it to a footnote.

Cover's exile of this "deeper" violence within the framework of a discussion of the law's violence suggests that the body intrinsically attracted to pain and suffering cannot be explained by theorists who expose the centrality of bodily pain to the ideological maintenance of the ostensibly nonviolent structures of modern societies. My point is that both Scarry and Cover do not address sexuality at all, and render questions about sexualized bodies (in this case about sadomasochistic desire) and the law illegitimate or unthinkable even as they posit the existence and importance of sexual desire intrinsic in the law's very rationality and exercise. Scarry in particular does not discuss female bodies, as if women were not part of the social body (however regulated), as if women were never "in pain." This absence proves particularly problematic, because men's fears about the body-dissolving properties of female sexuality or "feminine" desire were and are central to fashioning the modern male self. Thus by not addressing sexuality or inadvertently presuming an asexual body, they reiterate a clear-cut boundary between the law and violence, even as they insist on the violence that infuses the law.[11] If violence legitimately exists in ostensibly nonviolent institutions, it is crucial to know more about its operations in order to ensure that the law does not inadvertently or knowingly violate those rights it claims to protect. But if the law's operations are infused with sexual desire and affect, that desire must be accounted for instead of relegated to the realm of sexual pathology.

11. See, for an alternative view that does not conflate power and violence, but raises other problems, Hannah Arendt, *On Violence* (New York: Harcourt, Brace, 1970).

In Scarry and Cover, the distinction between violence and the law can only be persuasively and neatly made if sexualized bodies do not enter into the relationship between them. They must be assigned to psychiatric manuals, which classify those people who do not understand the distinction and for whom that misapprehension constitutes a pathology. In their work, when the sexualized body appears, it appears as deviant, pathological sexuality that falls outside the theoretical framework of classical and more recent versions of liberalism. Must the sexualized body then always be a sexually deviant, feminized body? Is the sexualized body, to go back to the original question, antithetical to liberalism's investment in an impermeable, integral body, and how? And if so, how does normative heterosexuality escape stigmatization? Most important, does the sexual deviant operate as a privileged figure of that which destroys the idea of a normative ethical community grounded in the material integrity of the body? And to go back to another earlier question, are the language of bodily integrity and the language of sexual rights (and hence the language of liberalism more generally) then incompatible?

And, to go further, might not the liberal humanist resistance to the historian Michel Foucault's work be interpreted as the repudiation of the sadomasochistic logic (for lack of a better term) that is in many ways its centerpiece? That is, Foucault argued that sexuality was constituted by a force he termed "power" that expanded for the sake of its own expansion, with no rhyme or reason other than the pleasure of its own exercise:

> The power which thus took charge of sexuality set about contacting bodies, caressing them with its eyes, intensifying areas, electrifying surfaces. . . . It wrapped the sexual body in its embrace. There was undoubtedly an increase in effectiveness and an extension of the domain controlled; but

also a sensualization of power and a gain of pleasure. This produced a twofold effect: an impetus was given to power through its very exercise; an emotion rewarded the overseeeing control and carried it further; the intensity of the confession renewed the questioner's curiosity; the pleasure discovered fed back to the power that encircled it.[12]

Foucault's own fashioning of this image of power after an unanchored but always intensifying sadomasochism derives from his refusal to make a distinction between violence and the law, because, in his view, discipline produces rather than represses historical subjects. The threat of sadomasochism in this context is nothing less than the loss of referentiality and causation (why does "power" produce subjects the way it does other than for its own pleasure?). How, in this context, can we determine why and how institutional formations like sexuality are formed the way they are? My point is thus not to celebrate this analysis of power, but again, to understand the theoretical and practical consequences of neglecting questions about historical figurations of sexualized bodies, including their relation to gender and their important role in producing and defining the relationship between bodies and politics. The point is not to condemn sexual pathology as the cause of anti-liberal politics or of Foucault's brilliant but gloomy portrait of a world full of human agents who have no agency, but to interpret it.

Recall that interwar critics were primarily concerned to prevent metaphorical bodily degradation from becoming an object of fascination or pleasure, as it arguably does in Foucault's work under the aegis of "power."[13]

---

12. Michel Foucault, *The History of Sexuality*, vol. 1: *An Introduction* (New York: Random House, Vintage Books, 1980), 45.

13. Remember that the premise of Foucault's later work collapses the two: the attraction exerted by power is identical with the law that is supposed to protect us from abuse.

Their concerns are also the same ones that Cover addresses when he both presumes that "violence" is an object of pleasure (and repulsion) and yet refuses to interpret that attraction. In so doing, he refuses interpret sexual deviance, or at the least, excludes it from his theoretical framework. But again, why does that deviance require no interpretation, even though it is universal? If the attraction to violence cannot, as Cover insists, simply be repressed or domesticated, since it infuses the law itself, how do we protect ourselves from its consequences? By analyzing in a rigorously focused fashion how interwar French critics addressed pornography and homosexuality in the context of this question about deviance and the social body—for they were the first to suggest the continuity between sexuality and its regulation—we might begin to understand why the repression of desire no longer seems so self-evident.[14] For why is the postwar social body so bloodless, so emptied of desire, so abstract? Why does that metaphorical body have to be so rigorously regulated through the creation of repositories of abjection that symbolize its violation, that rhetorically drain it of its sexuality not by repressing desire but by foreclosing it entirely? More specifically, we might historicize our investments in fashioning the social body the way we do.[15]

14. Foucault's work is the most salient example of the power of this insight.

15. The extent of this preoccupation with the relationship between sexuality and civilization by reference to sadomasochism has moved beyond the ranks of poststructuralists to include the liberal literary critic Mark Edmunson; see his *Nightmare on Main Street: Angles, Sadomasochism, and the Culture of Gothic* (Cambridge, Mass.: Harvard University Press, 1997). He insists we interpret sadomasochism, which, he claims, expresses itself through Gothic narrative conventions in a vast array of cultural production. His argument is humane, although his historical explanation for the presumed predominance of sadomasochism is relatively facile (the "unleashing" of anxiety produced by the 1960s). Historians will be surprised that Edmunson has found no adequate chroniclers of the 1960s, given the

Perhaps, then, after the Great War, universal "man" was revealed to be so forcefully embodied, so prosaic and particular in his desires and aspirations that he could no longer be the creation of an optimistic and hopeful era. Instead, he seems to be the uninspiring resolution to the problem of the collapse of older notions of universalism effected by that war and other modernizing forces.

This book uses production of fantasies about pornography and homosexuality to reveal one part of the process by which, at a particular historical moment, the "born" body does or does not become a rights-bearing citizen. It seeks to understand how violence to the social body is imagined at a specific time and place.[16] As some historians have shown, the ideally dignified humanity that serves to protect our rights relies for its existence on the exclusion of the "birth" rights of others, in this case those deemed sexually deviant and emblematic of bodily violation. This book aspires to continue this historical work, to nuance and defend it in the name of a perhaps utopian commitment to justice for all.

---

voluminous historiography of the period, but the book's general concern is one that historians don't give much thought to and perhaps should.

16. Here again I take up Giorgio Agamben's insistence on the original fluidity of the social body and the inseparability of *homo sacer* and the citizen: "And the root of modern democracy's secret biopolitical calling lies here: he who will appear later as the bearer of rights and, according to a curious oxymoron, as the new sovereign subject [meaning he is also subject to the law] . . . can only be constituted as such through the repetition of the sovereign exception and the isolation of *corpus*, bare life, in himself" (Agamben, *Homo Sacer: Sovereign Power and Bare Life* [Stanford, Calif.: Stanford University Press, 1998], 124). The only things Agamben fails to demonstrate are the historical process by which that repetition occurs and how it is historically specific (he associates it with "modernity").

Select Bibliography

Primary Sources

Unpublished Material

Archives de la Préfecture de Police de Paris, Series BA.

Printed Sources

Alibert, Dr. *Tribadism and Saphism*. Paris: New Edition, 1921.

Allendy, René. "Sentiment d'infériorité, homosexualité, et complex de castration." *Revue française de Psychanalyse* 3 (1927): 505–48.

Anquetil, Georges. *Satan conduit le bal*. Paris: Georges-Anquetil, 1925.

Apertus, Dr. *La Flagellation dite passionelle*. Paris: Collection des Orties blanches, 1927.

Arnot, Camille. *Des Violettes pour Renée Vivien*. Paris: Sansot, 1910.

Autrec, Lionel d'. *L'Outrage aux mœurs*. Paris: L'Epi, 1923.

Baldwin, James. *Giovanni's Room*. New York: Laurel Press, 1956.

Balkis. *Personne.* Paris: Edgar Malfere, 1922.

Bascoul, J. M. F. *La Chaste Sappho des Lesbos et le Mouvement Féministe à Athènes au IVème siècle av. J.C.* Paris: Weltner, 1911.

Bérénger, René. "La Traite des blanches et le commerce de l'obscenité: Conférences diplomatiques internationales du 15 juillet 1902 et du 18 avril 1910." *Revue des Deux Mondes* 58 (1 July 1910): 75–111.

Bethléem, Louis, Abbé. *La Littérature ennemie de la famille.* Paris: Blond & Gay, 1923.

———. *Romans à lire et romans à proscrire.* Cambrai: Masson, 1908.

Bizard, Léon. *La Vie des filles.* Paris: Grasset, 1934.

Bloch, Iwan. *Sexual Life in England Past and Present.* Translated by William H. Forstern. London: Aldor, 1938.

Bonmariage, Sylvain. *Les Plaisirs de l'Enfer.* Paris: Raoul Saillard, 1938.

Bonneau, Alcide. *Curiosa: Essais critiques de littérature ancienne ignorée ou mal connue.* Paris: Liseux, 1887.

Bourget, Paul. *Essais de psychologie contemporaine.* Paris: Lemerre, 1883.

Bricon, Etienne. "Pornographie." In *La Grande Encyclopédie,* vol. 27. Paris: Société Anonyme de la Grande Encyclopédie, 1895.

Cabanès, Dr. *La Flagellation dans l'histoire et la littérature.* Clermont: Daix Frères, 1899.

Caresses . . . ou les mémoires intimes de Jacqueline de R. Paris: Couvre Feu, 1933.

Caufeynon Dr. [Jean de Fauconney, pseud.]. *Les Vices féminins.* Paris: Librairie artistique, 1928.

Céline [Louis-Ferdinand Destouches]. *Voyage au bout de la nuit: Roman.* Paris: Denoël & Steele, 1932. English translation by Ralph Manheim under the title *Journey to the End of the Night* (London: John Calder, 1983).

Charles-Etienne. *La Bouche fardeé.* Paris: Curio, 1926.

———. *Les Désexués: Roman des mœurs.* Paris: Curio, 1924.

———. *Notre-Dame de Lesbos: Roman de mœurs*. Paris: Curio, 1919.

Charles-Etienne and Odette Dulac. *Le Bal des folles*. Paris: Curio, 1930.

Charonsay, G. de [Jean de Mézerette, pseud.]. *Orgies galantes et scènes saphiques*. Paris: Éditions du Vert-Logis, 1939.

Charpentier, René. Review of *La Folie et la guerre, 1914–1918*, by A. Rodiet and A. Fribourg-Blanc. *Annales médico-psychologiques* 1 (February 1931): 211.

Choisy, Maryse. *L'Amour dans les prisons: Reportage*. Paris: Montaigne, 1930.

———. "Dames seules." *Le Rire*, 21 May 1932. Reprinted with an introduction by Nicole Albert. *Cahier Gai Kitsch Camp* 23 (1993): 25–47.

Claiborne, William. "'Outing' Former Sex Offenders on the Midway: California Officials Defend the Use of a Country Fair Booth Showing Where Convicted Felons Live." *Washington Post National Weekly Edition*, 29 September 1997, 30.

Colette, Sidonie-Gabrielle. *Ces Plaisirs*. Paris: J. Ferenczi & fils, 1932.

Curnovsky. "Sur la progrès de la pornographie." *La Vie parisienne*, 11 November 1905, 904.

Cygielstrejch, Adam. "La Psychologie de la panique pendant la guerre," *Annales médico-psychologiques* 7 (April 1916): 172.

———. "Séance du 26 Juin 1916: De l'utilisation des indisciplines en temps de guerre," *Annales médico-psychologiques* 7 (October 1916): 526–29.

Deherme, Georges. *Les Classes moyennes: Etude sur le parasitisme social*. Paris: Perrin, 1912.

Delcourt, Pierre. *Le Vice à Paris*. Paris: Librairie française, 1888.

Del Noiram, Rita. *Des accords sur le luth*. Saint Raphael: Des Tablettes, 1920.

Delteil, Joseph. *Sur le fleuve amour*. Paris: Gallimard, 1933.

Delvadès, Manuel. *La Guerre dans l'acte sexuel*. Paris: Pacifisme scientifique, 1936 [1934].

Desnos, Robert. *De l'érotisme considéré dans ses manifestations écrites et du point de vue de l'esprit moderne.* 1923. Reprint. Paris: Cercle des Arts, 1952.

Drouin, Henri [Dr. François Nazier, pseud.]. *L'Anti-Corydon: Essai sur l'inversion sexuelle.* Paris: Editions du Siècle, 1924.

———. *Femmes damnées.* Paris: La Vulgarisation scientifique, 1945.

———. *Trois entretiens sur la sexualité.* Paris: Editions du Siècle, 1926.

DuBarry, Armand. *Les Flagellants.* Paris: Chameul, 1898.

———. *Les Invertis (Le Vice allemand).* Paris: Chamuel, 1896.

DuCoglay, Michel. *Chez les mauvais garçons (choses vues).* Paris: Raoul Saillard, 1938.

———. *Sous le col bleu.* Paris: Raoul Saillard, 1938.

Dumur, Louis. *Nach Paris!* Paris: Payot, 1919.

Dupuy, Dr. L. R. *The Strangest Voluptuousness: The Taste for Lascivious Corrections.* Paris: Medical Library, n.d.

Eliot, T. S. "Ulysses, Order, and Myth." *The Dial,* November 1923. Reprinted in *Selected Prose of T. S. Eliot,* ed. Frank Kermode (New York: Harcourt Brace Jovanovich, 1975).

Ellis, Havelock. *More Essays of Love and Virtue.* London: Constable, 1931.

———. *Studies in the Psychology of Sex,* vol. 2: *Sexual Inversion* Philadelphia: F. A. Davis, 1904.

Englisch, Paul. *L'Histoire de l'érotisme en Europe.* French adaptation Jacques Gorvil. Paris: Aldor, 1933.

Estève, Louis. "L'Amour androgyne." *Le Bon Plaisir,* February 1923, 45.

———. "L'Amour romantique et ses aberrations dans notre littérature." *Le Bon Plaisir,* June 1922–April 1923.

———. *L'Enigme de l'androgyne.* Paris: Monde moderne, 1927.

———. Preface to *Le Troisième Sexe,* by Willy [Henri Gauthier-Villars]. Paris: Paris Editions, 1927.

Eulenburg, Albert. *Algolania: The Psychology, Neurology, and Physiology of Sadistic Love and Masochism.* Translated by Harold Kent. New York: New Era, 1934. Originally published as *Sadismus und Masochismus,* Grenzfragen des

Nerven und Seelenlebens, vol. 19. (Wiesbaden: Bergmann, 1902).

Exner, Franz. *Krieg und Kriminalität in Österreich.* Vienna: Holder-Pichler-Tempsky; New Haven, Conn.: Yale University Press for the Carnegie Endowment for International Peace, 1927.

Eyquem, Albert. *De la repression des outrages à la morale publique et aux bonnes mœurs, ou de la pornographie au point de vue historique, juridique, législatif et social.* Paris: Marchal & Billard, 1905.

Fabri, Marcello. *L'Inconnu sur les villes: Roman des foules modernes.* Paris: J. Povolozky, 1921.

Flake, Otto. *Le Marquis de Sade.* Translated by Pierre Klossowski. Paris: Grasset, 1933.

Fleury, Maurice. *L'Angoisse humaine.* Paris: Editions de France, 1918.

Fonsegrive, Georges. *Art et pornographie.* Paris: Blond, 1911.

Forel, Auguste. *La Question sexuelle exposée aux Adultes cultivés.* Paris: Steinheil, 1906.

Freud, Sigmund. *The Complete Letters of Sigmund Freud to Wilhelm Fliess, 1877–1904.* Translated and edited by Jeffrey Moussaieff Masson. Cambridge, Mass.: Harvard University Press, 1985.

———. *Three Essays on the Theory of Sexuality.* New York: Basic Books, 1975.

Fursac, Rogues de. *Manuel de psychiatrie.* Paris: Felix Alcan, 1917.

Gagey, Roland. *Le Visage sexuel de l'Inquisition.* Paris: Chez l'auteur, 1932.

Galiléah, Salma Zakia. "Renée Vivien." *Les Muses: Revue féminine* (1910): 11.

Gand, Maurice. *Guide juridique et pratique pour la lutte contre la license des rues.* Paris: Librairie de Recueil Sirey, 1932.

———. *Une Forme moderne d'esclavage: La Traite des femmes.* Lyon: Chronique sociale de France, 1930.

Gaultier, Paul. *Leçons morales de la guerre.* Paris: Flammarion, 1919.

————. *Le Sens de l'art.* Paris: Hachette, 1911.

Gêllo. *Harmonies et poèmes.* Paris: Albert Messin, 1926.

Germain, André. *Renée Vivien.* Paris: G. Crès, 1917.

Ghilini, Hector. *Le Secret du Dr. Voronoff.* Paris: Eugene Fasquell, 1926.

Gide, André. *Corydon.* Paris: Nouvelle revue française, 1924.

Gourmont, Rémy de. *Lettres à l'Amazone.* 1914. Reprint. Paris: Mercure de France, 1988.

Guénolé, Pierre. *L'Etrange Passion: La Flagellation dans les mœurs d'aujourd'hui.* Paris: Office central de Librairie, 1904

Hall, Radclyffe. *The Well of Loneliness.* 1928. Reprint. New York: Avon Books, 1981.

Hamel, Maurice. "La Pornographie au café-concert." *Le Courrier français,* 15 February 1913, 8.

Haraucourt, Edmond. *La Démoralisation par le livre et par l'image.* Paris: Ollendorff, 1917.

Hedges, Chris. "Dejected Belgrade Embraces Hedonism but Still, Life Is No Cabaret." *New York Times,* 19 January 1998, sec. 1.

Hesnard, A. "Psychologie de l'homosexualité masculine." *Evolution psychiatrique 1* (October 1929).

Humbert, Pierre. *Homosexualité et psychopathies: Etude clinique.* Paris: G. Doin, 1935.

Huot, Louis, and Paul Voivenel. *La Psychologie du soldat.* Paris: La Renaissance du livre, 1918.

Jacobus X [Augustin Cabanès]. *Crossways of Sex: A Study in Eroto-Pathology.* Translator not noted. New York: American Anthropological Society, 1934.

————. *Le Marquis de Sade devant la science médicale et la littérature moderne.* Paris: Carrington, 1901.

Jean-Desthieux, François. *Femmes Damnées.* Paris: Editions Ophrys Gap, 1937.

Ladame, Paul. "Inversion sexuelle et pathologie mentale." *Bulletin de l'Académie de médecine* 70 (21 October 1917): 226–29.

Laforgue, René. "La Pratique psychanalytique." *Revue française de Psychanalyse* 2 (1928): 239–304.

Lalo, Charles. *La Beauté et l'instinct sexuel*. Paris: Flammarion, 1922.

———. *L'Expression de la vie dans l'art*. Paris: Felix Alcan, 1933.

Lamazelle, M. de. *Fédérations des sociétés contre la pornographie: Assemblé*, 21 May 1908.

Lapeire, Paul. *Essai juridique et historique sur l'outrage aux bonnes mœurs par le livre, l'écrit, et l'imprimé*. Lille: Douriez-Bataille, 1931.

Larnac, Jean, and Robert Salmon. *Sappho*. Paris: Rieder, 1934.

Lauris, J. *Les Amies perverses*. Paris: F. Schmid, 1933.

Le Dantec, Yves-Gérard. *Renée Vivien: Femme damnée, femme sauvée*. Aix-en-Provence: Editions du Feu, 1930.

Lemercier d'Erm, Camille. Reviews of *L'Album de Sylvestre* and *Sillages*, by Renée Vivien. *Argonautes* 9 (1908): 26; ibid. 10 (1909): 28.

Les Marges (March–April, 1926). Reissued in *Cahiers Gai Kitsch Camp* 19 (Paris, 1993).

Lorulot, André. *Barbarie Allemande et barbarie universelle: Le Livre Rouge des Atrocités mondiales*. Paris: L'Idée libre, 1921.

———. *La Flagellation et les perversions sexuelles*. Paris: L'Idée libre, 1948.

———. *Ma "pornographie" et . . . la Votre! Réponse à l'Abbé Bethléem*. Herblay: L'Idée libre, 1930.

———. *La Véritable Education sexuelle*. 1926. Reprint. Paris: L'Idée libre, 1945.

Louÿs, Pierre, Natalie Barney, and Renée Vivien. *Correspondances croisées: Suivies de deux lettres inédites de Renée Vivien à Natalie Barney et de divers documents*. Edited by Jean-Paul Goujon. Paris: Muizon à l'Ecart, 1983.

MacOrlan, Pierre [Pierre Dumarchey, pseud.]. *Le Masochisme en Amérique; suivi de la Petite marquise de Sade*. Paris: J. Fort, 1910.

———. [Pierre Jersange, pseud.]. *La Comtesse au fouet*. Paris: Collections des Orties blanches, 1911.

Mairobert, Pidansat de. *L'Espion anglais, ou Correspondance secrète entre Mylord All'Eye et Mylord All'Ear*. Vol. 10. London: John Adamson, 1774.

————. *La Secte des anandrynes: Confession de Mlle Sapho.* 1784. Paris: Bibliothèque des curieux, 1920.

Malherman. *Le Plaisir dans la souffrance.* Translated by Charles Wincker. Paris: A. Quignon, 1929.

Marchand, Henry. *Sex Life in France.* New York: Panurge Press, 1933.

Margueritte, Victor. *La Garçonne.* 1922. Reprint. Paris: Flammarion, 1978.

————. "Pourquoi j'ai écrit *La Garçonne* et *Ton corps est à toi.*" *Grand Guignol* 40 (Winter 1927–28): 265–66.

Maurras, Charles. *Le Romantisme féminin.* 1905. Reprint. Paris: Cité des livres, 1926.

McGrath, Patrick. Review of *Live Girls,* by Beth Nugent. *New York Times Book Review,* 14 April 1997.

Mézerette, Jean. *Les Amours d'Hitler: Reportage.* Paris: Jean Mézerette, 1935.

Milhyris. *La Douceur ancienne.* Paris: Caravelle, 1931.

Minvielle, Anne. *Sappho la Lesbienne.* Paris: Eugène Figuière, 1923.

Mirtel, Héra. "Renée Vivien." *La Vie moderne: Journal des lettres et des artistes* 31 (July 1910), n.p.

Morel, Bénédict-Auguste. *Traité des dégénérences physiques, intellectuelles et morales de l'espèce humaine.* Paris: Ballière, 1857.

"The New Pornography." *Time* 85 (16 April 1965): 29.

Nordau, Max. *Degeneration.* 1892. English translation. New York: Appleton, 1895. Reprint. Lincoln: University of Nebraska Press, 1993.

Nourrisson, Paul. *Etude de la répression des outrages aux bonnes mœurs au point de vue de la nature de l'infraction, de la penalté et de la jurisdiction.* Paris: J. B. Sirey, 1905.

Parent-Duchâtelet, Alexandre. *De la prostitution dans la ville de Paris.* 2 vols. Paris: Baillère, 1836.

Parnon, C. I. "Phénomenes d'inversion sexuelle ou d'intersexualité psychique et somatique, en rapport avec des altérations de la région infundibulo-hypophysaire." *Annales médico-psychologiques* 2 (June 1931): 91–93.

Paulhan, Frédéric. *Les Transformations sociales des sentiments.* Paris: Flammarion, 1920.

Porché, François. *L'Amour qui n'ose pas dire son nom.* Paris: Grasset, 1927.

Pourésy, Emile. *Le Bilan de la pornographie.* Paris: Bibliothèque nationale, 1934.

———. *Sous la fléau de l'immoralité: Cris d'alarme.* Paris: Relèvement Social, 1936.

Raffalovich, Dr. Marc-André. *Uranisme et unisexualité: Etude sur différentes manifestations de l'instinct sexuel.* Paris: Masson, 1896.

Ramuz, Charles-Ferdinand. *Présence de la mort.* Geneva: Georg, 1922. Reprint, Lausanne: L'Aire, 1978.

Rebell, Hugues. *Le Culte des idoles.* Paris: Bernard, 1929.

Recueil des Gazettes des Tribunaux, 1920–1936.

Réja, Marcel. "La Révolte des hannetons." *Mercure de France* 13 (1 March 1928): 334.

Renard, Charles-Noël. *Les Androphobes.* St. Etienne: Imprimerie spéciale, 1930.

Riolan, Dr. *Pédérastie et homosexualité.* Paris: Librairie artistique et médicale, 1927.

Romilly, Edouard. *Sappho, la passionnante, la passionnée.* Paris: Eugène Figuière, 1931.

Royer, Charles-Louis. *Le Club des damnés.* Paris: Editions de France, 1934.

Saint-Alban. "Chronique des mœurs." *Mercure de France* 105 (1 August 1928): 674.

Saint-Hélène, C. de. Letter to Ernest Armand. In *La Camaraderie amoureuse.* Paris: Edition de l'en-dehors, 1930.

Samuel, Dr. *La Flagellation dans les maisons de tolérance.* Paris: Maurice Wandnoel, n.d.

Sarcey, Robert. "Un Grain de pornographie." *XIXe Siècle* 4 (October 1881), n.p.

Sartre, Jean-Paul. "Qu'est-ce qu'un collaborateur?" *Situations,* vol. 3. Paris: Gallimard, 1949.

Ségard, Achille. *Les Voluptueux et les hommes d'action.* Paris: Société d'editions littéraires et artistiques, 1900.

Spiess, Camille. *Ceux qui l'attaquent et ceux qui le comprennent: Opinions diverses et commentaires suivis d'une étude de C. Spiess sur A. Gide et le problème de l'inversion sexuelle.* Paris: Annales d'Hermétisme, 1930.

———. *Pédérastie et homosexualité.* Paris: H. Daragon, 1917.

Tailhade, Laurent. *La Médaille qui s'efface.* Paris: G. Crès, 1924.

Tardieu, Dr. Ambroise. *Etude médico-legale sur les attentats aux mœurs.* Paris: J. B. Baillière & fils, 1858

Taxil, Léo [Gabriel Jogand-Pagès]. *La Prostitution contemporaine.* Paris: Librairie populaire, 1884.

Téry, Gustave. *L'Ecole des garçonnes.* Paris: L'Oeuvre, 1923.

Théry, Adolphe. *Manuel pratique de lutte antipornographique.* Paris: Spes, 1927.

Thoinot, Dr. L. *Attentat aux mœurs et perversions des sens génital.* Paris: Octave Doin, 1898.

United Nations Convention on the Prevention and Punishment of the Crime of Genocide. GAOR 260A (III), December 9, 1948.

Uzanne, Octave. "Du Saphisme en poésie." *Les Marges* 20 (15 March 1921).

Vachet, Dr. Pierre. *L'Inquiètude sexuelle.* Paris: Grasset, 1927.

Vignon, Charles-Louis. *Histoire du sexe.* Paris: Pierre Gara, 1935.

Vignons, Max. *Frédi à l'école: Le Roman d'un inverti.* Paris: Librairie artistique, 1929.

Villiot, Jean de [Hugues Rebell]. *En Virginie: Episode de la guerre de sécession. Précédé d'une étude sur l'esclavage et les punitions corporelles en Amérique.* Paris: Carrington, 1901.

———. *Etude sur la flagellation aux points de vue médical et historique.* Paris: Carrington, 1899.

———. *Femmes chatiées.* Paris: Mercure de France, 1994.

———. *Le Fouet à Londres.* Paris: Viviane Hamy, 1992.

———. *Les Mystères de la maison de la Verveine, ou Miss Bellasis Fouettée pour vol (tableau de l'education des jeunes Anglaises), traduit de l'anglais par Jean de Villiot.* Paris: Carrington, 1901.

Vivien, Renée. *L'Album de Sylvestre.* Paris: E. Sansot, 1908.

———. *Une Femme m'apparut.* 1904. Reprint. Paris: Desforges, 1977.

Voivenel, Paul. "A Propos de Sacher Masoch: Les Allemands et le marquis de Sade." *Progrès medical* 1 (6 January 1917), and 7 (17 February 1917).

———. *Le Génie littéraire.* Paris: Alcan, 1912.

Weininger, Otto. *Sex and Character.* London: Heinemann, 1910. Originally published as *Geschlecht und Charakter: Eine prinzipielle Untersuchung* (1903).

Willette, Henriette. *Le Livre d'Or de Renée Viven.* Paris: Livre d'Or, 1927.

Witoswki, G., and Lucien Nass. *Le Nu au théâtre depuis l'antiquité jusqu'à nos jours.* Paris: Paragon, 1909.

Witry, Dr. "Lettre de deux prêtres homosexuels. Guérisons après fièvre typhoide. Homosexualité et traumatisme." *Annales médico-psychologiques* 1 (May 1929): 398–419.

Zévaès, Alexandre. *Les Procès littéraires au XIXème siècle.* 3d ed. Paris: Perrin, 1924.

Zola, Emile. Preface to *Thèmes psycholoqiques,* by Dr. G. St. Paul. Paris: Vigot Frères, 1930.

Secondary Sources

Abelove, Henry, Michèle Aina Barale, and David M. Halperin, eds. *The Gay and Lesbian Studies Reader.* New York: Routledge, 1993.

Adorno, Theodor. *Minima Moralia.* London: Verso, 1974.

Agamben, Giorgio. *Homo Sacer: Sovereign Power and Bare Life.* Translated by Daniel Heller-Roazen. Stanford, Calif.: Stanford University Press, 1998. Originally published as *Homo sacer: Il potere sovrano e la nuda vita* (Turin: Giulio Einaudi Editore, 1995).

Albert, Nicole. "Sappho Mythified, Sappho Mystified, or the Metamorphoses of Sappho in Fin-de-Siècle France." In *Gay Studies from the French Cultures: Voices from France, Belgium, Brazil, Canada and the Netherlands,* ed. Rommel

Mendès-Leite and Pierre Olivier de Busscher, 87–104. New York: Haworth Press, 1993.

Aldrich, Robert. *The Seduction of the Mediterranean: Writing Art, and Homosexual Fantasy.* London: Routledge, 1993.

Apter, Emily S. *André Gide and the Codes of Homotextuality.* Saratoga, Calif.: Anma Libri, 1987.

Arendt, Hannah. *Eichmann in Jerusalem: A Report on the Banality of Evil.* New York: Viking, 1957.

———. *On Violence.* New York: Harcourt, Brace, 1970.

Aron, Jean-Paul, and Roger Kempf, *La Bourgeoisie, le sexe, et l'honneur.* Brussels: Editions complexes, 1984.

Audoin-Rouzeau, Stephane. *Men at War: National Sentiment and Trench Journalism in France During the First World War.* Providence, R.I.: Berg, 1992.

Baecque, Antoine de. *Le Corps de l'histoire: Métaphores et politique (1770–1800).* Paris: Calmann-Lévy, 1993.

Banks, Olive. *Faces of Feminism: A Study of Feminism as a Social Movement.* New York: St. Martin's Press, 1981.

Bard, Christine. *Les Filles de Marianne: Histoire des féminismes 1914–1940.* Paris: Fayard, 1994.

———. *Les Garçonnes: Modes et fantasmes des années folles.* Paris: Flammarion, 1998.

Barney, Natalie Clifford. *Adventures of the Mind.* Translated by John Spalding Gatton. New York: New York University Press, 1992.

Bécourt, Daniel. *Livres condamnés, livres interdits, régime juridique du livre, liberté ou censure?* Paris: Cercle de la Librairie, 1972.

Benstock, Shari. *Women of the Left Bank: Paris, 1900–1940.* Austin: University of Texas Press, 1986.

Berger, Maurice, Brian Wallis, and Simon Watson, eds. *Constructing Masculinity.* New York, Routledge, 1995

Bersani, Leo. *The Freudian Body.* New York: Columbia University Press, 1986.

———. *Homos.* Cambridge, Mass.: Harvard University Press, 1995.

Berubé, Allan. *Coming Out under Fire: The History of Gay Men and Women in World War Two.* New York: Plume, 1990.

Bonnet, Marie-Jo. *Les Relations amoureuses entre les femmes.* Paris: Odile Jacob, 1995.

Boswell, John. *Christianity, Social Tolerance, and Homosexuality: Gay People in Western Europe from the Beginning of the Christian Era to the Fourteenth Century.* Chicago: University of Chicago Press, 1980.

Bourke, Joanna. *Dismembering the Male: Men's Bodies, Britain, and the Great War.* Chicago: University of Chicago Press, 1996.

Boxer, Marilyn J., and Quaertet, Jean H., eds. *Connecting Spheres: Women in the Western World, 1500 to the Present.* Oxford: Oxford University Press, 1987.

Bremmer, Jan, ed. *From Sappho to de Sade: Moments in the History of Sexuality.* New York: Routledge, 1989.

Brennan, Teresa. *History after Lacan.* New York: Routledge, 1993.

Bronfen, Elisabeth. *Over Her Dead Body: Death, Femininity, and the Aesthetic.* New York: Routledge, 1992.

Brown, Wendy. *States of Injury: Power and Freedom in Late Modernity.* Princeton, N.J.: Princeton University Press, 1995.

Burgin, Victor. *In/Different Spaces: Place and Memory in Visual Culture.* Berkeley and Los Angeles: University of California Press, 1996.

Burke, Peter. *History and Social Theory.* Ithaca, N.Y.: Cornell University Press, 1992.

———. *Varieties of Cultural History.* Ithaca, N.Y.: Cornell University Press, 1997

Butler, Judith. *Bodies That Matter: On the Discursive Limits of Sex.* New York: Routledge, 1993.

———. *Gender Trouble: Feminism and the Subversion of Identity.* New York: Routledge, 1990.

———. *The Psychic Life of Power.* New York: Routledge, 1997.

Cairns, Lucille. "Gide's *Corydon:* The Politics of Sexuality and Sexual Politics." *Modern Language Review* 91.3 (July 1996): 582–96.

Chartier, Roger. *On the Edge of the Cliff: History, Language, and Practices.* Translated by Lydia G. Cochrane. Baltimore: Johns Hopkins University Press, 1997.

Chauncey, George. *Gay New York: Gender, Urban Culture, and the Making of the Gay Male World, 1890–1940.* New York: Basic Books, 1994.

Condemni, Concetta. *Café-concerts: Histoire d'un divertissement.* Paris: Quai Voltaire, 1992.

Corbin, Alain. *Women for Hire: Prostitution and Sexuality in France after 1850.* Translated by Alan Sheridan. Cambridge, Mass.: Harvard University Press, 1990.

Cover, Robert M. *Narrative, Violence, and the Law: The Essays of Robert Cover.* Edited by Martha Minow, Michael Ryan, and Austin Sarat. Ann Arbor: University of Michigan Press, 1992.

Darnton, Robert. *Edition et sédition: L'Univers de la littérature clandestine au XVIIIe siècle.* Paris: Gallimard, 1991.

Dean, Carolyn J. *The Self and Its Pleasures: Bataille, Lacan, and the History of the Decentered Subject.* Ithaca, N.Y.: Cornell University Press, 1992.

———. *Sexuality and Modern Western Culture.* New York: Twayne, 1996.

DeJean, Jean. *Fictions of Sappho, 1546–1937.* Chicago: University of Chicago Press, 1989.

Dellamora, Richard. *Masculine Desire: The Sexual Politics of Victorian Aestheticism.* Chapel Hill: University of North Carolina Press, 1990.

Derrida, Jacques. "Force of Law: The 'Mystical Foundation of Authority.'" In *Deconstruction and the Possibility of Justice.* Special Issue of the *Cardozo Law Review* 11 (July–August 1990): 919–1046.

Dijkstra, Bram. *Evil Sisters: The Threat of Female Sexuality in Twentieth-Century Culture.* New York: Owl Books, 1996.

———. *Idols of Perversity: Fantasies of Feminine Evil in Fin-de-Siècle Culture.* New York: Oxford University Press, 1986.

Dollimore, Jonathan. *Sexual Dissidence*. New York: Oxford University Press, 1993.

Douglas, Mary. *Purity and Danger: An Analysis of the Conception of Pollution and Taboo*. New York: Routledge, 1995.

Dowling, Linda. *Hellenism and Homosexuality in Victorian Oxford*. Ithaca, N.Y.: Cornell University Press, 1994.

Drescher, Seymour, David Sabean, and Allan Sharlin, eds. *Political Symbolism in Modern Europe: Essays in Honor of George L. Mosse*. New Brunswick, N.J.: Transaction Books, 1982.

Duggan, Lisa. "Theory in Practice: The Theory Wars, or Who's Afraid of Judith Butler." *Journal of Women's History* 10 (Spring 1998): 9–19.

Dworkin, Andrea. *Pornography: Men Possessing Women*. New York: Putnam, 1981.

Edmunson, Mark. *Nightmare on Main Street: Angles, Sadomasochism, and the Culture of Gothic*. Cambridge, Mass.: Harvard University Press, 1997.

Epstein, Julia, and Kristina Straub, eds. *Body Guards: The Cultural Politics of Gender Ambiguity*. New York: Routledge, 1991.

Felski, Rita. "The Counterdiscourse of the Feminine in Three Texts by Wilde, Huysmans, and Sacher-Masoch." *PMLA* 5 (1991): 1094–1105.

Feher, Marc, ed. *Fragments for a History of the Human Body*. 3 vols. New York: Zone Books, 1989.

Ferguson, Frances. "Sade and the Pornographic Legacy." *Representations* 36 (Fall 1991): 1–21.

Foucault, Michel. *The History of Sexuality*. Translated by Robert Hurley. Vol. 1: *An Introduction*. New York: Random House, Vintage Books, 1978. Vol. 2: *The Use of Pleasure*. New York: Random House, 1985. Vol. 3: *The Care of the Self*. New York: Pantheon Books, 1986. Originally published in 3 vols. as *Histoire de la sexualité* (Paris: Gallimard, 1976–84).

———. "Rituals of Exclusion." In *Foucault Live (Interviews, 1966–84)*. Translated by John Johnston. New York: Semiotext(e), 1989.

Fraisse, Geneviève. *Reason's Muse: Sexual Difference and the Rise of Democracy*. Translated by Jane Marie Todd. Chicago: University of Chicago Press, 1994.

Freud, Sigmund. "The Psychogenesis of a Case of Homosexuality in a Woman." In *Sexuality and the Psychology of Love*. New York: Collier, 1963.

Fuss, Diana. *Identification Papers*. New York: Routledge, 1995.

Gaetens, Moira. *Imaginary Bodies, Ethics, Power and Corporeality*. New York: Routledge, 1996.

Garréta, Anne. "In Light of Invisibility." *Yale French Studies* 90 (1996): 205–13.

Garréta, Anne, and Josyane Savigneau. "A Conversation." *Yale French Studies* 90 (1996): 214–34.

Gilbert, Sandra, and Susan Gubar. *No Man's Land: The Place of Women Writers in the Twentieth Century*. New Haven, Conn.: Yale University Press, 1988.

Grosz, Elizabeth. *Volatile Bodies: Toward a Corporeal Feminism*. Bloomington: Indiana University Press, 1994.

Guilleminault, Gilbert, ed. *Le Roman vrai des années folles, 1918–1930*. Paris: Denoël, 1975.

Halttunen, Karen. "Humanitarianism and the Pornography of Pain in Anglo-American Culture." *American Historical Review* 2 (April 1995): 303–34.

Harris, Ruth. "The 'Child of the Barbarian': Rape, Race and Nationalism in France During the First World War." *Past and Present* 141 (November 1993): 170–206.

Hause, Steven, and Anne Kenney. *Women's Suffrage and Social Politics in Third Republic France*. Princeton, N.J.: Princeton University Press, 1984.

Hawthorne, Melanie, and Richard J. Golsan. *Gender and Fascism in Modern France*. Hanover, N.H.: University Press of New England, 1997.

Hewitt, Andrew. *Political Inversions: Homosexuality, Fascism, and the Modernist Imaginary*. Stanford, Calif.: Stanford University Press, 1996.

Higonnet, Margaret R., Jane Jenson, Sonya Michel et al., eds. *Behind the Lines: Gender and the Two World Wars*. New Haven, Conn.: Yale University Press, 1987.

Huas, Jeanine. *L'Homosexualite au temps de Proust*. Dinard: Danclau, 1992.

Hunt, Lynn, ed. *The Invention of Pornography: Obscenity and the Origins of Modernity, 1500–1800*. New York: Zone Books, 1991.

Hunter, Ian, David Saunders, and Dugald Williamson. *On Pornography: Literature, Sexuality, and Obscenity Law*. New York: St. Martin's Press, 1993.

Hyde, H. Montgomery. *A History of Pornography*. New York: Farrar, Straus & Giroux, 1964.

Jay, Karla. *The Amazon and the Page: Natalie Clifford Barney and Renée Vivien*. Bloomington: Indiana University Press, 1988.

Kalifa, Dominique. *L'Encre et le sang: Recits de crimes et société à la Belle Epoque*. Paris: Fayard, 1995.

Kaplan, Alice Yaeger. *Reproductions of Banality: Fascism, Literature, and French Intellectual Life*. Minneapolis: University of Minnesota Press, 1986.

Kaplan, Morris B. *Sexual Justice: Democratic Citizenship and the Politics of Desire*. New York: Routledge, 1997.

Katz, Jonathan Ned. *The Invention of Heterosexuality*. New York: Dutton, 1995.

Kendrick, Walter. *The Secret Museum: Pornography in Modern Culture*. New York: Penguin Books, 1987.

Kent, Susan K. *Making Peace: The Reconstruction of Gender in Interwar Britain*. Princeton, N.J.: Princeton University Press, 1993.

Krauss, Rosalind, Yves Bois, Hal Foster et al. "The Politics of the Signifier II: A Conversation of the *Informe* and the Abject." *October* 67 (1994): 3–21.

LaCapra, Dominick. *History and Criticism*. Ithaca, N.Y.: Cornell University Press, 1985.

———. "Violence, Justice, and the Force of Law." *Cardozo Law Review* 11 (July–August, 1990): 1071–73.

Ladenson, Elisabeth. "Colette for Export Only." *Yale French Studies* 90 (1996): 25–46.

LaPlanche, Jean. *Problématiques III: La Sublimation*. Paris: Presses universitaires de France, 1980.

Laqueur, Thomas. *Making Sex: Body and Gender from the Greeks to Freud.* Cambridge, Mass.: Harvard University Press, 1990.

Ledge, Sally, and Scott McCracken, eds. *Cultural Politics at the Fin de Siècle.* Cambridge: Cambridge University Press, 1995.

Leed, Eric. *No Man's Land: Combat and Identity in World War One.* Cambridge: Cambridge University Press, 1979.

Leroy-Forgeot, Flora. *Histoire juridique de l'homosexualité en Europe.* Paris: Presses universitaires de France, 1997.

Lo Duca, Giuseppe Maria. *L'Histoire de l'érotisme.* Paris: Le Jeune Parque, 1969.

Loth, David Goldsmith. *The Erotic in Literature: A Historical Survey of Pornography as Delightful as It Is Indiscreet.* New York: Dorset, 1961.

Loubet de Bayle, J. L. *Les Non-Conformistes des années 30: Une tentative de renouvellement de la pensée politique française.* Paris: Seuil, 1969.

MacKinnon, Catharine. *Feminism Unmodified: Discourses on Life and Law.* Cambridge, Mass.: Harvard University Press, 1989.

———. *Only Words.* Cambridge, Mass.: Harvard University Press, 1993.

———. "Rape, Genocide, and Women's Human Rights." *Harvard Women's Law Journal* 17 (Spring 1994): 5–16.

———. *Toward a Feminist Theory of the State.* Cambridge, Mass.: Harvard University Press, 1989.

Marcus, Steven. *The Other Victorians: A Study of Sexuality and Pornography in Mid-Nineteenth-Century England.* New York: Norton, 1964.

Marks, Elaine, and George Stambolian, eds. *Homosexualities and French Literature.* Ithaca, N.Y.: Cornell University Press, 1979.

Martin, Biddy. *Femininity Played Straight: The Significance of Being a Lesbian.* New York: Routledge, 1996.

Maza, Sarah. *Private Lives and Public Affairs: The Causes Célèbres of Prerevolutionary France.* Berkeley and Los Angeles: University of California Press, 1993.

McLaren, Angus. *The Trials of Masculinity: Policing Sexual Boundaries, 1870–1930.* Chicago: University of Chicago Press, 1997.

McLintock, Anne. *Imperial Leather: Race, Gender and Sexuality in the Colonial Context.* New York: Routledge, 1995.

Merrick, Jeffrey, and Ragan, Bryant T., eds. *Homosexuality in Modern France.* Oxford: Oxford University Press, 1996.

Morel, J. H. *La Police des mœurs sous la Troisième République.* Paris: Seuil, 1992.

Moses, Claire Goldberg. *French Feminism in the Nineteenth Century.* Albany, N.Y.: SUNY Press, 1984.

Mosse, George L. *Fallen Soldiers: Reshaping the Memory of the World Wars.* Oxford: Oxford University Press, 1990.

———. *The Image of Man: The Creation of Modern Masculinity.* Oxford: Oxford University Press, 1996.

———. *Nationalism and Sexuality: Respectability and Abnormal Sexuality in Modern Europe.* New York: H. Fertag, 1985.

———. Preface to *Degeneration* by Max Nordau. Lincoln: University of Nebraska Press, 1993.

———. *Toward the Final Solution: A History of European Racism.* Madison: University of Wisconsin Press, 1978.

Noyes, John K. *The Mastery of Submission: Inventions of Masochism.* Ithaca, N.Y.: Cornell University Press, 1997.

Nye, Robert. *Masculinity and Male Codes of Honor in Modern France.* Oxford: Oxford University Press, 1993.

Ory, Pascal, ed. *La Censure en France à l'ère démocratique.* Brussels: Editions complexes, 1997.

Otis, Laura. *Organic Memory: History and Body in the Late Nineteenth and Early Twentieth Centuries.* Lincoln: University of Nebraska Press, 1994.

Pateman, Carole. *The Sexual Contract.* Stanford, Calif.: Stanford University Press, 1988.

Paulhan, Jean. *Le Marquis de Sade et sa complice, ou, Les revanches de la pudeur.* Brussels: Editions complexes, 1987.

Payne, Stanley. *A History of Fascism, 1914–1945.* Madison: University of Wisconsin Press, 1995.

Penniston, William A. "Love and Death in Gay Paris: Homosexuality and Criminality in the 1870s." In Jeffrey Merrick and Bryant T. Ragan, Jr., eds., *Homosexuality in Modern France* (Oxford: Oxford University Press, 1996), 129–30.

———. "'Pederasts and Others': A Social History of Male Homosexuals in the Early Years of the French Third Republic." Ph.D diss., University of Rochester, 1997.

Perrot, Phillipe. *Le Travail des apparences: Le Corps féminin XVIIIe–XIXe siècle.* Paris: Seuil, 1984.

Pollard, Patrick. *André Gide: Homosexual Moralist.* New Haven, Conn.: Yale University Press, 1991.

Praz, Mario. *The Romantic Agony.* Oxford: Oxford University Press, 1933. Reprint, 1970.

Rearick, Charles. *The French in Love and War: Popular Culture in the Era of the World Wars.* New Haven, Conn.: Yale University Press, 1997

Reynolds, Siân. *France between the Wars: Gender and Politics.* New York: Routledge, 1996.

Roberts, Mary Louise. *Civilization without Sexes: Reconstructing Gender in Postwar France, 1917–1927.* Chicago: University of Chicago Press, 1994.

Robinson, James. *Pornography: The Polluting of America.* Wheaton, Ill.: Tyndale House, 1982.

Robinson, Paul. *The Modernization of Sex: Havelock Ellis, Alfred Kinsey, William Masters and Virginia Johnson.* 1976. Ithaca, N.Y.: Cornell University Press, 1989.

Rosario, Vernon. *The Erotic Imagination: French Histories of Perversity.* Oxford: Oxford University Press, 1997.

Rose, Jacqueline. *States of Fantasy.* Oxford: Oxford University Press, Clarendon Press, 1996.

Rosenfeld, Alvin H. "Another Revisionism: Popular Culture and the Changing Image of the Holocaust." In *Bitburg in Moral and Political Perspective,* ed. Geoffrey Hartman. Bloomington: University of Indiana Press, 1986.

Roudebush, Marc. "A Battle of Nerves: Hysteria and Its Treatment in France during World War I." Ph.D diss., University of California, Berkeley, Department of History, 1995.

Rubenstein, William B., ed. *Gay Men, Lesbians, and the Law: A Reader.* New York: New Press, 1993.

Santner, Eric. *My Own Private Germany: Daniel Paul Schreber's Secret History of Modernity.* Princeton, N.J.: Princeton University Press, 1996.

Scarry, Elaine. *The Body in Pain: The Making and Unmaking of the World.* Oxford: Oxford University Press, 1985.

Schlesinger, Arthur M., Jr. *The Vital Center: The Politics of Freedom.* 1949. Reprint. New York: De Capo Press, 1988.

Schneider, William H. *Quality and Quantity: The Quest for Biological Regeneration in Twentieth-Century France.* Cambridge: Cambridge University Press, 1990.

Scott, Joan. *Gender and the Politics of History.* New York: Columbia University Press, 1988.

——. *Only Paradoxes to Offer: French Feminists and the Rights of Man.* Cambridge, Mass.: Harvard University Press, 1996.

Sedgwick, Eve Kosofsky. *Epistemology of the Closet.* Berkeley and Los Angeles: University of California Press, 1990.

——. *Tendencies.* Durham, N.C.: Duke University Press, 1993.

Seltzer, Mark. *Bodies and Machines.* New York: Routledge, 1992.

Shapiro, Anne-Louise. *Breaking the Codes: Female Criminality in Fin-de-Siècle Paris.* Stanford, Calif.: Stanford University Press, 1996.

Sherman, Daniel. "Monuments, Mourning and Masculinity in France after World War I." *Gender and History* 1 (April 1996): 83–107.

Silverman, Deborah. *Art Nouveau in Fin-de-Siècle France.* Berkeley and Los Angeles: University of California Press, 1990.

Smith, Bonnie, Jonathan Dewald, William Sewell, and Roger Chartier. Discussion. *French Historical Studies* 21 (Spring 1998): 213–64.

Solomon-Godeau, Abigail. "The Legs of the Countess." *October* 39 (1986): 65–108.

Sontag, Susan. "The Pornographic Imagination." In *Styles of Radical Will.* New York: Farrar, Straus & Giroux, 1969.

Sorel, Georges. *Reflections on Violence.* Translated by T. E. Hulme. New York: Free Press, 1950. Originally published as *Réflexions sur la violence* (1908).

Soucy, Robert. *French Fascism: The Second Wave, 1933–1939.* New Haven, Conn.: Yale University Press, 1995.

Spackman, Barbara. *Decadent Genealogies: The Rhetoric of Sickness from Baudelaire to D'Annunzio.* Ithaca, N.Y.: Cornell University Press, 1990.

Stafford, Barbara Maria. *Body Criticism: Imaging the Unseen in Enlightenment Art and Medicine.* Cambridge, Mass.: MIT Press, 1991.

Steiner, Wendy. *The Scandal of Pleasure.* Chicago: University of Chicago Press, 1995.

Sternhell, Zeev. *The Birth of Fascist Ideology.* Translated by David Maisel. Princeton, N.J.: Princeton University Press, 1994.

———. *Ni droite ni gauche: L'Idéologie fasciste en France.* Paris: Seuil, 1983.

Stoler, Ann Laura. *Race and the Education of Desire: Foucault's History of Sexuality and the Colonial Order of Things.* Durham, N.C.: Duke University Press, 1995.

Stora-Lamarre, Annie. *L'Enfer de la Troisième République: Censeurs et pornographes, 1880–1914.* Paris: Imago, 1990.

———. "Plaisirs interdits: L'Enfer de la Bibliothèque nationale." In Pascal Ory, ed., *La Censure en France à l'ère démocratique,* 43–52. Brussels: Editions complexes, 1997.

Stychin, Carl. *Law's Desire: Sexuality and the Limits of Justice.* New York: Routledge, 1995.

Tartar, Maria. *Lustmord: Sexual Murder in Weimar Germany.* Princeton, N.J.: Princeton University Press, 1995.

Thébaud, Françoise, ed. *A History of Women: Toward a Cultural Identity in the Twentieth Century.* Cambridge, Mass.: Harvard University Press, 1994.

Theweleit, Klaus. *Male Fantasies.* 2 vols. Minneapolis: University of Minnesota Press, 1987.

Thomas, Kendall. "Beyond the Privacy Principle." *Columbia Law Review* 92 (October 1992): 1431–1516.

————. "Corpus Juris (Hetero) Sexualis: Doctrine, Discourse, and Desire in Bowers v. Hardwick." *Gay and Lesbian Quarterly* 1 (1993): 33–51.

Tonnet-LaCroix, Elaine. *Après-Guerre et sensibilités littéraires (1919–1924)*. Paris: Publications de la Sorbonne, 1991.

————. *La Littérature française de l'entre-deux-guerres, 1919–39*. Paris: Nathan, 1993.

Vanwelkenhuyzen, Gustave. *Histoire d'un livre:* Un Mâle, *de Camille Lemonnier.* Brussels: Palais des Académies, 1961.

Vigarello, Georges. *Histoire du viol*. Paris: Seuil, 1998.

Wagner, Peter, ed. *Erotica and the Enlightenment*, New York: Lang, 1990.

Warner, Michael, ed. *Fear of a Queer Planet: Queer Politics and Social Theory*. Minneapolis: University of Minnesota Press, 1993.

Weed, Elizabeth, and Schor, Naomi, eds. *Feminism Meets Queer Theory*. Bloomington: Indiana University Press, 1997.

Weeks, Jeffrey. *Sex, Politics, and Society: The Regulation of Sexuality since 1800*. London: Longman, 1981.

Westphal, Karl. "Die conträre Sexualempfindung." *Archiv für Psychiatrie und Nervenkrankheiten* 2.1 (August 1869): 73–108.

Williams, Linda. *Hard Core: Power, Pleasure, and the Frenzy of the Visible*. Berkeley and Los Angeles: University of California Press, 1989.

Žižek, Slavoj. *The Plague of Fantasies*. London: Verso, 1997.

Index

Lalo, Charles, 95; *La Beauté et l'instinct sexuel*, 91–94
L'Amant légitime (Anquetil), 56–57
L'Amitié magazine, 148
Lang, Etienne, 44
Lapeire, Paul, 83, 85–86
Laurent, Emile, 140
Lawrence, D. H., 85n
League Against Puritanism, 87, 96
League for the Liberty of Art, 37
Le Club des damnés (Royer), 190–191, 193–194
Le Dantec, Yves-Gérard, 204
Le Génie littéraire (Voivenel and Rémond), 75–79
legislation: anti-abortion, 6, 188; anti-contraception, 188; anti-pornography, 29–31, 32–33, 34–35, 42, 51, 60–62, 61n; anti-sodomy, 12, 131; anti-suffrage, 6; censorship, 30–31, 35
Le Mensonge du féminisme (Joran), 69
Lemonnier, Camille, 84; *Un Mâle*, 74
L'Entremetteuse (Daudet), 96–97
Le Pur et l'impur (Colette), 199, 200
lesbianism, 173–215; detecting, 191–195; distinguishing normal women from, 184, 197n; feminine vs. masculine, 177n, 185n, 186–187, 197; femininity and, 177n, 180, 181–182, 184–185, 184n; feminism and, 177–180; flagellation and, 109, 193, 197–198; as gender inversion, 181, 183–185, 186–187; interwar, 169n, 187–195; invisibility of, 131, 174n, 175, 176–177, 190–195, 196, 212–215;

medical opinion on, 176n, 181, 182–186, 196–197, 199; pervasiveness of, 147, 189–190, 195–196; prostitution and, 182, 185, 191, 192; sadomasochism and, 194; secret clubs of, 193–195; use of term, 18n, 177n; writings by lesbians on, 199–212. *See also* homosexuality
Les Flagellants (DuBarry), 104, 107–108
Le Troisième Sexe (Gauthier-Villars), 148, 166n, 190–191, 193
liberal political theory, body as viewed by, 1–2
literature, 17–18; avant-garde, 69–72, 94–95; by degenerate writers, 69–72; erotic, vs. pornography, 61–62, 89–90, 96–97; homosexual, 149; as masculine, 71, 75–76, 77–79; pornographic, 28, 28n, 49, 53, 54–59, 56, 75–80, 81, 82; pornography redefined as, 95, 97, 98; sadomasochistic, as regenerative, 120–126, 127–128; sexuality and, 79–82, 85–87, 85n, 93–95; vs. pornography, 26n, 37–38, 66, 66n
Live Girls (Nugent), 9, 10
Locke, John, 1, 25
Lo Duca, Giuseppe, 25, 97
Lombroso, Cesare, 76n, 198
Lorrain, Jean, 72–73
Lorulot, André, 89; on homosexuality, 149, 158; on sado-masochism of Great War, 112, 113, 117–118, 122
Loth, David, *The Erotic in Literature*, 64
Loüys, Pierre, 85–86

262   Index

Solomon-Godeau, Abigail, 66n
Sontag, Susan, 26n
Sorel, Georges, 143–144; *Reflections on Violence*, 130
Sous le Col Bleu (DuCoglay), 144–145, 145n
Spiess, Camille, 163–164, 164n, 166; *Pédérastie et homosexualité*, 165
state, relationship between body and, 1–3, 3n
Sternhell, Zeev, 164
Stora-Lamarre, Annie, 27–28, 36, 50
suffrage, laws against, 6
Sur le fleuve amour (Delteil), 114
Swinburne, Algernon Charles, 70
Symonds, John, 165

Tailhade, Laurent, 69, 204
Taine, Hippolyte, 74
tantes, 154, 154n
Tardieu, Ambroise, 134–136, 135n, 137, 140; *Etude médico-legale sur les attentats aux moeurs*, 134–135
Tarn, Pauline. *See* Vivien, Renée
Taxil, Léo, 135, 139–140, 185–186
Téry, Gustave, 41, 45, 49
Théry, Adolphe, 47–48, 49, 51
Thoinot, L., 135–136, 140, 184
tribades, 181, 185, 197

Ulrichs, Karl Heinrich, 138
Un Mâle (Lemonnier), 74
uranists, 139, 161. *See also* homosexuality
Uzanne, Octave, 75, 192

Vachet, Pierre, 189
Valéry, Paul, 86

Valois, Georges, 143–144
Verlaine, Paul, 74
Vignon, Charles-Louis, 149
Villeneuve, Jérome Pétion de, 158n
Villiot, Jean de. *See* Rebell, Hugues
violence: eroticized, 105n; as pornography, 8–9, 9n; sexual deviance as, 223–224; sexual pleasure associated with, 108–109; state, and human body, 220–228. *See also* flagellation; sadomasochism
Visage du vice (Fabri), 114
Vivien, Renée, 180, 201–211, 203n, 215; Colette on, 202–203; Sappho and, 202, 203, 204, 205n, 206, 208
Voivenel, Paul, 112–113, 118; *Le Génie littéraire*, 75–80, 81, 82

war: sadomasochism and, 112–118; as spiritually cleansing, 110. *See also* Great War
Watteau, Antoine, 35, 207; *Embarquement pour Cythère*, 35
Weininger, Otto, *Sex and Character*, 67n
The Well of Loneliness (Hall), 146n
Westphal, Karl, 138
white slave trade, 59n
Wilde, Oscar, 164
Willette, Henriette, 205, 207, 209
Williamson, Dugald, 66n
Willy. *See* Gauthier-Villars, Henri
Wilmot, John, 74
Winckelmann, Johannes, 163n
Wollstonecraft, Mary, 179n
women, in social body, 6, 6n
World War I. *See* Great War

Text:	11/14 Aster
Display:	Frutiger
Composition:	G & S Typesetters, Inc.
Printing and binding:	Thomson-Shore, Inc.
Index:	Jean Mann